A Guide to the

WITHDRAWN

...juide to the Trade Marks Act 1994

A Guide to the Trade Marks Act 1994

Christopher Morcom, MA
One of Her Majesty's Counsel

Butterworths
London, Dublin, Edinburgh
1994

United Kingdom	Butterworth & Co (Publishers) Ltd, Halsbury House, 35 Chancery Lane, LONDON WC2A 1EL and 4 Hill Street, EDINBURGH EH2 3JZ
Australia	Butterworths, SYDNEY, MELBOURNE, BRISBANE, ADELAIDE, PERTH, CANBERRA and HOBART
Canada	Butterworth Canada Ltd, TORONTO and VANCOUVER
Ireland	Butterworth (Ireland) Ltd, DUBLIN
Malaysia	Malayan Law Journal Sdn Bhd, KUALA LUMPUR
New Zealand	Butterworths of New Zealand Ltd, WELLINGTON and AUCKLAND
Puerto Rico	Butterworth of Puerto Rico, Inc, SAN JUAN
Singapore	Butterworths Asia, SINGAPORE
South Africa	Butterworths Publishers (Pty) Ltd, DURBAN
USA	Butterworth Legal Publishers, CARLSBAD, California; SALEM, New Hampshire

A CIP catalogue record for this book is available from the British Library.

ISBN 0 406 04581 X

Printed and bound in Great Britain by Mackays of Chatham plc, Kent.

∞This text paper meets the requirements of ISO 9706/1994. Information and Documentation—paper for documents—requirements for permanence.

Preface

The purpose of this book is to provide a guide to the Trade Marks Act 1994, which makes radical changes to the law relating to registered trade marks in the United Kingdom. The 1994 Act replaces the Trade Marks Act 1938, as amended by the Trade Marks (Amendment) Act 1984, and the Patents, Designs and Marks Act 1986 which introduced registration of service marks as from 1 October 1986. It received Royal Assent on 21 July and is expected to come into force on 31 October 1994.

An important purpose of the Act is to implement the EC Directive which approximates the laws of the Member States relating to trade marks, although it goes considerably further than is necessary for compliance with the Directive and also contains provisions to enable the United Kingdom to ratify the Madrid Protocol for the international registration of trade marks. Another important development is the adoption, on 21 December 1993, of the Community Trade Mark Regulation, several of the provisions of which are very similar to provisions of the Directive. However the unitary system which will be established under the Regulation is in a number of respects significantly different from the national trade mark registration systems which will continue to exist in accordance with the Directive. The implementing regulations for the Community Trade Mark have still to be finalised and the Community Trade Mark Office is not expected to start receiving applications until 1996. In the circumstances it has been decided not to cover the Community Trade Mark in this book.

As under the previous law, many procedural and other matters will be governed by rules. At the time of writing this guide, the rules had not been finalised. It is understood that they will be laid before Parliament not later than 10 October 1994.

The aim of this book is to explain the new law, comparing it as far as practicable with the previous law. It must be emphasised however that any views expressed as to the meaning and effect of the new law, which are generally my own views, are in many instances tentative. Although the 1994 Act is generally speaking well drafted, and is in rather simpler language than some parts of the 1938 Act, the new system for the registration and protection of trade marks will be significantly different from the old system, which has remained fundamentally the same for many years, despite important changes from time to time.

There are not many provisions in relation to which case law under the 1938 Act and its predecessors is of much assistance. This applies particularly to those provisions which are based on the Directive, some of which are derived from the Benelux trade mark law. In due course many of these provisions are likely to be affected by rulings of the European Court of Justice, on references from other Member States as well as from UK courts. This book is not intended to be a full exposition or analysis of the new law, but I hope that it will be of assistance to those who are required to advise their clients and employers on how to operate under the 1994 Act.

Finally I would like to thank all those who have assisted in the preparation of this book. These include members of my own Chambers, who have offered advice and suggestions at various times, and Butterworths, whose staff have helped considerably with the presentation of my work and its early publication.

CM
September 1994

Contents

Table of statutes

Table of EC legislation

Table of Cases

<h2 style="text-align:center">Y</h2>

1 Introduction

BACKGROUND TO THE 1994 ACT

Previous UK trade mark legislation

1.1   Trade mark registration in the UK is over 100 years old. Throughout much of this period the general nature of trade mark law has not altered very much. The previous law, contained in the Trade Marks Act 1938, which was in force for nearly 50 years, was not amended significantly. In 1974 the Report of the Mathys Committee[1] recommended the extension of the law to allow registration of marks for services. The registration of service marks—itself an important step towards bringing the UK law up to date and more in keeping with the needs of industry—was introduced in 1986, by the Trade Marks (Amendment) Act 1984, with some further amendment by the Patents, Designs and Marks Act 1986.

[1]   Cmnd 5601.

The effects of EC membership

1.2   In the meanwhile, the effects of Britain's membership of the EC were beginning to be seen in the world of industrial property, more especially perhaps in the field of trade marks. Not only have the provisions of the Treaty of Rome, in particular Articles 30–36 and 85 and 86, made considerable impact on the way in which trade mark rights may be protected and enforced; the Common Market itself has provided the impetus for proposals for the harmonisation of trade mark laws in the member states, by means of a Directive, and a unitary Community Trade Mark system, under which a single registration will have effect throughout the whole of the EC. The Directive, made under Article 100 of the Treaty of Rome, to approximate the laws of the member states relating to trade marks, was adopted on 21 December 1988.[1] This contains provisions which are mandatory, ie they *must* be included in national laws of member states, and other provisions which are optional, ie they may be included if member states so wish. Under Article 16 of the Directive, member states were originally required to make the necessary changes to their trade mark laws not later than 28 December 1991. The Council was empowered to defer the date for implementation until 31 December 1992, and this was in fact done. The Community Trade Mark Regulation,[2] made under Article 235 of the Treaty, was adopted on 20 December 1993, having been long delayed by a failure to reach agreement on two questions, namely the location of the Office and the language or languages in which the Office was to work. These matters have now been resolved, and it has been agreed that the Office will be in Spain, although the particular location chosen by the Spanish Government (Alicante) is not perhaps ideal for an important international intellectual property office.

[1]   Council Directive 89/104/EEC: OJ L40 11.2.1989, p 1. See Appendix 2.
[2]   Council Regulation 40/94/EEC: OJ L11 14.1.1994, p 1.

International registration under the Madrid Agreement

1.3   Another event, which provided a further cause for legislation, was the signing of a Protocol to the Madrid Agreement Concerning the International Registration of Marks on 28 June 1989. The purpose of the Protocol, which was signed by the UK, together with a number of other countries including the other member states of the EC which are not parties to the original Madrid Agreement,[1] was to overcome certain difficulties which had prevented the UK and others from becoming parties to the Madrid Agreement.

---

[1]   Denmark, Eire and Greece.

The White Paper

1.4   In September 1990 the Government published a White Paper[1] proposing comprehensive reforms, in particular to implement the Directive (including the provisions which were only optional as well as those which were mandatory), and to enable the UK to ratify the Madrid Protocol. A number of other necessary changes were also proposed. When the deadline for complying with the Directive passed on 31 December 1992, there was discussion about the possibilities of invoking the mandatory provisions of the Directive immediately. However, this became more or less academic with the announcement, on 18 November 1993, of the introduction of the Trade Marks Bill in the House of Lords.

---

[1]   Reform of Trade Marks Law (Cm 1203).

The Paris Convention

1.5   Another aspect of the White Paper proposals was the meeting of certain international obligations under the Paris Convention for the Protection of Industrial Property of 20 March 1883, as revised or amended from time to time. Although the UK is a party to the Paris Convention, there have long been some obligations which the UK, at least arguably, did not meet. The 1994 Act contains several provisions[1] the purpose of which is to meet some of those obligations. These are considered in detail below, but one in particular is worth mentioning here. Section 56 makes special provision for the protection of trade marks which are 'well-known' within the meaning of Article 6bis of the Paris Convention, and should meet the difficulties of the kind encountered by the owners of such trade marks which have not been used in trade in the UK, which were highlighted, for example, by the decision of the Court of Appeal in the *Budweiser* case.[2]

---

[1]   See ss 55–60.
[2]   *Anheuser-Busch Inc v Budejovicky Budvar* [1984] FSR 413 *Narodni Podnik, Budweiser Case*, CA.

The Trade Marks Bill

1.6   The Bill was the subject of a great deal of consultation, with the interested professions and other organisations. This undoubtedly helped to produce legislation which could be expected to be non-controversial and indeed it has had a generally easy passage through parliament. The Bill was read for the first time in the House of Lords on 24 November 1993 and received Royal Assent on 21 July 1994. The UK now has what may fairly be described as a modern trade mark law to meet the needs of industry. It has been announced that the Act will come into force on 31 October 1994.

The Copyright, Designs and Patents Act 1988

1.7   Some reference should be made here to certain parts of the Copyright, Designs and Patents Act 1988, concerning trade marks and trade mark practice. As is only too well known, in recent years there has been a considerable increase in trade mark piracy, as well as piracy of other forms of intellectual property. Attempts have been made, and continue to be made, to deal with the problem both nationally and internationally. At national level, s 300 of the 1988 Act, which came into force on 1 August 1989[1] introduced new ss 58A–58D into the Trade Marks Act 1938 creating a new offence of 'fraudulent application or use of trade mark' and providing machinery for enforcement. Sections 58A–58D of the 1938 Act (and s 300 of the 1988 Act) have been repealed by the 1994 Act. Section 92 of the 1994 Act, which replaces s 58A of the 1938 Act, is significantly different, and is hoped that it will be more effective in prosecuting dealers in counterfeit goods. Section 93, which is concerned with enforcement, is very similar to s 58D of the 1938 Act, but the provisions of ss 97 and 98, relating to forfeiture of counterfeit goods, are significantly different from the previous provisions of ss 58B and 58C of the 1938 Act. Also, new provisions were included in the 1988 Act for establishing a register of trade mark agents and for granting professional privilege for communications with trade mark agents.[2] These provisions are substantially re-enacted by ss 83, 84 and 87 of the 1994 Act. Section 86 is new, and enables trade mark agents to use the term 'trade mark attorney', thus bringing the position of trade mark agents generally into line with that of patent agents.[3]

---

[1] Copyright, Designs and Patents Act 1988 (Commencement No 1) Order 1989, SI 1989/816.
[2] Sections 282–284 of the 1988 Act, with similar provisions relating to patent agents, in ss 274–280, which all came into force on 13 August 1990.
[3] See the Patents Act 1977, s 85 and now, ss 277–279 of the 1988 Act.

Purpose of this guide

1.8   The main purpose of this guide is to explain the new law relating to trade marks and service marks (now all to be called 'trade marks') in the UK under the 1994 Act. The common law of passing off is expressly preserved by s 2(2) of the 1994 Act, although in many areas it may be much less needed than under the previous law. It is not covered in detail here. For some purposes, existing trade marks registered or applied for under the 1938 Act will still be governed by that Act, and these matters, which are dealt with by the transitional provisions in Sch 3, are also discussed.

THE ROLE OF TRADE MARKS TODAY

1.9   In view of the fact that the 1994 Act introduces some fundamental changes, in particular the relaxation of the restrictions on licensing and assignment of trade marks, which might have been considered revolutionary when the Mathys Committee reported 20 years ago, it is appropriate to consider how far, if at all, the role of trade marks will be changed. The traditional function of a trade mark was the indication of the origin, or trade source, of goods. This was made clear, for instance, by the House of Lords in *Aristoc Ltd v Rysta Ltd*.[1] The emphasis no doubt has changed somewhat, owing to some relaxation of the very strict rules, which before 27 July 1938 applied to the licensing of any trade mark, or its assignment separately from the business in which it was used; also, in more recent years, owing to the frequency of company takeovers, in which the effective ownership of trade mark rights can be transferred without any actual assignment.

---

[1] [1945] 62 RPC 65; see in particular per Viscount Maugham at p 74 line 31 and per Lord Wright at p 82 line 36.

1.10   In spite of these developments, the function of a trade mark remained essentially the same. As it was put in the Memorandum on the creation of an EEC trade mark[1]—

'Both economically and legally the function of the trade mark as an indication of origin is paramount. It follows directly from the concept of a trade mark as a distinctive sign, that it serves to distinguish trade marked products originating from a particular firm or group of firms from the products of other firms. From this basic function of the trade mark are derived all the other functions which the trade mark fulfils in economic life. If the trade mark guarantees that the commercial origin is the same, the consumer can count on a similarity of composition and quality of goods bearing the trade mark; and the advertising value of the trade mark requires that between the trade marked goods and the owner of the trade mark there is a definite legal relationship. Although the quality function predominates in the mind of the consumer and the publicity function predominates in the mind of the producer, so far as the legal aspect is concerned the decisive criterion is the function of the mark as an indication of origin. Only if the proper purpose of the trade mark is maintained, namely to distinguish the trade marked goods from goods of different origin, can it fulfil its further role as an instrument of sales promotion and consumer information; and only then does the trade mark right perform its function of protecting the proprietor against injury to the reputation of his trade mark.'

---

[1] Bulletin of the European Communities, Supplement 8/76, adopted by the Commission on 6 July 1976; see para 68.

1.11   These observations apply equally to service marks, and they point also to the role of the trade mark in commerce, a matter mentioned earlier in the Memorandum[1]—

'The consumer is faced . . . with a large and . . . considerable number of consumer goods of the same kind; and these are not distinguished, like raw materials and many agricultural products, by natural or technical features alone, but have numerous variations and differences in quality, special properties, taste and appearance. To make the right choice, the consumer needs to be able to identify and distinguish these goods according to their origin and to recognise a connection between a particular product, its quality and its reputation.'

'Trade marks facilitate this process of identification and choice. . . . The consumer needs a clear and unambiguous distinguishing mark for each required article. Thus trade marks assist the consumer in the first instance when consumer goods of the same kind are offered for sale, facilitate a further purchase of the same article and enable the consumer to distinguish, according to his wishes, between the various goods offered for sale. The same is true in respect of the provision of services.'

'To an economic system directed towards the needs of consumers, trade marks are thus indispensable. They play an important role in the public interest in the distribution of goods and services, and should therefore be given legal protection.'

---

[1]   Paragraphs 11–13.

1.12   By removing all restrictions on the licensing and assignment of trade marks the 1994 Act goes even further than the 1938 Act. However, given the obvious reasons why we have trade marks at all, and the strong incentive upon traders to preserve the distinguishing power and thus the value of their trade marks, it is not thought that the new law will lead to a fundamental change in the traditional function of a trade mark as described above. This is considered further at para 2.4.

1.13   It is but a short step from the foregoing passages in the Memorandum to the conclusion, again expressed in the Memorandum, that trade marks stimulate trade. It is observed[1] that—

'By virtue of their role as an indicator of origin and quality and as a means of advertising, trade marks are indeed an indispensable means of promoting trade and in doing so assist the further interpenetration of national markets. They help manufacturers to acquire new markets and thus help to promote the expansion of economic activity beyond national borders.'

It follows that, if it is desired to abolish altogether trade in any particular product, one means of achieving this is to prohibit the use of trade marks for such products. This principle can be illustrated by some recent national laws aimed at curbing trade in tobacco products; these are coming close to a prohibition of the use of trade marks and proposals have been made in some countries which do go that far. Similarly a recent Canadian law has prohibited (with few exceptions) the use of the same trade mark for tobacco products as for other goods, and vice versa. It is hard to imagine any clearer demonstration of the role of trade marks.

---

[1]   Paragraph 21.

1.14   One result of the recognition of the importance of trade marks in stimulating trade, is the growing practice of placing substantial values on brand names in the balance sheets of companies. This interesting, but still controversial, development is outside the scope of this book, but is mentioned here because it represents another demonstration of the continuing, indeed increasing, importance of trade marks in modern business.

1.15 As will be seen below (para 2.1), the definition of a 'trade mark', in s 1 of the 1994 Act, requires a trade mark to be 'capable of distinguishing goods or services of one undertaking from those of another'. Thus it seems that the role of the trade mark will remain essentially the same, although perhaps a secondary function of some trade marks, namely distinguishing different products of one proprietor, may become more significant with the greater ease of registration.

THE DIRECTIVE AND THE 1994 ACT

1.16 It is a matter of considerable practical importance that a major purpose of the 1994 Act is to implement the EC Directive. The Directive itself can be the subject of interpretation by the European Court of Justice (ECJ) under Article 177 of the Treaty of Rome. Although this procedure may be of less relevance in instances in which the 1994 Act is not in identical terms to the Directive, it is to be noted that the draftsman of the Act has in fact kept very close to the wording of the Directive; in many instances the wording is identical or virtually so. Therefore it is inevitable, as a practical matter, that courts in the UK will need to pay close attention to the interpretation placed on provisions of the Directive by the ECJ, and to be ready to request rulings from that court. Rulings of the ECJ on references from other member states will also have to be considered and applied where relevant.

1.17 In interpreting the provisions of the Directive, there is another document which may have to be considered, although it has not yet been formally published. The document is referred to as an 'Annex' and contains 'Statements' for entry in the minutes of the Council Meeting at which the Directive was adopted. In this book it is referred to as 'the Annex'. Each paragraph commences with the words 'The Council and the Commission consider that . . . ', followed by statements as to the meaning and effect of a number of provisions in the Directive, not necessarily obvious from the provisions themselves. A similar document annexed to the Community Trade Mark Regulation is to be found in the *ECTA Law Book* published in March 1994 by the European Communities Trade Mark Association, referred to below as 'the Annex' to the Regulation. It is not yet known what approach the courts in England or elsewhere in the UK will adopt in respect of 'the Annex' if it is referred to. In the past they would simply have refused to take such a document into consideration for the purpose of construing the Directive or a national law implementing it. However, it would be surprising if the ECJ were to do other than take 'the Annex' into account when requested to interpret the Directive. In these circumstances it is to be expected that the UK courts could do the same, at least for the purpose of deciding whether or not to make a reference to the ECJ. It should be emphasised that in the event that 'the Annex' can be referred to, it could only be regarded as a guide in interpreting and applying statutory provisions based on the Directive, and would not necessarily be regarded as conclusive.

GENERAL OBSERVATIONS ON THE APPROACH OF THE NEW LAW

1.18 It may be helpful to draw attention to some of the significant differences between the 1938 Act and the 1994 Act in their general approach to trade marks. First of all, with few exceptions, the general approach is to leave it to proprietors of trade marks to look after their own interests. Hence the removal of restrictions on licensing and assignments of trade marks. Secondly, whereas the onus under the 1938 Act was on the applicant for registration to show that his mark ought to be registered, the 1994 Act (ss 3, 4, 46 and 47) follows the Directive in adopting the opposite approach by setting out grounds for refusal or invalidity, creating a presumption that a mark ought to be registered unless there is some specific objection to it.[1] The same general approach applies to the 'relative' grounds for refusal (or invalidation) based on earlier rights (ss 5 and 47). It should also be noted that the registrar's discretion, which has been part of the law since 1883, to refuse registration where there is no statutory ground for objection, or to refuse to remove a mark from the register even when statutory grounds for removal are established, has ceased to exist; all the grounds for refusal or invalidation are set out in the 1994 Act.[2] Another difference in approach concerns the treatment of concurrent rights. In the Bill as published, there was no provision corresponding to s 12(2) of the 1938 Act, which enabled an objection, based upon a prior registration or application, to be overcome by establishing 'honest concurrent use' or 'other special circumstances'. However, following representations made to the government, the doctrine of 'honest concurrent use' has now been incorporated into the 1994 Act, albeit in a more restricted form (see para 4.7).

---

[1] See the White Paper, paras 3.06 and 3.07.
[2] See the White Paper, paras 3.10–3.12.

1.19   The position regarding refusal of registration on the relative grounds merits special mention. Although the Community Trade Mark Regulation contains no provision enabling an application to be refused by the Office on such grounds, the matter being left to be considered in opposition proceedings, the 1994 Act, as indicated above, retains the possibility for the registrar to refuse an application which conflicts with earlier rights. However, s 8 of the Act does give the Secretary of State the necessary powers, after 10 years have elapsed since the Community Trade Mark Office starts to receive applications, to remove the registrar's power to raise objections on relative grounds (see para 4.1).

DIFFERENT KINDS OF TRADE MARK REGISTRATIONS

Abolition of two parts of the register

1.20   One change in the law, which was recommended by the Mathys Committee in 1974, is the abolition of the two parts of the register, Part A and Part B. The separation of the register into two parts has never been of any real significance, save in rare instances. Under the 1994 Act registrations in both parts will be placed into a single register of trade marks, and in future will all be treated in the same way.

Defensive trade mark registrations

1.21   Defensive trade mark registrations, under s 27 of the 1938 Act, are few in number, owing to the great difficulty, encountered in practice, in obtaining registration. Their significance will be greatly reduced under the 1994 Act, in view of the broader scope of protection given to ordinary registrations and to the special protection for well-known trade marks under s 56. Existing defensive registrations will, after five years from the commencement of the 1994 Act, become open to revocation on the ground of non-use.[1]

---

[1] Under s 46; see Sch 3, para 17(2).

Certification trade marks

1.22   Certification trade marks will continue to be registrable under the 1994 Act, and will be extended to services, for which there was no provision under the 1984 and 1986 Acts. An important change in the procedure is that the regulatory functions of the Department of Trade and Industry have been transferred to the registrar. The relevant provisions are contained in s 50 and Sch 2 (see Chapter 11).

Collective trade marks

1.23   Under the 1994 Act, collective trade marks, which will also be capable of registration under the Community Trade Mark Regulation, are introduced for the first time in the UK. The relevant provisions are contained in s 49 and Sch 1 (see Chapter 12).

2 Definition of a trade mark

TRADE MARK

2.1   In contrast to the 1938 Act, which defined 'mark' and 'trade mark' (and, when amended, 'service mark') separately[1] and which contained separate provisions in ss 9 and 10 laying down what marks were registrable, the 1994 Act contains a comprehensive definition of 'trade mark' in s 1, covering marks for both goods and services, followed by provisions in ss 3 and 4 setting out what is not registrable. Section 1(1), which follows closely the wording of Article 2 of the Directive, is as follows—

> 'In this Act a 'trade mark' means any sign capable of being represented graphically which is capable of distinguishing goods or services of one undertaking from those of other undertakings.
>
> A trade mark may, in particular, consist of words (including personal names), designs, letters, numerals or the shape of goods or their packaging.'

Section 1(2) provides that references in the Act to a trade mark include, unless the context otherwise requires, references to a certification mark or collective mark. The special provisions for these two kinds of mark, which are to be found respectively in s 50 and Sch 2, and s 49 and Sch 1, are discussed in Chapters 11 and 12.

---

[1]   Section 68(1) of the 1938 Act and the Trade Marks (Amendment) Act 1984, s 1(7) (as amended by the Patents, Designs and Marks Act 1986).

'ANY SIGN'—QUALIFICATION FOR REGISTRATION AS A TRADE MARK

2.2   The expression 'sign' is very broad, and is only qualified by the requirement of being 'capable of being represented graphically'. The words 'may, in particular consist of . . .' indicate that the list of examples of trade marks is not intended to be exhaustive. As pointed out in the White Paper,[1] the definition is a flexible definition intended to serve the needs of commerce and is open-ended so as to be capable of adapting to changes in trading practices. The categories of signs specifically mentioned confirm that a trade mark may be three-dimensional. In addition to signs in these categories, devices and logos, and indeed everything that could be a 'mark' for the purposes of the 1938 Act will be a 'sign' for the purposes of the definition. For instance the colour combinations which were held to be 'marks' in the case of *Smith, Kline & French Laboratories Ltd's Trade Mark Applications*[2] may also qualify as trade marks under the new law.[3] The inclusion of the shape of goods or their packaging makes it clear[4] that the decision of the House of Lords in *Coca-Cola Trade Marks*,[5] that the distinctive shape of a bottle was not a 'mark' for the purposes of the 1938 Act, is no longer applicable. There is nothing in the definition to suggest (any more than there was in the 1938 Act)[6] that anything capable of protection under design law is excluded. In each case the guiding principle, endorsed in the White Paper,[7] is that if a sign functions in the market place as a trade mark, it is to be regarded as a trade mark.

---

1 Paragraph 2.06.
2 [1975] 2 All ER 578, [1976] RPC 511, HL.
3 This is understood to be confirmed by 'the Annex'; cf para 3 of 'the Annex' to the Regulation (See para 1.17).
4 This is also understood to be confirmed by 'the Annex'; cf para 3 of 'the Annex' to the Regulation (See para 1.17).
5 [1986] RPC 421.
6 See *Smith, Kline & French Laboratories Ltd* [1976] RPC 511 at p 537.
7 At para 2.06.

'CAPABLE OF BEING REPRESENTED GRAPHICALLY'

2.3   There has been some discussion about other things which might, now or in the future, be held to be signs and therefore trade marks. In particular sounds, smells and tastes are mentioned in the Commission's Explanatory Memorandum on the Regulation.[1] The real issue, in such cases, would seem to be whether the 'sign' is capable of being represented graphically. What in particular should be required, it is suggested, is that the sign should be capable of being represented in such manner that other traders can see precisely what the trade mark is. Ultimately the courts, including the ECJ, will have to determine these questions. For the moment it is perhaps sufficient to say that there could well be sounds which are capable of graphical representation, for example by musical notation;[2] on the other hand, it is difficult to see how particular smells or tastes could be graphically represented. Attention should also be drawn to s 103(2) of the 1994 Act,[3] which greatly extends the meaning of 'use' of a mark beyond visual representations. It is difficult to see that, without such a provision, registration of a sound or a smell could have had any practical use.

---

1 Bulletin of the European Communities, Supplement No 5/80, para 56. This is understood to be confirmed by 'the Annex'; cf para 3(a) of 'the Annex' to the Regulation (see para 1.17), which states that Article 4 of the Regulation does not rule out the possibility of registering sounds as trade marks in the future; smells however are not mentioned.
2 Eg the first three notes of 'Three Blind Mice' could be represented either by the notes E, D and C shown on a musical stave, or even perhaps by 'Me-Ray-Doh'.
3 Introduced during the passage of the Bill through the House of Lords at Report Stage (HL Report, 24 February 1994).

THE FUNCTION OF A TRADE MARK

2.4   Some further comment is appropriate on the function of a trade mark under the new law. Although, as already mentioned (see paras 1.9 to 1.15) the traditional object of a trade mark was to denote the trade origin of goods, it was never necessary that the identity of the proprietor of the mark should be known.[1] This was expressly confirmed in the definition of a 'trade mark' in s 68(1) of the 1938 Act. There is no reason to suppose that the new law changes the position in this respect. The earliest trade mark statutes did not attempt to define a trade mark in terms of its function. It was defined for the first time in the Trade Marks Act 1905, s 3, which referred to use 'upon or in connection with goods for the purpose of indicating that they are the goods of the proprietor'; particular kinds of relationship with the goods (manufacture, selection, certification, dealing with, or offering for sale) were specified. The 1938 definition adopted the general term 'connection in the course of trade', which included all the kinds of connections previously specified. When the law was extended in 1986 to cover service marks, the definition of 'service mark'[2] required an indication 'that a particular person is connected in the course of business, with the provision of those services'. 'Provision' in this context was defined as 'provision for money or money's worth'; this itself gave rise to certain difficulties, which are mentioned below. The concept of distinguishing the goods or services of the proprietor from those of others was to be found in the requirements for a mark to be registrable.[3] Essentially, whatever the wording used, a trade mark or a service mark was an indication which enabled the goods or services from a particular source to be identified and thus distinguished from goods or services from other sources. In adopting a definition of 'trade mark' which simply describes the function in terms of capability of 'distinguishing the goods or services of one undertaking from those of other undertakings' the new law is really saying precisely the same thing.

1   See *Birmingham Vinegar Brewery v Powell* [1987] AC 710 at p 715, 14 RPC 720 at p 729 and 750; also
     the observations of Slade LJ in Re *Dee Corpn plc* [1990] RPC 159 at p 181 line 26 to p 182 line 4.
2   See para 2.1, note 1.
3   Trade Marks Act 1938, ss 9, 10.

'CAPABLE OF DISTINGUISHING THE GOODS OR SERVICES OF ONE UNDERTAKING FROM THOSE OF OTHER UNDERTAKINGS'

2.5   Although the words 'capable of distinguishing' are familiar enough to trade mark practitioners, in the context of the requirement for registration of a trade mark in Part B of the register under s 10 of the 1938 Act, the effect of the words in the new definition of a trade mark in the 1994 Act is significantly different. In the 1938 Act, the terms 'capable of distinguishing' and the corresponding requirement for a Part A registration in s 9 of being 'adapted to distinguish' were defined with reference not only to factual distinctiveness, acquired through use, but also to 'inherent' distinctiveness, which had to be present in the mark to at least some extent.[1] Successive decisions of the courts resulted in the conclusion[2] that the meaning of the references to the inherent qualities of the mark was that, in order to be registrable at all (however distinctive in fact) a mark must be adapted to distinguish or be capable of distinguishing (as the case might be) *in law*—a concept which businessmen have, not surprisingly, found hard to comprehend. This conclusion was equated with the requirement that the right to registration should—

> 'largely depend upon whether other traders are likely, in the ordinary
> course of their business and without any improper motive, to desire to
> use the same mark, or some mark nearly resembling it, upon or in
> connection with their own goods.'[3]

The intention of the Directive and the new law, in using the term 'capable of distinguishing' in place of the more complex wording of the 1938 Act, is to abolish the requirement that a mark be registrable in law. That is not to say that the interests of other bona fide traders will be ignored. The 1994 Act contains several provisions designed to safeguard honest traders in the use of non-distinctive matter and in certain other respects. These include the 'absolute grounds' for refusal of registration, set out in s 3, and other provisions set out in ss 10(6) and 11, limiting the effect of a registered trade mark. In future, subject only to the absolute grounds for refusal, any trade mark which is shown to be distinctive in fact will be regarded as distinctive in law and thus capable of registration.[4]

---

1 See *Yorkshire Copper Works Ltd v Trade Marks Registrar* (1956) 71 RPC 150, at p 156 per Lord Asquith and *Blue Paraffin Trade Mark* [1977] RPC 473 at p 501, per Buckley LJ.
2 See eg the decision of the House of Lords in *York Trade Mark* [1984] RPC 231 at p 254.
3 Per Lord Parker in *Trade Marks Registrar v W and G du Cros Ltd* [1913] AC 624, 30 RPC 660 HL, approved (eg) by Lord Diplock in *Smith, Kline & French.*
4 See the White Paper at para 3.08.

THE NATURE OF THE PROPRIETOR'S TRADE OR BUSINESS ACTIVITY

2.6   Another question, which arose under the previous law, was whether, in order to be trading in goods, or providing services in the course of business, there had to be any payment of money. The original 1938 Act said nothing about whether trading in goods must necessarily involve some kind of consideration, monetary or otherwise. Some decisions supported the view that there could be no trade in goods without there being some monetary consideration.[1] However the position changed following a decision of the Supreme Court of Ireland in *Golden Pages Trade Mark*,[2] in which the goods concerned were a classified telephone directory issued free of charge, the applicants receiving their revenues from the advertising, as did the applicants in *UPDATE*. Subsequently, it became the registrar's practice to accept that marks used for 'free' publications could be 'trade marks'. Nevertheless, it probably remained the case that there must be some monetary or equivalent consideration in order to constitute a 'trade', although it did not matter who provided such consideration. By contrast, the amendment to the 1938 Act in 1986, for service marks, introduced a specific requirement of 'money or money's worth' in the case of services. In *Re Dee Corpn plc*[3] the Court of Appeal held that this meant that the services have to be charged for as such. Accordingly, it was held, a mark could not be registered for 'retail services', although the Court of Appeal appeared to accept that 'retailing' could properly be described as a 'service' in the ordinary sense of the word. The definition of a trade mark in the new law, which only refers to the distinguishing of goods or services, and makes no mention of 'money or money's worth', or any other reference to consideration, seems to leave it open to argue that the position has now changed and that so long as there are 'services' in the ordinary sense of the word, marks can be registered for such services. It must be noted that in 'the Annex' to the Regulation, the opinion is expressed that 'the activity of retail trading in goods is not as such a service for which a Community trade mark may be registered'. However, it is thought that no such opinion is to be found in 'the Annex' and, as already suggested, these opinions are to be considered, at most, as guides, and are not necessarily binding on the courts, which have the task of construing the words of the Directive. This point is considered further (at para 5.3), in connection with classification.

---

1   See *'Hospital World' Trade Mark* [1967] RPC 595 (Registry) and *UPDATE Trade Mark* [1979] RPC 166 (Board of Trade, Douglas Falconer QC). In both cases the goods were printed publications distributed free of charge, but in *UPDATE* there was a difference, ie the applicants received revenue from the advertisers.
2   [1985] FSR 27.
3   [1989] 3 All ER 948, [1990] RPC 159.

2.7   Another aspect which needs mentioning, is the position of charities, which have sometimes had difficulty in registering trade marks and service marks under the 1938 Act. No problem ever seems to have arisen where a charity has established a separate trading 'arm', perhaps a company, selling goods. But in other cases, especially when the law was extended to services in 1986, there have been difficulties for the reasons already explained. However that may have been, there does not appear to be any special difficulty, under the 1994 Act, for charities in registering trade marks for goods or services.

3 Registrability

ABSOLUTE GROUNDS FOR REFUSAL OF REGISTRATION

3.1   The term 'absolute grounds' is derived from the Directive, and is also used in the Community Trade Mark Regulation. It does not mean that the grounds are all 'absolute' in the sense that they cannot be overcome, but simply denotes grounds which are related to the mark or application itself, as opposed to grounds based on conflict with rights of other parties. The absolute grounds for refusal, set out in s 3 of the 1994 Act, fall into six categories. The first category comprises the four basic grounds, directed primarily at a lack of distinctiveness, which may be applied to any kind of mark. The second category comprises objections applicable only to marks consisting of shapes of goods. The third relates to matters of public policy or morality, and deceptiveness. Fourthly, registration may be refused in the case of marks whose use is prohibited by law. The fifth category comprises certain other specified cases, called 'specially protected emblems'. Finally, there are grounds for objection in cases of applications made in bad faith.

THE BASIC GROUNDS

3.2   Section 3(1) sets out the four basic grounds on which any mark may be refused registration. This section adopts the wording of Article 3.1(a)–(d) of the Directive, and provides that the following shall not be registered—

'(a) signs which do not satisfy the requirements of section 1(1),
(b) trade marks which are devoid of any distinctive character,
(c) trade marks which consist exclusively of signs or indications which may serve, in trade, to designate the kind, quality, quantity, intended purpose, value, geographical origin, the time of production of goods or of rendering of services, or other characteristics of goods or services,
(d) trade marks which consist exclusively of signs or indications which have become customary in the current language or in the *bona fide* and established practices of the trade:

Provided that, a trade mark shall not be refused registration by virtue of paragraph (b), (c) or (d) above if, before the date of application for registration, it has in fact acquired a distinctive character as a result of the use made of it.'

The four grounds need to be considered separately. It should be noted that, although the words 'shall not be registered' are used, the proviso applies to grounds (b)–(d), so that ground (a) is the only one which is incapable of being overcome. The proviso follows the first part of Article 3.3 of the Directive; the second part, in so far as it says that member states may permit reliance on acquisition of distinctive character after the date of application for registration, has not been adopted here.

SIGNS WHICH DO NOT SATISFY THE REQUIREMENTS OF S 1(1)

3.3   This provision needs little further comment. If in some respect the requirements of s 1(1) are not met, for example if the 'sign' is not one which can be represented graphically, then it cannot be registered, regardless of any distinctive character which is claimed to have resulted from use. It may be that the provision can be applied to signs which are completely incapable of distinguishing the applicant's goods or services, although such cases would normally fall under s 3(1)(b).

TRADE MARKS WHICH ARE DEVOID OF ANY DISTINCTIVE CHARACTER

3.4   There is a statement in 'the Annex' to the effect that a trade mark is devoid of distinctive character if it is not capable of distinguishing the goods or services of one undertaking from those of other undertakings. This is not very helpful, being a repetition of the definition of a 'trade mark' in Article 2 and in s 1(1) of the 1994 Act, and thus seems also to involve some overlap with s 3(1)(a). Trade marks which are 'devoid of any distinctive character' will include the generic names of goods and words which are purely laudatory, such as 'good' and 'perfect', as well as descriptions such as 'all wool'. Other examples of marks which might be refused under this head include 'king size' for cigarettes, and perhaps very common surnames might be included. However, the wording of s 3(1)(b) should not be equated with the old concept of 'lacking in inherent distinctiveness'. For example marks which were refused under the 1938 Act as being mere phonetic equivalents of descriptive words, such as 'Orlwoola', may not necessarily be regarded as 'devoid of distinctive character'. Even if a mark does fall within this ground it will in many cases, if not in every case, be possible to obtain registration under the proviso on the basis of evidence of distinctiveness acquired as a result of use.

SIGNS DESIGNATING CHARACTERISTICS OF GOODS OR SERVICES

3.5   Section 3(1)(c) covers many signs which were excluded under s 9(1)(d) of the 1938 Act, as being marks having 'direct reference to the character or quality' of the goods or services, or being according to their ordinary signification, geographical names, including such marks which, under the 1938 Act, would have been rejected as being non-distinctive in law. However the word 'exclusively' should be noted. Composite marks, such as labels, will not be excluded by this provision although, while disclaimers of non-registrable matter will not now be required by the registrar by virtue of s 13, registration will by no means necessarily give rights to the non-registrable matter. If the mark consists exclusively of a sign of any of the kinds specified, or if such a sign is in essence the mark sought to be registered, then it will nevertheless be open to the applicant to file evidence in order to obtain registration under the proviso, by proving acquired distinctiveness. It should be noted that surnames are not specifically mentioned; as they would not usually be considered to designate any 'characteristics' of goods or services, it is difficult to see how there is any real scope for refusing registration of surnames under this head.

'GENERIC' SIGNS

3.6   Section 3(1)(d) is intended to enable applications for signs which have become generic or have come into general use in the trade to be refused. Such signs may be signs which have always been generic, as well as those which may once have been exclusively used by the applicant. An important point is that the words 'of the trade' appear to qualify the words 'which have become customary in the current language', as well as 'the bona fide and established practices'. Thus where, as not infrequently happens with some well-known trade marks which were first adopted for a new product, a trade mark is 'misused' by members of the public in the sense of being used as the name of the product, it is not thought that such a mark is to be regarded as being 'customary in the current language' for the purposes of s 3(1)(d). Only if the trade mark falls into descriptive use in the trade, for example through failure on the part of the proprietor to police it effectively, should the registrar be entitled to refuse registration under this provision. Although, as already indicated, the objection is subject to the proviso enabling it to be overcome by evidence of acquired distinctive character, the nature of the objection is such that it may well be very difficult to overcome in practice, unless of course the effect of the evidence is to demonstrate that the original objection was in fact unfounded. Again the word 'exclusively' indicates that composite marks incorporating such signs can be registered.

THE PROVISO—ACQUIRED DISTINCTIVE CHARACTER

3.7   It is expected that the registrar will lay down guidelines as to the way in which these grounds will be applied and as to what amount of acquired distinctive character is necessary to bring a case within the proviso. To some extent this will inevitably depend upon the facts of each case, in particular the nature of the mark and the goods and services concerned. Clearly an applicant will have some difficulty if he cannot prove distinctive character acquired through use *as a trade mark*. However, it seems unlikely that applicants will have to go as far, in every case, as was often necessary under the 1938 Act. The filing of a main declaration of use may well suffice in many cases, and the requirement of filing extensive trade evidence may be found to be the exception, particularly bearing in mind that the requirement of 'inherent' capability of distinguishing no longer exists.

3.8   One question which may arise from time to time, but which is not specifically covered by the Act, is whether the registrar can take into consideration, in favour of an applicant, the fact that he has a previous registration of the same mark for similar goods or services, or a similar mark for the same or similar goods or services. Under ss 9(3)(b) and 10(2)(b) of the 1938 Act, such matters could be taken into account as 'other circumstances'. Where, for example, an application is for a sign such as a label or a logo, or some other combined mark which incorporates a well established mark which is already on the register in the name of the applicant, there can be little if any justification, for requiring the applicant to file voluminous evidence of acquired distinctive character. In some instances, which would usually be cases involving objections under s 3(1)(b) or (c), the prior registration may properly be regarded as an indication that the mark is not 'devoid of distinctive character' or that the sign is not such as 'may serve, in trade', to designate any characteristics of the goods or services. Alternatively the existence of the registration, which may well have been obtained by filing evidence of use, may enable the registrar to allow the new application on the basis of a formal short declaration confirming that use has continued since the date of the existing registration.

OBJECTIONS RELATING TO SHAPES OF GOODS AND THEIR PACKAGING

3.9   Section 3(2) of the 1994 Act, the wording of which follows Article 3.1(e) of the Directive, contains grounds for objection which relate to marks which consist of shapes of goods; it provides that—

> 'a sign shall not be registered as a trade mark if it consists exclusively of—
>> (a) the shape which results from the nature of the goods themselves,
>> (b) the shape of goods which is necessary to obtain a technical result, or
>> (c) the shape which gives substantial value to goods.'

Again, as with s 3(1)(c) and (d) the word 'exclusively' should be emphasised. Marks are not precluded from registration under these provisions where they comprise a combination of a shape with other matter such as words or devices. It should be noted that, although these provisions do not apply in terms to the shape of packaging, the matter may not be as straightforward as that. On this point, a statement in 'the Annex' says that, where goods are packaged, the expression 'shape of goods' includes the shape of the packaging.[1] Even in the absence of such a statement, the courts would probably apply s 3(2) to 'packaging' that comprised a container that was an essential part of the 'goods' in the sense that they could not be marketed other than in a container. Beverages provide an obvious example.

---

[1]   Cf para 4 of 'the Annex' to the Regulation (See para 1.17).

3.10   It should be observed that an application must be refused if the shape in question falls within any of paras (a)–(c). The objection, if well-founded, cannot be overcome by proving acquired distinctive character, although evidence will be permissible to show that the ground of objection is not applicable. Under s 3(2)(a) an ordinary shaped bottle or other container, required to contain a liquid product, might be regarded as a shape which 'results from the nature of the goods themselves'; so also might a basic handle of an utilitarian article, such as a tool. On the other hand a container of distinctive appearance would not be so regarded. Under s 3(2)(b) the important word seems to be 'necessary'; if the product or container can be made in a number of possible shapes, as well as that claimed by the applicant, and still have the same function, it would seem that the shape was not one which resulted from the nature of the goods and was therefore not 'necessary' to achieve a technical result. The third ground of objection, contained in s 3(2)(c), is not so straightforward to apply. It would appear to be contrary to the purpose of the Directive to exclude shapes under this head merely because they are more attractive to customers, and which might in a sense be said to give 'substantial value to the goods'. It may be that the objection is to be understood as applying to something that makes a product a better product, in the functional sense. In general, looking at the overall purpose of the provisions, it may be suggested that what is intended to be excluded is the basic or fundamental shape of an article, even if it is capable of being made in other shapes. On the other hand, a shape adopted for the purpose of distinguishing goods, ie to serve the function of a trade mark, should not be refused on this ground.

3.11   Finally, it should be emphasised that objections to applications for shapes of goods and containers are not necessarily confined to the grounds set out in s 3(2). In cases in which the shape is essentially the fundamental shape of an article, or the goods are of a kind in which there is not much difference in design as between different manufacturers, objections might be raised, for example, under s 3(1)(a) on the ground of incapability of distinguishing or under s 3(1)(b) on the ground that the shape is devoid of distinctive character.

MARKS CONTRARY TO PUBLIC POLICY OR MORALITY, AND DECEPTIVE MARKS

3.12   Section 3(3) provides that a trade mark—

'shall not be registered if it is—
(a) contrary to public policy or to accepted principles of morality, or
(b) of such a nature as to deceive the public (for instance as to the nature, quality or geographical origin of the goods or service).'

In some respects this provision is quite similar to s 11 of the 1938 Act, for example, to the extent that objections under it were raised by the registrar at the examination stage. Section 11 prohibited the registration of marks 'the use of which would be disentitled to protection in a court of justice, by reason of its use being likely to deceive or cause confusion or otherwise, or would be contrary to law or morality'. Also excluded was 'any scandalous design'. Some marks were refused registration on the ground of deceptiveness as to such matters as the nature of the goods,[1] but objections of this kind were usually readily overcome by evidence of use, without any deception occurring, or any complaint being made, for example, under consumer legislation. The same is likely to be the case under the 1994 Act. A few applications were also refused under the 1938 Act provision, it seems, as being contrary to morality,[2] although in some of the cases it is not always clear whether refusal was on that ground or merely in the exercise of the registrar's discretion, which (for the purpose of refusing registration other than on the grounds set out in the 1994 Act) now no longer exists. In practice it is unlikely that this provision will be applied very often, and it may be that the ECJ will adopt a fairly broad minded approach.

---

[1]   See eg *CHINA-THERM Trade Mark* [1980] FSR 21.
[2]   See eg *Hallelujah Trade Mark* [1976] RPC 605. 'Jesus' is understood to have been refused for jeans on this ground; also 'Orgasm' and 'Poison' for perfume.

MARKS, THE USE OF WHICH IS CONTRARY TO LAW

3.13   Section 3(4) prohibits registration of a trade mark 'if or to the extent that its use is prohibited in the United Kingdom by any enactment or rule of law or by any provision of Community law'. UK enactments, which may be relevant for this purpose, include various consumer protection statutes, such as the Trade Descriptions Act 1968, and certain statutes implementing international obligations, such as the Anglo-Portuguese Commercial Treaty Acts 1914 and 1916, the "Anzac" (Restriction on Trade Use of Word) Act 1916 and the Geneva Conventions Act 1957. 'Rule of law' could perhaps cover a common law rule, although it is difficult to identify any such rule as might apply here; for example it probably is not intended to exclude a trade mark the use of which might constitute passing off, since that would come under 'relative grounds' for refusal, considered in Chapter 4 below. Also included among 'rules of law' for this purpose might be subordinate legislation such as statutory instruments. The term 'any provision of Community law' is potentially very broad, covering not only the Treaty of Rome and the subsequent treaties, but also the many Directives and Regulations adopted by the Council. So far as trade marks are concerned, particular instances which come to mind include the wine regulations[1] and the recent Regulation 'on the protection of geographical indications and designations of origin for agricultural products and foodstuffs'.[2]

---

[1]   See eg Council Regulation 823/87, applied by the Court of Appeal in the 'Elderflower Champagne' case *Taittinger SA v Allbev Ltd* [1993] 2 CMLR 741, [1993] FSR 641.
[2]   Council Regulation 2081/92/EEC: OJ L208, 24.7.92, p 1.

SPECIALLY PROTECTED EMBLEMS

3.14   Section 3(5) provides that a 'trade mark shall not be registered in the cases specified, or referred to, in section 4, (specially protected emblems)'. Under the 1938 Act, the main provisions for refusal of registration of marks in these categories were contained in the Trade Marks and Service Marks Rules 1986 (SI 1986/1319), rr 16–18. Under the 1994 Act the main provisions are to be found in the Act itself. The categories of emblems are set out in detail in s 4, subsection (3) of which in turn refers to ss 57 and 58. It is not necessary to set out the provisions of any of the sections in detail here; they appear in Appendix 1.

3.15   Section 4(1) is concerned with trade marks consisting of or containing the Royal arms or other matters suggesting Royal patronage or authorisation, including representations of the Royal crown or any of the Royal flags, representations of Her Majesty or other members of the Royal family. Registration of such marks is prohibited unless it appears to the registrar that the appropriate consent has been given.

3.16   Section 4(2) prohibits registration of trade marks consisting of or containing any representation of the 'Union Jack' or the flags of England, Wales, Scotland, Northern Ireland or the Isle of Man, but only if it appears that the use of the trade mark would be 'misleading or grossly offensive'. No guidance is offered as to the meaning of these words, but it is not thought that they are likely to be applied in many cases. The giving of consent is not mentioned, but may presumably have some bearing on whether the use would in fact be misleading or grossly offensive.

3.17   The provisions of ss 57 and 58, referred to in s 4(3), are included in compliance with the UK's obligations under Article 6ter of the Paris Convention, and relate respectively to national emblems, official signs and hallmarks of Convention countries and to emblems, abbreviations and names of certain international intergovernmental organisations. Section 59 imposes certain conditions which must be met before the restrictions of ss 57 and 58 can be invoked. In the case of s 57, the country in question must notify the UK, in accordance with Article 6ter(3) of the Convention, that it desires to protect the emblem, sign or hallmark in question, the notification must still be in force, and any objection to the notification must have been withdrawn. The same conditions apply as to notifications for the purposes of s 58, in respect of the emblems, abbreviations and names of the international organisations in question. In either case, notifications have effect only in relation to applications for registration made more than two months after receipt of the notification. Section 59(4) requires the registrar to keep and make available for public inspection a list of the state emblems, abbreviations and hallmarks, and the emblems, abbreviations and names of international organisations, which are for the time being protected by virtue of notification under Article 6ter(3).

3.18   Section 4(4) contains a power to provide by rules for the prohibition, in such cases as may be prescribed, of the registration, without the appropriate consent, of a trade mark consisting of, or containing, personal arms or insignia so nearly resembling such arms as to be likely to be mistaken for them. It is expected that the new rules will simply enact the provision as such.

APPLICATIONS MADE IN BAD FAITH

3.19   Section 3(6) requires registration to be refused 'if or to the extent that the application is made in bad faith'. This provision is based upon Article 3.2(d) of the Directive, but neither there, nor anywhere in the 1994 Act, is there any actual indication of what is 'bad faith' for these purposes. The term is capable of covering cases in which the applicant seeks to register a trade mark which he knows does not belong to him, although such cases may well be covered by s 5[1] or by the provisions of s 60 relating to 'acts of agent or representative'. The registry itself has said that applications made without any bona fide intention to use the mark applied for would be covered by s 3(6). In this connection, it is to be noted that s 32 (Application for registration) requires an applicant to state that the trade mark is being used by the applicant or with his consent, in relation to the goods or services concerned, or that he has a bona fide intention that it should be so used; also that s 47(4) gives the registrar himself the right to apply to the court for a declaration of invalidity in case of bad faith in the registration of a trade mark. It is likely that applications for registration of 'ghost' trade marks,[2] with a view to securing protection against the use of some other mark, would be regarded as having been made in bad faith within the meaning of s 3(6).

---

[1]   See s 6(1)(c) and s 56, relating to 'well-known' trade marks.
[2]   See eg the NERIT case, *Imperial Group Ltd v Philip Morris & Co Ltd* [1982] FSR 72, CA.

4 Conflict with earlier rights

RELATIVE GROUNDS FOR REFUSAL

4.1   The term 'relative grounds', ie those grounds on which a trade mark may be refused registration, is derived from the Directive and refers to grounds based upon some conflict with the rights of another party. These grounds are set out in s 5 and are based either upon an 'earlier trade mark' or on some other 'earlier right'. Under the 1994 Act, for the time being at least, such grounds for refusal may be raised not only in opposition proceedings but by the registrar himself as was the case under the 1938 Act. A very important change however is that, under s 5(5), the registrar cannot now refuse registration on any relative ground if the proprietor of the earlier trade mark or other earlier right concerned consents to the registration. Previously the registrar may have taken consent into consideration, but was never bound by it. Section 8 should be mentioned here, although by virtue of subsection (5), the powers conferred by it cannot be invoked until after the end of the period of ten years from the day on which applications for Community trade marks may first be filed. It will be possible then for the Secretary of State to provide, by statutory instrument (subsections (1), (5)), that registration of a trade mark may not be refused on relative grounds, other than following opposition by the proprietor of the earlier trade mark or other earlier right. Unless and until that happens, the registrar is obliged to examine applications and for that purpose to carry out a search of earlier trade marks, although it should be noted that the latter obligation is qualified by the words 'to such extent as he considers necessary'.[1] It remains to be seen what searches the registrar will carry out, and there may be practical limits beyond which he cannot search. There may well be a need for proprietors of earlier trade marks to be more vigilant than before.

---

[1]   Section 37(2): see para 5.7.

MEANING OF 'EARLIER TRADE MARK'

4.2   The earlier trade marks, on which refusal of registration under s 5 may be based, are defined in s 6. Under s 6(1) these are: (a) a registered trade mark, an international trade mark (UK)[1] and a Community trade mark (as defined in s 51), all of which must have an application date earlier than that of the trade mark applied for (taking into account priorities claimed, where appropriate); (b) a Community trade mark having a valid claim to seniority from an earlier registered trade mark or international trade mark (UK), and (c) a trade mark which, at the date of application (or priority claimed) was entitled to protection under the Paris Convention as a well-known trade mark (see s 56). Also included, under s 6(2), are trade marks which have been applied for and which, if registered, would be earlier trade marks under subsection (1)(a) or (b), but subject to being so registered. Presumably, where a ground for refusal relied upon is based on an application, the application under objection will be suspended until the earlier application is finally granted, after which the refusal could be confirmed. Under subsection (3), where an earlier trade mark under subsection (1)(a) or (b) has expired, it remains a possible basis for refusal for a year, unless the registrar is satisfied that there was no bona fide use of the mark in the two years before the expiry.

---

[1] A trade mark entitled to protection in the UK under the Madrid Protocol—see s 53.

REFUSAL BASED ON 'EARLIER TRADE MARKS'

4.3   It should be noted that the grounds for refusal based upon earlier trade marks, set out in s 5(1)–(3), are reflected in the definition of infringement in s 10(1)–(3). Thus, where registration is refused on the ground of conflict with an earlier registered trade mark, or an international trade mark (UK), there will also be infringement. That was not always the case under the 1938 Act. There are three different situations in which registration must be refused, unless consent is given by the proprietor of the earlier trade mark. The first is where the trade mark applied for is identical to the earlier mark and the goods or services are identical to those for which the earlier mark is protected. If the specifications are not identical, the objection will apply to the items which are the same. In these cases there is no need for any likelihood of confusion.

4.4   The second situation is that in which the trade marks are the same or similar, and the goods or services are the same or similar, to those for which the earlier trade mark is protected. The word 'protected' is used in subsections (1) and (2) to cover the case of a well-known trade mark, which is necessarily not registered in the UK. Under subsection (2), refusal can only be justified where there exists a likelihood of confusion on the part of the public, which includes the likelihood of association with the earlier trade mark. Several points need to be made regarding the application of subsection (2). First of all, the likelihood of confusion has to be determined in the light of all the relevant factors, which include the identity or similarity of the marks and the identity or similarity of the goods or services. Under the 1938 Act, if the mark applied for was identical or confusingly similar to the earlier trade mark and there was the required overlap of goods or services,[1] then registration would be refused. There is no guidance as to when marks are similar, or as to when goods or services are to be regarded as 'similar'. Although it has been suggested that the question of the similarity of goods and services should be determined in the same way as the question, under the 1938 Act, as to whether the goods or services are 'of the same description'[2] as any of those covered by the earlier trade mark, it may be doubted whether this is necessarily the right approach. There is also the question of similarity between goods and services. It is understood that there is a statement in 'the Annex' to the effect that for the purposes of Articles 4(1)(b) and 5(1)(b) of the Directive which are essentially the same as ss 5(2) and 10(2) of the 1994 Act), goods may be considered to be similar to services in appropriate circumstances. This seems to a reasonable interpretation of the words used. What the new provisions require is an appraisal of the likelihood of confusion of the public in all the circumstances of each case, rather than considering the separate questions, whether the marks, or the goods or services, are 'similar'. The nature of the mark is clearly a relevant factor; there is in general a greater likelihood of confusion in the case of more distinctive marks. The reference to 'likelihood of association' may also be important. According to 'the Annex' this is a concept which in particular has been developed by Benelux case-law.[3] In fact, it is understood that the concept has been developed in infringement cases, there having been no provision for refusal or opposition on relative grounds under the Benelux law. In one leading case,[4] the Benelux Court of Justice stated that—

> 'There is similarity between a mark and a sign when, taking into account the particular circumstances of the case, such as the distinctive power of the mark, the mark and the sign, each looked at as a whole and in correlation, show such a resemblance phonetically, visually or conceptually that by this resemblance alone, associations between the sign and the mark are evoked.'

A good example of this approach is a decision of the Dutch Supreme Court,[5] in which it was decided, applying the concept of likelihood of association, that 'Anti-Monopoly' (used for a game) was an infringement of the registration of 'Monopoly', because of the simple fact that the public, when seeing or hearing 'Anti-Monopoly' in connection with a game, would think of 'Monopoly'.

---

1 Ie goods or services the same or of the same description, or goods and services 'associated'—see the Trade Marks Act 1938, (as amended), s 12.
2 See in particular the decision of Romer J in *Jellinek's Application* (1946) 63 RPC 59, which was generally used as being the correct approach.
3 Cf para 5 of 'the Annex' to the Regulation (see para 1.17).
4 Decision of 20 May 1983, case nr A 82/5, Nederlandse Jurisprudentie 1984, 72 *Henri Julien BV v Norbert Verschuere.*
5 Decision of 24 June 1977, Nederlandse Jurisprudentie 1978, 83, *Edor Handelsonderneming BV v General Mills Fun Group.*

4.5   In the third situation, under s 5(3), an application to register a trade mark will be refused (again, in the absence of consent from the proprietor of the earlier trade mark) if it is identical with, or similar to, the earlier mark, notwithstanding that the goods or services are not similar to those covered by the earlier mark, if or to the extent that, the earlier trade mark has a reputation in the UK (in the case of a Community trade mark, in the European Community) and the use of the mark applied for, being 'without due cause would take unfair advantage of, or be detrimental to, the distinctive character or the repute of the earlier trade mark'. It appears from these words, that this provision is concerned with what, in some jurisdictions, is sometimes called 'dilution' of trade marks. The purpose of the words 'without due cause' is not clear; they may simply mean in the absence of authority, such as some form of licence, or perhaps the absence of some otherwise legally justifiable reason for adopting the mark for the goods or services in question. The requirements of unfair advantage or detriment raise questions which will essentially be questions of fact. Clearly the nature of the earlier mark will be a significant factor. It is thought that the provision does not require proof of any particular degree of reputation. What has to be considered in each case is whether, having regard to the marks themselves and to the nature of the goods or services covered by the earlier mark and by the application, the reputation of the earlier mark is such that either of the consequences, of unfair advantage or detriment, can be expected to follow.

REFUSAL BASED UPON OTHER EARLIER RIGHTS

4.6   Section 5(4) provides that a trade mark shall not be registered—

> 'if, or to the extent that, its use in the United Kingdom is liable to be prevented—
>> (a) by virtue of any rule of law (in particular, the law of passing off) protecting an unregistered trade mark or other sign used in the course of trade, or
>> (b) by virtue of an earlier right other than those referred to in subsections (1) to (3) or paragraph (a) above, in particular by virtue of the law of copyright, design right or registered designs.'

A person thus entitled to prevent use of the mark is referred to as the proprietor of an 'earlier right'. Section 5(4)(b) needs no comment, and probably represents no change in the law.[1] Section 5(4)(a) however, is significantly narrower than the ground for objection based upon prior use of a conflicting mark under s 11 of the 1938 Act. As was clear from the authorities, in particular the decision of the House of Lords in *Bali Trade Mark*,[2] it was not necessary for an opponent, or applicant for rectification, relying on s 11 of the 1938 Act, to make out a passing off case. Established use of the conflicting trade mark, even over quite a short period, was sufficient. Section 5(4) serves to underline the importance of registering trade marks under the 1994 Act.

---

[1]   See *'Karo Step' Trade Mark* [1977] RPC 255, decided under s 11 of the 1938 Act.
[2]   [1969] 2 All ER 812, [1969] RPC 472.

HONEST CONCURRENT USE

4.7   The UK concept of 'honest concurrent use' in s 12(2) of the 1938 Act, which could be invoked by applicants to register marks where there was an objection based on an earlier registration, is not mentioned in the Directive and had no place in the Bill as originally published. However as a result of representations made at a later stage a new clause, now s 7, was introduced, to allow reliance on honest concurrent use to a limited extent. It applies to any case in which there is an objection under s 5(1), (2) or (3) based on an earlier trade mark and to cases in which the objection is based upon another earlier right, under s 5(4). Where honest concurrent use (which by subsection (3) is such use, by the applicant or with his consent, as would have amounted to honest concurrent use of the purposes of s 12(2) of the 1938 Act)[1] is established to the satisfaction of the registrar, the registrar cannot refuse registration by reason of the existence of the earlier trade mark or other earlier right, 'unless objection on that ground is raised in opposition proceedings by the proprietor of that earlier trade mark or other earlier right'. The words quoted from subsection (2) show that the provision is likely to be of rather limited practical use, unless the owner of the earlier right fails to see the publication of the application in time to oppose and allows more than five years to pass before seeking a declaration of invalidity under s 47(2).[2] This last point is emphasised by subsection (4), which also says that refusal on absolute grounds is unaffected. Furthermore, under subsection (5) the provision will cease to apply if there is a statutory instrument in force under s 8.[3]

---

[1] Previous decisions such as *Pirie's Application* (1933) 50 RPC 147 at p 294 per Tomlin J should be referred to—see also Kerly's Law of Trade Marks and Trade Names, 12th Edition, pp 10–18.
[2] See s 48 (effect of acquiescence) which is confined to acquiescence in use of a registered trade mark.
[3] See para 4.1.

---

5 The application for registration

THE APPLICATION

5.1   Section 32 contains provisions as to what information must be provided in the application form. In addition to the obvious particulars required by subsection (2) (which include a statement of the goods or services and a representation of the mark), subsection (3) (see para 3.19) requires that the application state that the trade mark is being used, by the applicant or with his consent, in relation to the goods or services, or that he has a bona fide intention that it should be so used. This represents a change in the practice followed under the 1938 Act in recent years, and is said to have been included because of the provision of the Directive (ie Article 3.2(d), which was implemented by s 3(6) of the 1994 Act), that an application may be refused registration if made in bad faith. Section 32(4) provides for the payment of an application fee and such class fees as may be appropriate. These will be provided for by rules under s 79. An important feature of the new law is that it will now be possible to apply to register a trade mark in a number of different classes of goods and services.

DATE OF FILING

5.2   Under s 33, the date of filing of an application is the date on which documents containing everything required by s 32(2) are furnished to the registrar; if the documents are furnished on different days, the filing date is the last of those days. Under subsection (2), references to the date of an application for registration are to the date of filing; this represents no change.

CLASSIFICATION

5.3   Under s 34(1) goods and services are to be classified, for the purpose of the registration of trade marks, according to a prescribed system of classification. The existing system, which will be prescribed, is the international classification under the Nice Agreement of 15 June 1957, as subsequently revised. Section 34(2) follows the 1938 Act in providing that any question as to the class within which any goods or services fall, is to be determined by the registrar, whose decision is final. It may be remarked that, at least arguably, this is to be understood as imposing an obligation on the registrar to allocate any 'goods' or 'service' to some class. If indeed there is such an obligation on the registrar, it could be material, for example, if any question arises regarding an application to register for 'retailing services' (see para 2.6), which are not currently listed in the international classification.

PRIORITY

5.4 Claims to priority of applications, based on applications made previously in other countries, are the subject of ss 35 and 36, the former being concerned with priority claimed from applications in countries which are parties to the Paris Convention and the latter relating to priority claimed from applications in other countries. For the purposes of s 35, a 'Convention country' is defined (in s 55) as a country, *other than the UK*, which is a party to the Paris Convention, and 'Convention application' is to be construed accordingly, as an application made in a 'Convention country'. A person who has duly filed a Convention application to register a trade mark has a right to priority for the purposes of registering the same mark under the 1994 Act for some or all of the same goods or services, for a period of six months from the date of filing of the first Convention application. Under subsection (4), a subsequent Convention application concerning the same subject as the first application filed in the same Convention country may serve as the first Convention application if, at the time of the subsequent application the previous application has been withdrawn, abandoned or refused, and has not yet served as a basis for claiming a right to priority. Under subsection (3), any filing which, in a Convention country is equivalent to a regular national filing, under its domestic legislation or an international agreement, is treated as giving rise to the right to priority. 'Regular national filing' is defined as meaning a filing which is adequate to establish the date of filing in the country concerned, whatever the fate of the application. If the application under the 1994 Act is made within the six-month period then, under subsection (2), the date of filing of the first Convention application is the relevant date for establishing which rights take precedence, and registrability is not affected by any use of the mark in the UK between the date of the first Convention application and the date of the application in the UK. It should be noted that by virtue of Sch 3, para 13, an application made after the commencement of the 1994 Act may claim priority from a Convention application made before commencement. Subsection (6) provides for the possibility of assignment or transmission of a right of priority, either with the application or independently. It may be observed that the definition of 'Convention country' mentioned above, excludes the possibility of claiming 'internal priority' on the basis of an earlier UK application.

5.5 In the case of s 36, provisions for conferring rights to priority are made by rules,[1] and can only be made in respect of the Channel Islands or a colony, or other countries which have entered into a treaty, convention, arrangement or engagement with the UK Government, for the reciprocal protection of trade marks.

---

1 It appears that the existing rules, ie the Trade Marks and Service Marks (Relevant Countries) Order 1986 (SI 1986/1303) as subsequently amended on a number of occasions, will continue in force. See the Interpretation Act 1978, ss 17(2)(b), 22(1), Sch 2.

5.6 In the case of applications filed before commencement in a relevant overseas country within the meaning of s 39A of the 1938 Act, which is not a Convention country, (a 'relevant overseas application') Sch 3, para 14 makes detailed provisions, which follow the provisions of s 35 of the 1994 Act.

REGISTRATION PROCEDURE

5.7   Section 37 requires the registrar to examine whether an application satisfies the requirements of the Act, including any requirements imposed by rules. For this purpose he must carry out a search of earlier trade marks. As already mentioned this is qualified by the words 'to such extent as he considers necessary'. It is not yet known how extensive the search will be, although it would seem that in practice the registrar is not generally going to be an a position to raise objections under s 5(3) (marks having a reputation), or of course, under s 5(4). If it appears to the registrar that the requirements for registration are not met, he must inform the applicant and give him an opportunity to make representations or to amend the application. If the applicant fails to satisfy the registrar, or to amend the application so as to meet the requirements, or does not respond within the time to be prescribed by rules, then the registrar must refuse the application. If the requirements are met, he will accept the application.

5.8   Under s 38 the next step, as under the 1938 Act, is for the application to be published in the Trade Marks Journal (see s 81). Section 38(2) provides that any person may give notice of opposition within the prescribed time from publication. It is expected that the period for opposition will be three months and will, in contrast to the position under the 1938 Act, be *non-extendable*. As before, the notice must be in writing and must include a statement of the grounds of opposition. Subsection (3) introduces a new practice, sometimes followed informally under the 1938 Act; after publication any person may, at any time before registration, make written observations to the registrar as to whether the mark should be registered. The registrar must inform the applicant of any such observations. A person making any such observations does not become a party to the proceedings.

5.9   Section 39(1) provides for withdrawal of the application, or restriction of the goods or services, at any time. Re-publication is required if the application has already been published. Subsection (2) makes provision for amendment of the application, but only in very limited respects, considerably narrower than under the pervious practice. The only amendments allowed are the correction of the applicant's name or address, errors of wording or copying, or obvious mistakes, but even then the amendment must not substantially affect the identity of the trade mark or extend the goods or services covered. In accordance with subsection (3) the rules will provide for publication of any amendment which affects the representation of the mark or the goods or services covered, and for objections by third parties claiming to be affected by the amendment.

5.10   Section 41 which relates to the registration of a series of trade marks and the division and merging of applications or registrations, contains some important new provisions (which will be implemented by rules). Registration of a series of trade marks was possible under s 21(1) of the 1938 Act; the definition of a series, in s 41(2) of the 1994 Act, is less detailed than the corresponding provision of the 1938 Act, simply specifying that the marks should 'resemble each other as to their material particulars and differ only as to matters of a non–distinctive character not substantially affecting the identity of the trade mark'. Probably there is no significant change involved here. The provisions for division will be particularly useful where application is made to register a series of marks and the registrar objects on the ground that the marks do not constitute a series within the meaning of the definition. Instead of deleting one or more of the marks, it will now be possible to divide the application into several applications. A registration can be similarly divided, which might be considered appropriate in the event of another party seeking a declaration of invalidity. Apart from these specific situations, the provisions for division and merging of applications and registrations introduce a welcome flexibility into the procedure. Further comment cannot be made until the details of the rules, to be made under subsection (3) are known.

5.11   As under the 1938 Act, once an application has been accepted and no notice of opposition has been given within the prescribed time, or all opposition proceedings are withdrawn or decided in the applicant's favour, s 40(1) provides that the registrar must register the mark unless it appears to him that the application was accepted in error. However, there is a material difference from the 1938 Act, in that the registrar can only come to the view that the application was accepted in error 'having regard to matters coming to his notice since he accepted the application'. It is likely that he cannot now change his mind, on the basis of a change of opinion as to the relevance of an earlier registered mark, because all registered marks are within his knowledge. Although there may be cases where new facts are discovered which go to registrability from the point of view of absolute grounds, there should generally be very much less scope, after acceptance, for one official in the registry to overturn a decision reached by another official. Subsection (2) provides that the appropriate fee must be paid before a trade mark can be registered; if it is not paid within the period prescribed the application is deemed to be withdrawn. Subsection (3) provides that the trade mark shall be registered as at the date of the application for registration, which is deemed to be the date of registration; this is the same as under the 1938 Act. Under subsection (4) the registration is published and a certificate of registration issued to the applicant.

CONVERSION OF APPLICATIONS PENDING AT COMMENCEMENT

5.12   Under Sch 3, para 10 applications made under the 1938 Act, pending at commencement, are dealt with under the old law. However the rule making powers under s 78 of the Act are exercisable in relation to such applications. Schedule 3, para 10(3) provides that the requirements for associated trade marks, under s 23 of the 1938 Act, are to be disregarded. Where an application under the 1938 Act, which is pending at the commencement of the 1994 Act, has not then been advertised under s 18 of the 1938 Act, Sch 3, para 11 provides that the applicant may give notice to the registrar, in the prescribed form, claiming to have the registrability of the mark determined in accordance with the provisions of the 1994 Act. The notice must be given no later than six months after commencement. The notice is irrevocable and has the effect that the application is to be treated as if made immediately after commencement. Although the original date is then lost, the effect of Sch 3, para 13 appears to be that priority, based upon a Convention application made not more than six months before commencement, is retained.

6 Registered trade marks and applications as rights of property

THE NEW PROVISIONS

6.1   In the past, there has been a fair amount of discussion as to whether a trade mark is a right of property. The 1994 Act finally settles the question. Section 2(1) states clearly that a registered trade mark is a property right obtained by registration of the trade mark under the Act. Section 22 states that a registered trade mark is personal property (in Scotland, incorporeal moveable property). Section 22 is followed by a series of provisions, in ss 23 to 26, which are concerned with registered trade marks as objects of property rights. Sections 28 to 31 relate to licensing. These provisions thus cover all aspects of the ownership of, and dealings with, trade mark rights. An important provision is s 27, which states that the provisions of ss 22 to 26 apply, with the necessary modifications, in relation to an application for the registration of a trade mark, as in relation to a registered trade mark. Under the 1938 Act the registrar would not record a new proprietor of a pending application, and recordal had to await registration; now there is no difficulty. One consequence of these provisions is that the use of a trade mark as a security interest, which was always a difficult and complex matter under the 1938 Act, is now much more straightforward, as far as the registry is concerned. The question, which parties considering accepting registered trade marks as security will always consider in each case, namely whether the trade mark is a sufficient security, is outside the scope of this guide.

CO-OWNERSHIP

6.2   Section 23 makes potentially quite significant changes in respect of co-ownership of registered trade marks. Under s 63 of the 1938 Act (as amended) joint registration was only possible where the relationship between the applicants was such that no one of them was entitled as between himself and the other or others of them to use it except (a) on behalf of both or all of them, or (b) in relation to an article with which both or all of them were connected in the course of trade or (as the case might be) services with the provision of which both or all of them were connected in the course of business. Section 23(1) states that where a registered trade mark is granted to two or more persons jointly, each of them is entitled, subject to any agreement to the contrary, to an equal undivided share in the registered trade mark; by s 27(2) this provision also applies to· cases of joint applications for registration. In the case of registrations in joint names under the 1938 Act, Sch 3, para 7 of the 1994 Act provides that s 23 shall apply, but so long as the relations between the joint proprietors are such as one described in s 63 of the 1938 Act, there is deemed to be an agreement to exclude the operation of subsections (1) and (3) of s 23. Subsection (2) applies the provisions that follow to cases of joint ownership; they impose some restrictions upon the exercise of rights by the joint owners. Under subsection (4), one co-proprietor cannot, without the consent of the other or others, licence the use of the trade mark or assign or charge his share in it (or in Scotland, cause or permit security to be granted over it). Subsection (5) ensures that, unless the leave of the court is given, all co-proprietors are parties to any infringement proceedings, and thus bound by any decision in the proceedings, although a single proprietor may apply for interlocutory relief. If a co-proprietor does not agree to be joined as a plaintiff, he must be made a defendant, although he will not be liable for any costs unless he actually takes part in the proceedings. However, it is clear from subsection (3) that, notwithstanding these restrictions, each co-proprietor may use the trade mark freely without reference to the other(s), unless they agree otherwise. In practice, there may well be risks involved if co-proprietors do exercise their rights independently of one another. This matter is considered in para 10.8.

ASSIGNMENT

6.3   In clear (and intentional) contrast with the position under the 1938 Act, the 1994 Act places no restrictions on the assignment of registered trade marks or applications for registration. Furthermore, where under the 1938 Act registered marks were 'associated' (under s 23), which prevented their assignment other than together, the associations are removed by the transitional provisions contained in Sch 3, para 2(3).[1] Section 24 (which as mentioned above applies also to applications for registration) provides, in subsection (1), that a registered trade mark is transmissible by assignment, testamentary disposition or operation of law in the same way as any other personal or moveable property, and whether in connection with the goodwill of a business or separately. Subsection (2) permits a partial assignment or transmission, limited to only some of the goods or services covered by the registration, and in relation to the use of the mark in a particular manner or in a particular locality. Under subsection (3) the assignment (or assent) must be in writing and signed by or on behalf of the assignor (or personal representative); it does not however need to be signed by the assignee or transferee. Except in Scotland,[2] the requirement may be satisfied where the assignor or personal representative is a body corporate, by the affixing of its seal. Subsection (4) confirms that the provisions apply to an assignment by way of security as in relation to any other assignment. Under subsection (5), a registered trade mark may be the subject of a charge (in Scotland, security) in the same way as other personal or moveable property. Finally, subsection (6) provides that nothing in the Act is to be construed as affecting the assignment or other transmission of an unregistered trade mark as part of the goodwill of a business. This confirms the common law position, that the transfer of the goodwill of a business included the trade marks used in the business. An 'unregistered' trade mark is still not assignable separately from the business in which it is used, although this of course does not apply to a trade mark which is the subject of a pending application, because of s 27.

---

1   This does not apply to a series of marks registered in a single registration.
2   As to which, see the Companies Act 1985, s 36B.

TRUSTS AND EQUITIES

6.4   Section 26 provides that no notice of any trust shall be entered in the register, and the registrar shall not be affected by any such notice. But this does not affect the enforcement of equities (in Scotland, rights) in a registered trade mark as for other personal or moveable property, subject to the provisions of the Act. Essentially this provision is the same as under s 64 of the 1938 Act, but, by s 27, is also expressly applied to applications for registration. The effect is that, if a situation arises where a proprietor or applicant for registration is to be regarded as holding the registration or application in trust for another party, then the trust can be enforced by that party against him, even though the there is no notice of the trust on the register.

LICENSING OF REGISTERED TRADE MARKS

The approach of the new law

6.5   The trade marks statutes before the 1938 Act made no provision for the licensing of registered trade marks. In 1938 the possibility was introduced of recording other parties, who were licensees although not so described, as 'registered users' of registered trade marks. Under s 28(4) of the 1938 Act some degree of control was required, by the proprietor over the use of the mark by the registered user, and if this was absent, the registrar might refuse to record the user, on the ground that to do so might tend to facilitate 'trafficking' in a trade mark.[1] In the case of *Bostitch Trade Mark*[2] it was held that the requirements of s 28 of the 1938 Act were only optional, not mandatory, so that use of a trade mark could be licensed; so long as the proprietor exercised sufficient control over the use, the registration of the mark was not invalidated. The 1994 Act repeals all the previous provisions, and places no restrictions on the licensing of registered trade marks. Although it is certain that the 1938 rules regarding 'trafficking' have been abolished,[3] it should not be assumed that licensing can never involve any risk to the validity of a registration of the licensed mark, and it may be that the new provisions relating to revocation (s 46—see para 10.8) mean that as much if not more care will need to be taken to ensure that use of a registered mark by a licensee is properly controlled.

1   See s 28(6) and eg *Holly Hobbie Trade Mark* [1984] RPC 329.
2   [1963] RPC 183.
3   See the White Paper, paras 4.40–4.43.

The basic provisions for licensing

6.6   Section 28(1) provides that a licence to use a registered trade mark may be general or limited. A limited licence may, in particular,[1] apply in relation to some but not all of the goods or services covered by the registration, or in relation to use of the mark in a particular manner or in a particular locality. The only formal requirement[2] (under subsection (2)) is that, in order to be effective, the licence must be in writing and signed by the grantor (the licensor). Except in Scotland,[3] this requirement may be satisfied, where the proprietor is a body corporate, by the affixing of its seal. It is to be noted that 'licence' is to be distinguished from mere 'consent' to the use of a trade mark, which for some purposes[4] may be oral or implied, as for instance between a holding company and a subsidiary. An important provision, in subsection (3), is that unless the licence otherwise provides, it is binding on a successor in title to the grantor's interest. It will generally be better, from a licensee's point of view, if his licence continues notwithstanding that the registered trade mark is assigned to a new proprietor. If the licensor does not want this to happen automatically, then he will have to ensure that the terms of the licence are drawn to provide otherwise. Subsection (3) further says that references in the Act to doing anything with, or without, the consent of the proprietor of a registered trade mark shall be 'construed accordingly'. This means that where a licence is binding on a new proprietor under the subsection, use of the mark by the licensee will be treated as being use by the new proprietor. Another new provision is subsection (4), which relates to sub-licensing, something which was discouraged under the 1938 Act.[5] Where the licence so provides, the licensee may grant a sub-licence. References in the Act (in particular ss 29–31) to licence or licensee include a sub-licence or sub-licensee. The Act makes different provision for exclusive and non-exclusive licences. For the purposes of the Act s 29 provides that 'exclusive licence' means a licence (whether general or limited) authorising the licensee to the exclusion of all other persons, including the grantor, to use the trade mark in the manner authorised by the licence. This follows what has long been understood as the meaning of 'exclusive licence' in relation to intellectual property rights. Section 29(2) should be noted; it states that an exclusive licensee has the same rights against a successor in title who is bound by the licence as he has against the grantor. This would however, seem to follow from s 28(3), whether the licence is exclusive or non-exclusive, but the provision is perhaps included to make it clear that the licence remains exclusive, after assignment of the registered trade mark, as against the new proprietor.

---

1   These words appear to be intended to have the same meaning as the Latin term 'inter alia', thus indicating that other kinds of limited licence are possible.
2   Apart from the registration of the licence, discussed at paras 6.11 to 6.15, which while being voluntary may generally be regarded as advisable.
3   As to which see the Companies Act 1985, s 36B.
4   Eg s 9 (infringement), s 12 (exhaustion of rights), s 46(1)(a) and (b) (revocation for non-use).
5   See s 28(12).

6.7   Schedule 3, para 9 makes it clear that ss 28 and 29(2) only apply to licences granted after the commencement of the Act. Therefore, if the parties wish to take advantage of any aspect of the new law, a new licence is required.

Exclusive licences

6.8   The Act creates much greater possibility for exclusive licensees to take their own action to protect their interests in the licensed trade mark, but the extent of their rights is dependent upon the terms of their licence. Section 31(1) provides that an exclusive licence may provide that the licensee shall have, 'to such extent as may be provided by the licence, the same rights and remedies in respect of matters occurring after the grant of the licence as if the licence had been an assignment'. The exclusive licensee is thereby entitled to bring infringement proceedings, against any person other than the proprietor, in his own name. Under s 103(1), 'infringement proceedings' includes proceedings for delivery up under s 16. Subsection (2) provides that the rights and remedies of the exclusive licensee are concurrent with those of the proprietor, and that references in the Act to infringement are to be construed accordingly. As would be expected, by virtue of subsection (3), any defendant to an action for infringement brought under these provisions can avail himself of any defence which would have been available to him if the action had been brought by the proprietor. Subsection (4) aims to ensure that the proprietor and the exclusive licensee, where their rights are concurrent, are bound by any decision. Neither may proceed with the action without the leave of the court, unless the other is joined as a plaintiff or added as a defendant (except for the purposes of the granting of interlocutory relief). Under subsection (5) the proprietor or licensee, if added as a defendant, is not liable for any costs unless he takes part in the proceedings. Subsection (6) contains further provisions requiring the court, in assessing damages, to take into account the terms of the licence and any pecuniary remedy already awarded or available to either of them in respect of the infringement. The reference to a remedy being 'available' would cover the case in which an inquiry as to damages or an account of profits had been ordered but no assessment had taken place. Subsection (6) also excludes the directing of an account of profits where there has already been a pecuniary remedy ordered in favour of the other party (whether an award of damages or an account of profits), and the court is required to apportion any profits between them, subject to any agreement between them. These provisions apply whether or not the proprietor and the exclusive licensee are both parties to the action; if they are not, the court is empowered to direct the one party to hold the proceeds of any pecuniary remedy on behalf of the other, to such extent as the court thinks fit. Subsection (7) makes separate provision in the case of an application for delivery up under s 16; the proprietor, before making an application, must notify an exclusive licensee having a concurrent right of action, and the licensee is entitled to apply to the court, which may make such order as it thinks fit, having regard to the terms of the licence. Finally, subsection (8) states that the provisions of subsections (4) to (7) have effect 'subject to any agreement to the contrary between the exclusive licensee and the proprietor'. To the extent that these provisions appear to be intended to ensure that any decisions regarding the registered trade mark are binding on both the proprietor and the exclusive licensee, and any assessment of damages or profits is made between all the parties (so as to avoid the possibility of defendants being made to pay twice over) the giving of a general right to the proprietor and licensee to nullify these provisions, either in the licence or by subsequent agreement, seems surprising. It remains to be seen how the courts will deal with any situations which may arise, where proprietors and exclusive licensees seek to exclude any of these provisions.

Licences in general

6.9   Section 30 contains general provisions concerned with the rights of licensees in cases of infringement. The relationship of these provisions with s 31, regarding the rights of exclusive licensees, is not clear. Subsection (1), which says that the section has effect with respect to the rights of a licensee in relation to infringement of a registered trade mark, continues by stating that the provisions 'do not apply where or to the extent that, by virtue of section 31(1) . . . the licensee has a right to bring proceedings in his own name'. However, subsection (7) seems, at first sight at least, to say the opposite. It says that 'the provisions of this section apply in relation to an exclusive licensee if or to the extent that he has, by virtue of section 31(1), the rights and remedies of an assignee as if he were the proprietor'. It has been suggested that the purpose of subsection (7) is to cover the position of the exclusive licensee as putative assignee (under s 31(1)) so that if, for example, he grants a licence to a third party the relationship between him and that third party is governed by the provisions of s 30(2)–(6). However, in spite of this possible explanation, it cannot be said that the matter is altogether clear.

6.10   Turning to the provisions of s 30(2)–(6) it is to be noted that, whereas in the case of s 31(1) the licence must make express provision for the exclusive licensee to have any of the rights there set out, s 30(2) entitles the licensee to take infringement proceedings in his own name in the circumstances set out, unless his licence (or any licence through which his interest is derived) provides otherwise. Thus, if the grantor does not wish the licensee to be in a position to take proceedings in his own name, he must ensure that the licence excludes the rights set out in s 30. The right given to the licensee by subsection (2) is to call on the proprietor to take infringement proceedings (which, by virtue of s 103(1), includes proceedings under s 16 for delivery up) in respect of any matter which affects the licensee's interests. By virtue of Sch 3, para 6, s 30 applies to licences granted before the commencement of the Act but only in respect of infringements committed after commencement. Under subsection (3), if the proprietor refuses to take proceedings or fails to do so within two months after being called upon, the licensee can bring proceedings in his own name, as if he were the proprietor. A significant difference between this provision and the similar provision in s 28(3) of the 1938 Act is that the right to take proceedings arises immediately if the proprietor expressly refuses to do so; previously, the licensee had in any event to wait until the end of the two-month period specified. As in the case of exclusive licensees, the non-exclusive licensee may not proceed with the action, without the leave of the court, unless the proprietor is joined as a plaintiff or added as a defendant. However, interlocutory relief may be granted on an application by the licensee alone and, in cases where the proprietor is joined as a defendant, subsection (5) will exempt him from costs unless he actually takes part in the action. Subsection (6) requires the court, in any infringement proceedings brought by a proprietor, to take into account any loss suffered or likely to be suffered by licensees; the court is also given power to give directions as to the extent to which the proprietor is to hold the proceeds of any pecuniary remedy on behalf of licensees.

REGISTRATION OF TRANSACTIONS AFFECTING REGISTERED TRADE MARKS

General observations

6.11   While dealings in registered trade marks, including assignment and licensing, have been made considerably easier, s 25 of the 1994 Act contains provisions for the registration of transactions affecting registered trade marks. While registration under s 25 is voluntary, it is clear that in practice there may be significant risks involved, or at least disadvantages of a financial nature, if a transaction is not registered.

Definition of registrable transaction

6.12   Registrable transactions are defined in s 25(2). They are—
        '(a)   an assignment of a registered trade mark or any right in it;
        (b)   the grant of a licence under a registered trade mark;[1]

> (c) the granting of any security interest (whether fixed or floating) over a registered trade mark or any right in or under it;
>
> (d) the making by personal representatives of an assent in relation to a registered trade mark or any right in or under it;
>
> (e) an order of a court or other competent authority transferring a registered trade mark or any right in or under it.'

As already mentioned, s 26 applies the provisions of s 25 to applications for registration.

---

1   Which includes a sub-licence.

Registration of the transaction

6.13   Under s 25(1) the persons who may apply to the registrar for particulars (which are to be prescribed by rules) of a registrable transaction to be entered in the register or, by virtue of s 27(3), give notice to the registrar of such particulars, are persons claiming to be entitled to an interest in, or under, a registered trade mark by virtue of a registrable transaction, or persons claiming to be affected by such a transaction. The transitional provisions in Sch 3 should be noted. Paragraph 8 makes provision regarding previously recorded assignments and pending applications to record assignments, treating them generally as if under s 25 of the 1994 Act. Under Sch 3, para 9(2) existing entries of registered users are transferred to the register and have effect as if made under s 25, and under Sch 3, para 9(3), pending applications to record registered users are also treated as applications to register under s 25.

The consequences of non-registration or delayed registration

6.14   Section 25(3) emphasises the importance of promptness in applying to register the particulars of a registrable transaction. Until that is done, the transaction is ineffective as against a person acquiring a conflicting interest in, or under, the registered trade mark in ignorance of it. Furthermore, any person claiming to be a licensee by virtue of the transaction does not have the rights and remedies which would otherwise be available to him under ss 30 and 31. The consequence of this provision is that, for example, if A assigns a registered trade mark to B and subsequently, before B has applied to register the assignment to him, A executes an assignment in favour of C, who was then unaware of the earlier assignment, then C will take free of B's interest, so long as he himself applies to register his title and does so before B applies. Or if X grants a licence to Y, who does not apply to register the licence, and then X assigns the registered trade mark to Z, Z is not bound by the licence to Y if at the date of the assignment to him Z was unaware of the licence. Although it might seem that s 28(3), which provides that a licence (unless it provides otherwise) is binding on a successor in title to the grantor's interest, conflicts with s 25(3), it would appear that the latter provision is intended to prevail. In the case of licensees' rights to take action in their own name under ss 30 or 31, the effect of s 25(3) is not so serious, although it is still advisable for licensees to apply to register their interests. Subsection (4) imposes a further disadvantage in infringement proceedings, on the person who becomes the proprietor or the licensee of a registered trade mark by virtue of a registrable transaction but fails to apply to register the particulars of the transaction within six months. Unless he satisfies the court that it was not practicable to apply before the end of the six month period and an application was made as soon as practicable thereafter, such person is not entitled to damages or an account of profits in respect of any infringement occurring after the date of the transaction and before the particulars of the transaction are registered. Clearly subsection (4) makes it advisable for an assignee or licensee to make the application to register within six months of the transaction, and subsection (3) will often dictate the making of the application even earlier.

Other provisions to be made by rules

6.15   Section 25(5) enables provision to be made by rules for the amendment of particulars relating to a licence, to reflect any alteration in the terms of the licence and for the removal of the particulars if the licence, being for a fixed period, appears to the registrar to have expired or where the registrar has notified the parties of his intention to remove the particulars after a prescribed period. Subsection (6) enables provision to be made for amendment or removal of particulars relating to a security interest on the application of, or with the consent of, the person who is entitled to the benefit of such interest.

TRANSITIONAL PROVISIONS

6.16   Schedule 3, para 9 makes provisions regarding licensees recorded as registered users under the 1938 Act or the subject of pending applications for recordal. Sections 28 and 29(2) of the 1994 Act apply only in relation to licences granted after commencement of the Act, and the 1938 Act continues to apply in relation to licences granted before commencement. Existing entries of registered users, under s 28 of the 1938 Act, are transferred to the register kept under the 1994 Act and have effect as if made under s 25 of the 1994 Act; the same applies to applications for registration as a registered user determined by the registrar before commencement but not 'finally determined' (meaning, presumably, not completed). Pending applications for recordal are treated as applications to register a licence under s 25(1). In cases where there is no written licence (such as would be required by s 28), for example if a company has applied to record a subsidiary as a registered user, it would seem that this provision will still have the effect that the application is to be treated as made under s 25(1), although there would have been no possibility of s 25 applying in the absence of a written license. Finally, pending applications for variation or cancellation of registered users, under s 28(8) or (10) of the 1938 Act, are to be dealt with under the old law, any necessary alteration being made to the new register.

7 Infringement of registered trade mark

RIGHTS CONFERRED BY REGISTERED TRADE MARK

7.1 Section 9(1) provides that the proprietor of a registered trade mark has 'exclusive rights' in the trade mark, which are infringed by the use of the trade mark in the UK without his consent. Consent, for this purpose, clearly does not have to be written, as would be required for a formal licence, and may for example be oral. Subsection (1) refers to s 10 for acts which constitute infringement if done without the proprietor's consent. Subsection (2) states that references in the 1994 Act to infringement are to any such infringement of the rights of the proprietor. As under the 1938 Act, the rights of the proprietor have effect from the date of registration, which by s 40(3), is the date of filing of the application for registration; however, no infringement proceedings may be commenced, and no offence can be committed under s 92 in respect of 'unauthorised use' (the anti-counterfeiting provision), until the trade mark is actually registered. It appears that it is a requirement that the trade mark is validly registered. Although it is not specifically stated (as it was in s 4(1) of the 1938 Act) in the case of revocation or invalidation it would seem to follow that, at the date with effect from which a registered trade mark is revoked or declared invalid there can be no infringement (see ss 46(6) and 47(6)).

7.2 A question that may arise under s 9 and certain other provisions of the 1994 Act, is whether 'proprietor' means registered proprietor or whether a person who is the beneficial owner of a registered trade mark (for example an assignee whose title has not yet been registered under s 25) may bring proceedings for infringement. Under s 4(1) of the 1938 Act the words used suggested strongly that only a registered proprietor could take proceedings for infringement. Section 9 is not so explicit, and may therefore be open to a different interpretation. Decisions under the 1938 Act[1] indicated that 'proprietor' was not restricted to a registered proprietor. This may not matter so much now as it is expected that assignments will be much more speedily registered, but could perhaps be important if a new proprietor wished to make an immediate application for an injunction.

---

1 Eg under the non-use provisions of s 26; the same question could also arise under the provisions of s 46(1)(a) and (b) relating to revocation for non-use.

WHAT CONSTITUTES INFRINGEMENT

Relationship with relative grounds for refusal of registration

7.3 As already mentioned in para 4.3, the provisions defining infringement of a registered trade mark in s 10(1)–(3) of the 1994 Act reflect the provisions for refusal of registration of a trade mark on the relative grounds set out in s 5(1)–(3), based on 'earlier trade marks'. The only difference is that the provisions in s 10 refer to goods or services for which the trade mark is registered, since the question of infringement only arises where there is a registered trade mark, and not where a trade mark is 'protected' in some other way. Subject to this, the observations in paras 4.3 to 4.5 apply equally to s 10(1)–(3).

'Use' of a sign for the purposes of infringement

7.4   Subsection (4) gives examples of 'use' of a sign for the purposes of these definitions of infringement. The words 'in particular' again seem to mean 'inter alia' and indicate that there may be other kinds of infringing use as well as those specified. The types of infringement specified are: affixing to goods or their packaging; offering or exposing goods for sale, putting them on the market or stocking them for those purposes under the sign; offering or supplying services under the sign, importing or exporting goods under the sign, or using the sign on business papers or in advertising. An important change in the law is effected by s 103(2), which makes it clear that the infringing use does not have to be visual, or 'graphical', but may for example be oral and may also, it would seem, include use by storing on a computer.

Infringement in relation to labelling or packaging materials

7.5   Subsection (5) contains a new provision under which a person who applies a registered trade mark to material intended to be used for labelling or packaging goods, as a business paper, or for advertising goods or services, is to be treated as a party to any use of the material which infringes the registered trade mark in certain circumstances. These circumstances are that when he applied the mark he knew or had reason to believe that the application of the mark was not duly authorised by the proprietor or a licensee. Each case will depend upon its own facts, but a printer of such material may well be found to have reason to believe that the application of the mark was not duly authorised if the order comes from someone who is clearly not the proprietor or some person who might reasonably be thought to be an authorised agent. This may be the case particularly where the trade mark is very well known, and 'one-off' orders may well be found to be a sufficient reason for believing that the application was not duly authorised. It should however be observed that this provision is of comparatively limited use because it only applies to application of the registered mark and does not cover use of even a very similar mark, unless perhaps the differences are so slight as not to be noticeable in the market place.

WHAT IS NOT INFRINGEMENT

General observations

7.6   The 1994 Act does not follow the basic definition of infringement in s 4(1)(a) and (b) of the 1938 Act in defining any particular manner of use which is necessary in order to constitute infringement. Instead the new law defines infringing use in quite general terms, as use of a 'sign', which is identical with or similar to the registered mark, but then adds a number of provisions which limit the scope of infringement under ss 9 and 10. Some of these are similar to the limitations on the scope of infringement under the 1938 Act, but others are new.

Use in relation to the 'genuine' goods or services of the proprietor or a licensee

7.7   Section 10(6) excludes, from the scope of infringement, use in relation to what have often been called the 'genuine' goods or services of the proprietor of a registered trade mark, or a licensee. Thus, it is similar in some respects to the corresponding provision in s 4(3)(a) of the 1938 Act, but extends into the area of 'comparative advertising', which is not covered in any other provision.[1] Section 10(6) provides that nothing in the preceding provisions is to be construed as preventing the use of a registered trade mark by any person 'for the purposes of identifying goods or services as those of the proprietor or a licensee'. However, there are limitations to the kind of use which is to be protected under this provision. The protection will be lost if two requirements are satisfied. If the use is 'otherwise than in accordance with honest practices in industrial or commercial matters', then it is treated as infringing, if also 'the use without due cause takes unfair advantage of, or is detrimental to, the distinctive character or repute of the trade mark'. The reference to honest practices in industrial or commercial matters is also found in s 11(2) (see para 7.9) which is in turn derived from Article 6.1 of the Directive. These words originate in Article 10bis(2) of the Paris Convention. The application of these words in s 10(6) will depend upon the facts of each case, and may well be affected by any 'codes of practice' adopted by, or evidence of customary practices followed in, any particular field of commerce. The second requirement echoes the 'anti-dilution' provisions of ss 5(3) and 10(3), and is itself derived from Article 5.5 of the Directive. The aim of identifying goods or services of the proprietor is not of itself illegitimate, and the particular use must not be 'without due cause', which itself may depend upon whether there is any 'unfair advantage' or 'detriment' as required by the subsection. It will be a question of fact, depending upon the nature of the mark, its reputation, and the nature of the goods or services, whether the use takes 'unfair advantage', or is 'detrimental' for these purposes. It may well be that these requirements will be linked with the idea of 'honest practices', thus introducing an overall concept of 'fairness' in the use of a registered trade mark of another party. It is suggested that the recent case of *Chanel Ltd v Triton Packaging Ltd*[2] may be regarded as providing a good example of the kind of conduct which would be excluded by s 19(6); in that case the trial judge, Millett J described the defendants' material as 'freighted with the goodwill attached to the [plaintiffs'] brand names'. It should be noted that the wording of subsection (6) only refers to the 'proprietor or a licensee'. It may not be apt to extend to other companies associated with the proprietor; if that is so, then this provision cannot be used as a basis for a finding of 'exhaustion of rights' as was the case under s 4(3)(a) of the 1938 Act,[3] unless perhaps it can (for example) be argued that goods or services of a subsidiary are really goods of the parent which is the proprietor.

---

1   There is a published draft proposal of an Amended proposal for a European Parliament and Council Directive dealing (inter alia) with comparative advertising—COM(94) 151 final—COD 343, 21.04.1994. It may be some time before any such Directive is adopted, if at all.
2   [1993] RPC 32 (Court of Appeal), affirming the decision of Millett J sub nom *Chanel Ltd v L'Arome (UK) Ltd* [1991] RPC 335.
3   As applied in *Revlon Inc v Cripps & Lee Ltd* [1980] FSR 85, CA.

Use of own registered trade mark

7.8   Section 11(1) needs little explanation. As under s 4(4) of the 1938 Act, a registered trade mark cannot be infringed by the use of another registered trade mark which is validly registered for the goods or services in question. The express reference to s 47(6), which provides that a declaration of invalidity has the effect that the registration (to the extent of the declaration) is to be deemed never to have been made, prompts the question why is there no reference to revocation under s 46? Whatever the reason, it would seem clear that s 11(1) cannot apply to any use of a previously registered trade mark, which takes place after it ceases to have effect.

Use of own name, etc and descriptive and other indications

7.9   Section 11(2), which is derived wholly from Article 6.1 of the Directive, is similar to provisions in s 8 of the 1938 Act protecting bona fide use by any person of his name or address, or bona fide use of a description of the character or quality of goods or services. Three categories of use are covered, namely (a) use by a person of his own name or address; (b) the use of indications of various characteristics of goods or services; (c) the use of the trade mark where it is necessary to indicate the intended purpose of a product or service (in particular as accessories or spare parts). Each category is governed by the overriding proviso that the use be 'in accordance with honest practices in industrial or commercial matters'. It is likely that this will be applied in much the same way as the requirements of bona fide use under the 1938 Act. Subsection (2)(a) is fairly straightforward. For example, use of a name in a manner similar to that used by the proprietor of the registered mark would not be regarded as meeting the requirements of the provision. Comment should be made on 'the Annex',[1] in which (it is understood) the view is expressed that 'his own name' applies only in respect of natural persons. Having regard to the rule in English law, that 'person' includes any body of persons corporate or unincorporate,[2] it seems most unlikely that the courts would accept the view expressed. Subsection (2)(b) is very similar to s 3(1)(c), providing for refusal of registration of descriptive matter. The reference to 'intended purpose' might seem, at first sight, to overlap with subsection (2)(c). However, it will probably be limited to such use in the sense of a description of the purpose, and not with reference to spare parts or accessories, which is covered by subsection (2)(c). The effect of the proviso on subsection (2)(c), which requires that the use be 'necessary' to indicate the intended purpose, is likely to be similar to the requirement in s 4(3)(b) of the 1938 Act that the use be 'reasonably necessary' to indicate the purpose.

---

1   Cf para 7 of 'the Annex' to the Regulation (See para 1.17).
2   See the Interpretation Act 1978, s 5, Sch 1.

Use of an earlier right applying only in a particular locality

7.10   Section 11(3) is derived from Article 6.2 of the Directive but does not use exactly the same wording, which is understood to have been aimed at a particular kind of local situation which arises in German law. It is not immediately obvious how the subsection will be applicable in the UK. It provides that a registered trade mark is not infringed by the use in the course of trade 'in a particular locality' of an earlier right which applies only in that locality. For this purpose an 'earlier right' is said to mean an unregistered trade mark or other sign continuously used by a person (or a predecessor in title of his) from a date which is prior to the earlier of, the use of the registered trade mark by the proprietor (or a predecessor in title), or the registration of the trade mark. The earlier right is regarded as applying in a particular locality if, or to the extent that, its use in that locality is protected by virtue of any rule of law (in particular, the law of passing off). It is thought that this provision is unlikely to apply to marks used for goods, since such use is not normally local in character, and may really only apply to marks used for certain services of a local nature, such as launderettes, public houses and village stores. It is fairly clear that the owner of the 'earlier right' would not be permitted to expand the area of use and still avoid infringement. In view of this, and the uncertainty as to the scope of this provision, it may well be advisable for owners of such rights to consider opposition to any application to register trade marks, which they may infringe.

Exhaustion of rights

7.11   As mentioned in para 7.7, whereas a doctrine of international exhaustion was developed in infringement cases under the provisions of the 1938 Act protecting use for 'genuine' goods or services of the proprietor, the new provisions of s 10(6) may not necessarily provide scope for the continued existence of such a doctrine where the goods or services emanate not from the proprietor of the UK mark or a licensee, but from another company in the same group. In infringement cases the exhaustion of the proprietors' rights may only arise in the circumstances specified in s 12 of the Act, which is expressly limited in its operation to use in relation to goods put on the market in the European Economic Area by the proprietor or with his consent. This will no doubt be applied to goods marketed by another related company, as well as goods of licensees. Section 12(2) makes an exception to the general principle of exhaustion, by providing that subsection (1) does not apply where there exist legitimate reasons for the proprietor to oppose further dealings in the goods. In particular, where the condition of the goods has been changed or impaired after they have been put on the market. Although this provision may have the same effect as previous rulings of the ECJ on the interpretation of Article 36 of the EC Treaty in parallel import cases,[1] (in particular in the repackaging cases involving pharmaceutical preparations), it is not yet clear whether in fact it does have the same effect. References have recently been made[2] to the ECJ by a Danish court (in three cases) and by a German court (in three cases) which are expected to result in rulings which will need to be considered and, if appropriate, applied, by the courts in the UK when a question arises under s 12. Although the doctrine of international exhaustion in infringement cases will now be rather narrower than before, for the reasons explained, and because s 12 is limited to the European Economic Area, the common law doctrine of exhaustion, as developed in relation to the law of passing off[3] remains basically unchanged.

1   See in particular Case 102/77: *Hoffmann-La Roche & Co AG v Centrafarm Vertriebsgesellschaft Pharmazeutischer Erzeugnisse mbH* [1978] ECR 1139, [1978] 3 CMLR 217 ECJ and Case 3/78: *Centrafarm BV v American Home Products Corpn* [1978] ECR 1823, [1979] 1 CMLR 326, ECJ.
2   Under Article 177 of the Treaty; Cases C-427/93, C-429/93 and C-436/93: *Bristol-Myers v Paranova* (from the Danish Court); Cases C-71/94, C-72/94 and C-73/94:, *Eurim-Pharm Arzneinmittel GmbH v Beiersdorf AG* (from the German Court).
3   See eg, para 7.7 and footnote 3 above, and *Champagne Heidseick et Cie Monopole SA v Buxton* [1930] 1 Ch 330, 47 RPC 28.

Disclaimers

7.12   Although, as appears from s 13, the registrar will no longer be able to insist on disclaimers of non-distinctive matter appearing in a trade mark which is sought to be registered, subsection (1) does provide for applicants for registration voluntarily to accept a disclaimer, or a territorial or other limitation. Such disclaimers and limitations are likely only to be accepted by applicants following opposition, as a result of a term of settlement of a dispute. However, disclaimers and limitations imposed under the 1938 Act will continue to apply (see the transitional provisions in Sch 3, para 3(2)). Where, whether under the 1938 or the 1994 Act, a registration is subject to a disclaimer, the rights of the proprietor are accordingly limited by s 13(1).

TRANSITIONAL PROVISIONS AFFECTING INFRINGEMENT

7.13   From the commencement of the 1994 Act, the transitional provision in Sch 3, para 4(1) provides that ss 9 to 12 (effects of registration) apply in relation to existing registered marks, and that s 14 (action for infringement) applies in relation to infringements committed after commencement. Paragraph 4(2) contains limited protection for continued use of a sign after commencement of the Act, if the use did not constitute an infringement under the 1938 Act. However, this is seriously limited because para 4(2) only protects the continued use from a claim of infringement in respect of either an existing registered trade mark (as defined in Sch 3, para 1), or a registered trade mark of which the distinctive elements are the same, or substantially the same, as those of an existing registered mark and which is registered for the same goods or services. The last mentioned part of the provision prevents a proprietor from circumventing the first part by simply re-registering under the new law. However, if the registered trade mark allegedly infringed is a mark which could not be, or was not in fact registered under the 1938 Act, then the transitional provision offers no protection to the continuing user, and he will be left to defend the claim on the basis that if there has been no confusion, or unfair advantage or detriment, arising from his previous use, then there is no likelihood of confusion, and no unfair advantage or detriment within s 10(2) and (3), as the case may be. It may in fact be doubted whether this provision complies with Article 5.4 of the Directive, which appears to be framed so as to protect continuing users against infringement claims in respect of any trade marks, whether registered before or after implementation of the Directive. However, it is to be hoped that courts will try to mitigate any unjust effects by making appropriate findings of fact in relation to claims for infringement. The only situation in which it would seem, this cannot be done, is where the mark, and the goods or services, are identical to those for which the trade mark is registered.

8 Remedies

THE REMEDIES AVAILABLE

8.1   Section 14, which provides that an infringement of a registered trade mark is actionable by the proprietor of the trade mark, states that all such relief by way of damages, injunctions, accounts or otherwise, is available to the proprietor as is available in respect of the infringement of any other property right. No special discussion of these remedies is necessary here. The rules regulating their grant or refusal will apply as before. Although the remedies available under s 14 will often be sufficient, s 15 of the 1994 Act also makes specific provision for certain remedies. These are considered below.

INFRINGING GOODS, MATERIAL AND ARTICLES

8.2   Section 17 contains a comprehensive definition of 'infringing goods', 'infringing material' and 'infringing articles' for the purposes of the various remedies provided by the Act. In order to be 'infringing goods', the goods or their packaging must bear a sign which is identical or similar to the registered mark. In addition, subsection (2) requires that one of three other conditions be satisfied, namely that the application of the sign to the goods or packaging was an infringement, or, where the goods are proposed to be imported, that the application in the UK would be an infringement, or that the sign has 'otherwise been used in relation to the goods in such a way as to infringe the registered trade mark'. The last mentioned condition would cover such matters as infringing use in business papers and advertising (see s 10(4)), and thus makes it possible for the remedies under the Act to be directed at goods or packaging which does not bear an infringing sign. By way of exception in the case of goods proposed to be imported, subsection (3) expressly preserves the freedom of importation of goods which may lawfully be imported into the UK by virtue of an enforceable Community right. Such a right would, in particular, arise under the rules contained in Articles 30 to 36 of the EC Treaty regarding the free movement of goods between member states of the Community.

8.3   Like 'infringing goods', 'infringing material' as defined in subsection (4), must bear a sign identical or similar to the registered trade mark. Furthermore, the sign must either be used for labelling or packaging goods, as a business paper, or for advertising goods or services, in such a way as to infringe the registered trade mark, or it must be intended to be so used, and it is necessary that such use would infringe. Under subsection (5), 'infringing articles' are articles 'specifically designed or adapted for making copies of a sign identical or similar' to the registered mark concerned and 'which a person has in his possession, custody or control, knowing or having reason to believe that they have been or are to be used to produce infringing goods or material'. This should be compared with s 10(5) (see para 7.5); although in similar terms, s 17(4) is broader in that the sign need not be identical to the registered mark, but may be similar. This may have the effect that a person can be ordered under s 16 to deliver up infringing material although he himself is not an infringer.

ORDER FOR ERASURE, REMOVAL OR OBLITERATION OF OFFENDING SIGNS

8.4   Section 15 makes specific provisions giving the court power to order a person found to have infringed a registered trade mark to cause the offending (ie infringing) sign to be erased, removed or obliterated from any infringing goods, material or articles in his possession, custody or control. Where it is not reasonably practicable for the offending sign to be erased, removed or obliterated, the infringer may be ordered to secure the destruction of the goods, material or articles in question. Subsection (2) reinforces the court's powers by providing that if such an order is not complied with, or it appears likely that it would not be complied with, the court may order that the goods, material or articles be delivered to such person as the court may direct, for erasure, removal or obliteration of the sign, or for destruction, as the case may be. These remedies are available in addition to all the other remedies usually available, and may, because of the specific nature of the provisions, be more effective than traditional orders for obliteration or destruction, especially where the infringer is a counterfeiter or dealer in counterfeit goods.

PROCEEDINGS FOR DELIVERY UP OF INFRINGING GOODS, MATERIAL OR ARTICLES

8.5   Section 16 enables the proprietor of a registered trade mark to apply to the court for an order for the delivery up of any infringing goods, material or articles that a person has in his possession, custody or control in the course of a business. It appears that an application under s 16 may be made regardless of whether an action is brought for infringement. As indicated above, there can be infringing material where the person, in whose custody possession or control it is, is not an infringer.[1] Although s 16(1) only provides for the making of an application by the proprietor, the remedy is not so confined. As already noted (see para 6.10) s 30 enables a licensee to make such an application, such proceedings being included within the definition of 'infringement proceedings' in s 103(1). In the case of an exclusive licensee having rights and remedies as if the grant of the licence had been an assignment (under s 30(1)—see para 6.8), the position is the same; also s 31(7) makes specific reference to an application under s 16 by the proprietor.

---

1   This would be possible not only under s 17(4), but also in respect of infringing goods, under s 17(2)(c), and infringing articles under subsection (5).

8.6   Under s 20, proceedings under s 16, and under s 19, which makes related provisions with regard to orders for disposal of infringing goods, material and articles, may be brought in the sheriff court in Scotland, or in a county court in Northern Ireland. In the case of England and Wales there is no provision for the applications to be brought in a county court, although the Courts and Legal Services Act 1990 contains the power to make such provision, should this be considered appropriate. Under ss 16 and 19 the proceedings will be brought in the High Court, and s 20 also expressly preserves the jurisdiction of Court of Session in Scotland, and the High Court in Northern Ireland. Schedule 3 para 5 provides that s 16 applies to infringing goods, material or articles, whether made before or after commencement of the Act.

8.7   The order under s 16(1) may be for delivery up to the proprietor, or such other person as the court may direct. There is a time limitation for the making of an application under s 16, and there is a further provision in subsection (2), that an order for delivery up shall not be made at all, unless the court also makes an order under s 19 (for disposal, etc), or it appears that there are grounds for making such an order. In practice an application under s 19 would normally be made at the same time as the application under s 16. Where delivery up is to a person other than the proprietor of the trade mark, subsection (3) requires that such person must, if an order for disposal under s 19 is not made, retain the goods, material or articles pending the making of such an order, or a decision not to make such an order. The time limitation for an application under s 16 is set by s 18. It is normally a period of six years, in the case of infringing goods or material from the date on which the trade mark was applied to the goods (or their packaging) or the material, as the case may be or, in the case of infringing articles, from the date on which they were made. Subsection (2) makes an exception in cases of 'disability', or fraud or concealment preventing the proprietor from discovering the facts. 'Disability' is defined by reference to the meaning in the various Limitation statutes referred to in subsection (3). In such cases the period of six years does not start to run until the proprietor ceases to be under a disability or, as the case may be, could with reasonable diligence have discovered the facts.

8.8   Section 19 provides that where infringing goods, material or articles have been delivered up under s 16, an application may be made to the court for an order that they be destroyed, or forfeited to such person as the court may think fit, or for a decision that no such order should be made. In considering what order (if any) should be made, s 19(2) requires the court to have regard to whether other remedies available in an action for infringement would be adequate to compensate the proprietor and any licensee, and protect their interests. No doubt where the offending mark cannot be erased, removed or obliterated, the court will usually order the goods to be destroyed, or forfeited to the proprietor or to his order. But where the mark can be erased, removed or obliterated, or the material of which infringing goods or articles are made can be re-used for non-infringing purposes, particularly where the case is not one of counterfeiting, the court may be less prepared to order destruction or forfeiture under s 19(1). The same remarks apply with greater force where infringing goods (or packaging) do not even bear the offending mark. In such cases the court may decide that no order for destruction or forfeiture should be made, in which event subsection (5) provides that the person in whose possession, custody or control the goods, material or articles were before delivery up, is entitled to their return. Under subsection (3) procedural provisions are to be made by rules of court. In particular, provision must be made for the service of notice on persons having an interest in the goods, material or articles, and such persons are entitled to appear at the proceedings (whether or not served with notice), and to appeal against an order made, whether or not they appeared. By virtue of s 19(3) no order under s 19 can take effect until the expiry of the period for appealing, and if notice of appeal is duly given, the order remains suspended until the final determination or abandonment of the appeal. Under subsection (6), a person having an interest includes any person in whose favour an order could be made under the section or under ss 114, 204 or 231 of the Copyright, Designs and Patents Act 1988.[1] Where there is more than one interested person (for example in some circumstances a manufacturer and a distributor or retailer might claim an interest in the same goods, material or articles), subsection (4) enables the court to make such order as it thinks just.

---

1   Which make similar provision in relation to infringement of copyright, rights in performance and design right.

GROUNDLESS THREATS OF INFRINGEMENT PROCEEDINGS

8.9   For the first time in trade marks law in the UK, the 1994 Act provides a remedy in respect of certain groundless threats of infringement proceedings. Section 21 of the Act generally follows the current provisions in respect of patents and registered designs,[1] in limiting the availability of the action to persons who are not alleged to be 'primary infringers'. Thus, subsection (1) excludes the action for threats where the proceedings that are threatened are in respect of the application of a mark to goods or their packaging, the importation of goods to which, or to the packaging of which, the mark has been applied, or the supply of services under the mark. In the case of any threats other than the kinds excluded, any person aggrieved (ie anyone whose trade or business is or is likely to be in any way affected by the threats) may bring proceedings, seeking the relief set out in subsection (2), namely a declaration that the threats are unjustifiable, an injunction against continuance, and damages for any loss sustained by the threats. Liability is not confined to the proprietor; a solicitor or patent or trade mark agent issuing the threats may also be sued. The plaintiff is entitled to such relief unless the defendant justifies the threats, by showing that the acts, in respect of which the threats were made, constituted (or if done would constitute) infringement of the registered trade mark concerned. Subsection (3) provides that even if that the defendant can show such justification, the plaintiff is still entitled to relief if he shows that the registration 'is invalid or liable to be revoked in a relevant respect'. The words 'in a relevant respect' require some consideration. It would seem that the word 'relevant' indicates that the invalidity or liability to revocation is to be such that the acts, to which the threats were directed, would no longer be an infringement. That would be consistent with a similar situation under the patent and registered design provisions. But it is possible that the matter is not quite as simple as that, in cases of partial invalidity or liability to partial revocation, because of the very broad scope of the infringement provisions of s 10(2) and (3) of the 1994 Act. Each case will have to be considered on its facts. Finally, it should be noted that subsection (4), in line with the other threats provisions mentioned above, provides that the mere notification that a trade mark is registered, or that an application for registration has been made, does not constitute a threat for the purposes of the section.

---

1   See the Patents Act 1977, s 70, the Registered Designs Act 1949, s 26 and the Copyright, Designs and Patents Act 1988, Sch 4.

9 Duration, renewal and alteration

DURATION

9.1   Under s 42(1), a trade mark is registered for 10 years from the date of registration. Section 40(3) provides that a trade mark when registered, shall be registered as of the date of the filing of the application for registration. By s 42(2) renewal, under s 43, is for further successive terms of 10 years. This is simpler than the 1938 Act, under which registration was for a first term of seven years, with subsequent renewals for 14 year terms. The transitional provisions, in Sch 3, para 15(1), provide that s 42(1) applies in relation to registration of a mark applied for after commencement of the Act; this will include an application converted under para 11 of that Schedule. In the case of old applications, the original period will remain at seven years.

RENEWAL

9.2   Under s 43 a registration may be renewed at the request of the proprietor, subject to payment of a renewal fee. As before, the rules under subsection (2) will provide for the registrar to inform the proprietor before expiry, of the date of expiry and the manner in which the registration may be renewed. Subsection (3) requires the request for renewal to be made, and the fee paid, before the expiry date. However, subsection (3) also allows for renewal within such further period (not more than six months) as may be prescribed, but an additional renewal fee must also be paid within that period. Under subsection (4) renewal takes effect from the expiry of the previous registration. If a registration is not renewed in accordance with subsection (3), the registrar must remove the trade mark from the register. For the proprietor that is not necessarily the end of the matter, since under subsection (5) rules may provide for restoration, subject to such conditions as may be prescribed. As with the position under the 1938 Act, it is expected that further fees will be payable and that the registrar will be required to consider the circumstances of the failure to renew and be satisfied that it is just to restore the registration. Subsection (6) requires the renewal or restoration to be published in the prescribed manner. Schedule 3, para 15(2) provides that, where renewal falls due on or after commencement, ss 42(2) and 43 apply; in other cases the 1938 Act provisions still apply.

ALTERATION

9.3   Under the 1938 Act it was never easy to alter a registered trade mark, although it was possible, subject to the requirement in s 35, that the change must not substantially affect the identity of the mark. Section 44 of the 1994 Act is very much stricter even than that. Under subsection (1) it is provided that a registered trade mark 'shall not be altered in the register, during the period of registration or on renewal'. Nevertheless, under subsection (2) the registrar may, at the request of the proprietor, allow alteration where the mark includes the proprietor's name or address, if (and only if) the alteration is limited to altering that name or address 'and does not substantially affect the identity of the mark'. Under subsection (3), rules are to provide for publication of any alteration, and allowing for the making of objections by persons claiming to be affected. It will be seen therefore, that in most cases, alteration of a registered trade mark will be impossible. Where a proprietor alters a registered trade mark in use, then he will have the choice of relying on existing registrations if the alteration is not substantial, since they will not be likely to be open to attack on the ground of non-use under s 46(1), or obtaining new registrations of the altered form, and perhaps keeping the old registrations in force for at least some time afterwards. It should be noted that, under Sch 3, para 16, an application under s 35 of the 1938 Act for alteration of a registered trade mark, pending at commencement, will be dealt with under the provisions of that Act.

10 Surrender, revocation and invalidity

SURRENDER

10.1 Section 45 of the 1994 Act provides that a registered trade mark may be surrendered by the proprietor in respect of some, or all, of the goods or services for which it is registered. Subsection (2) allows for provision to be made by rules as to the manner and effect of a surrender and for protecting the interests of other persons having a right in the registered mark. This last provision may be important, not only because of the broader rights which licensees, particularly exclusive licensees, may have under the new law, but also because of the new possibilities for using registered marks as security interests, registrable under s 25. The rules will probably make provision for ensuring that any persons affected by the surrender, at least if their interest is registered under s 25, are notified and consent to the surrender.

REVOCATION

General remarks

10.2 Section 46(1) sets out four grounds on which the registration of a trade mark may be revoked. The first two involve non-use or use interrupted for five years, and subsections (2) and (3) contain further provisions relating to those grounds. The third ground relates to marks becoming generic, and the fourth to marks which become misleading. Generally speaking all registered trade marks, including 'existing registered marks' registered under the 1938 Act, will from the commencement of the 1994 Act be treated as if registered under that Act, and thus be subject to the new provisions (see Sch 3, para 2). There are other transitional provisions, which are mentioned below where they are relevant. Under subsection (4), an application may be made by any person (there is no longer the requirement for an applicant to be a 'person aggrieved' as there was in ss 26 and 32 of the 1938 Act, although in practice he usually will be) and may, with two exceptions, be made to the registrar or to the court. The exceptions are the same as in s 54 of the 1938 Act. When proceedings concerning the trade mark in question are pending in court, the application must be made to the court; and in any other case, if an application is made to the registrar, he may at any stage refer the application to the court. Under subsection (5), where grounds for revocation exist only in respect of some of the goods or services covered by the registration, revocation will relate only to those goods or services. Subsection (6) provides that revocation, whether in whole or only to the extent of some goods or services, has the effect that the rights of the proprietor shall be deemed to have ceased at the date of the application for revocation or at an earlier date if the tribunal is satisfied that the grounds existed then.

10.3 One final question, as to which there is possibly some doubt, is whether the use of the words 'may be revoked' import any discretion not to revoke where any of the grounds specified are established, or whether the tribunal must order revocation. The word 'may'[1] (Article 12 of the Directive uses the words 'shall be liable to revocation') suggests that there is a residual discretion. However, there are arguments to the contrary. For example, the references to 'proper reasons for non-use' in subsection (1)(a) and (b) suggest that if there are no such reasons then there should be no discretion to allow a registration to remain once the necessary non-use is proved. In addition, the use of the word 'shall' in subsection (5), with reference to partial revocation,[2] supports the view that 'may' is to be construed as meaning 'shall' in subsection (1).[3]

---

1   Which was also used in ss 26 and 32 of the 1938 Act, under which there was always a discretion not to remove or rectify, in appropriate circumstances.
2   See also Article 13 of the Directive.
3   See also para 10.8 regarding the same question in connection with the invalidation provisions of s 47.

Non-use

10.4   Section 46(1)(a) and (b) relate to two different non-use situations. The ground for removal under s 46(1)(a) is that 'within the period of five years following the date of completion of the registration procedure' (ie the date on which the trade mark was actually put on the register), the trade mark has not been put to genuine use in the UK by the proprietor or with his consent, in relation to the goods or services for which it is registered, and there are no proper reasons for non-use. It will be seen that, unlike under s 26(1)(a) of the 1938 Act, there is no requirement to establish a lack of bona fide intention to use, which may be the subject of an application for invalidation under s 47(1). Under s 46(1)(b) the ground is that genuine use of the trade mark (by the proprietor or with his consent) has been suspended for an uninterrupted period of five years, and there are no proper reasons for non-use. The term 'genuine use' is probably the same as 'bona fide use', in the sense in which the latter term has been interpreted by the courts under the 1938 Act. The use must be real commercial use, ie use with a specific commercial purpose in itself; if the use is merely for trade mark protection purposes, in particular if it is not intended to continue once any threat of revocation has receded, then it is unlikely to be regarded as 'genuine'[1] for the purposes of subsection (1)(a) or (b). It is clear from subsection (2) that the use does not have to be precisely in the form of the registered mark. Use in any form differing in elements which do not alter the distinctive character of the mark as registered is sufficient. Furthermore, applying the mark to goods or their packaging in the UK for export, is included in 'use' for the purposes of subsection (1). Use 'by the proprietor or with his consent' will include any use under a licence or, probably, a sub-licence, but also any other use by consent, such as use by a subsidiary or other company in the same group. An important change in the law relating to non-use cases is made by s 100, under which, in any civil proceedings in which a question arises as to the use to which a registered trade mark has been put, the burden of showing what use has been made of it is placed on the proprietor. There is no guidance as to what are 'proper reasons for non-use'. The phrase may be contrasted with s 26(3) of the 1938 Act which made an exception where the non-use is shown to have been due to 'special circumstances in the trade' and not to any intention not to use, or to abandon the trade mark. This was interpreted as referring to circumstances affecting the trade generally, as opposed to circumstances affecting only the proprietor and his trade. The new wording seems to be broader, and should permit justification of non-use on the basis of circumstances peculiar to the proprietor. For example, if an exclusive licensee ceased using the licensed mark, but refused to give up his exclusive rights, such situation might well be considered as providing the proprietor with a proper reason for non-use.

---

1   See for example *Concord Trade Mark* [1987] FSR 209, decided under s 26 of the 1938 Act, distinguishing on the facts the decision of the Court of Appeal in *Electrolux Ltd v Electrix Ltd* (1954) 71 RPC 23.

10.5   Subsection (3) makes special provision regarding cases in which use of a trade mark is commenced or resumed after the expiry of the five-year period referred to in subsection (1)(a) or (b). The general rule is that the registration will not then be revoked on the ground of the non-use; however, commencement or resumption of use after the expiry of the five-year period but within the period of three months before the making of an application for revocation is to be disregarded unless preparations for the commencement or resumption began before the proprietor became aware that the application might be made. A good example of a situation in which resumption of use would not have been disregarded under subsection (3), so that revocation would be refused under s 46, is provided by the case of *Hermes Trade Mark;*[1] although the preparations for resumption of use in that case were in fact held themselves to constitute bona fide use.

---

1   [1982] RPC 425.

Use of a trade mark as a common name in the trade

10.6   The third ground for revocation, under s 46(1)(c), is that in consequence of any acts or inactivity by the proprietor, the mark has become the common name in the trade for the product or service for which it is registered. The words 'in the trade' should be emphasised; as under s 15 of the 1938 Act mere descriptive use by members of the public, as opposed to traders, will not suffice. But the fact of generic use, even in the trade, will not of itself lead to revocation under subsection (1)(c). Such a result must be the consequence of acts or inactivity by the proprietor. In some comparatively rare cases, a proprietor has invalidated his trade mark rights by his own generic use; more usually this will result from inactivity, in particular a failure to police the use of the mark effectively. Such conduct is clearly capable of amounting to 'inactivity' for these purposes. On the other hand, a failure to take steps against misuse by traders, of which the proprietor was not even aware would not, it is thought, be held to be inactivity, 'in consequence of which' the misuse had occurred. By virtue of subsection (5) the registration will not, it seems, be revoked for any other goods or services on this ground, although in some situations the registration may be open to revocation on the next ground, ie under subsection (1)(d).

10.7   Some reference should be made to the transitional provisions in Sch 3. Whereas, under para 17(1) an application pending at the commencement of the 1994 Act, for removal on grounds of non-use under s 26 of the 1938 Act will be dealt with under those provisions, para 17(2) enables a new application to be made, under s 46(1)(a) or (b), at any time after commencement in respect of an existing registered mark. The only exception to this is in favour of defensive registrations under s 27 of the 1938 Act, in respect of which no application may be made until after five years from commencement.

Trade mark becoming misleading

10.8   Section 46(1)(d) provides for revocation where, as a consequence of the use made of the mark by the proprietor, or with his consent, in relation to the goods or services for which it is registered, the public is liable to be misled, particularly as to the nature, quality or geographical origin of those goods or services. The requirement that the liability to mislead the public must be 'in consequence of the use made of it by the proprietor or with his consent' probably amounts to the same as the requirement under s 11 of the 1938 Act, of some 'blameworthy conduct' on the part of the proprietor.[1] Again, use by licensees, sub-licensees and with consent in other cases, is covered. The likelihood of misleading the public must, it is considered, be a likelihood among a significant section of the relevant public, or (as it was put in decisions under the 1938 Act) a likelihood among a substantial number of persons. There is no requirement, as there was in s 11 of the 1938 Act, that the use of the mark be 'disentitled to protection in a court of justice'. Whether there is a likelihood of misleading the public is a question of fact; if it exists, then the ground for revocation is established. Although the provision only specifies a likelihood of the public being misled as to nature, quality or geographical origin, it is thought[2] that because of the word 'particularly', revocation may be possible if a mark becomes misleading in other respects, such as the identity of the manufacturer. What does seem to emerge from a consideration of the provision is that, generally speaking, although the new law has relaxed considerably the restrictions on the licensing and assignment of trade marks and the use of jointly owned trade marks, the need to maintain effective control, and in some cases of assignment to take steps to reduce any risks of trade marks becoming misleading, may well be no less than under the 1938 Act. Indeed, it may be easier for an application for revocation to succeed under s 46(1)(d) than it would have been under s 11 of the 1938 Act. Finally, it should be noted that under the transitional provisions of Sch 3, para 18, pending applications for rectification, including applications on grounds which are similar to those contained in s 46(1)(c) or (d), will be dealt with under the 1938 Act.

---

1   See *GE Trade Mark* [1973] RPC 297.
2   See also para 6.6, note 1.

DECLARATIONS OF INVALIDITY

The grounds for invalidity of a registration

10.9   Section 47(1) of the 1994 Act contains a general provision, that a registration of a trade mark may be declared invalid on the ground that the trade mark was registered in breach of s 3 or any of the provisions referred to in that section, ie if any of the absolute grounds for refusal applied at the date of the registration. Section 47(2) makes similar provision where relative grounds for refusal applied at the registration date, unless the proprietor of the earlier trade mark, or other earlier right, consented to the registration. As with s 46, the question may arise, whether the word 'may', in subsections (1) and (2), allows the exercise of any discretion to refuse a declaration of invalidity where one of the grounds referred to is proved. In the case of subsection (1) there is a provision that, where the ground relied upon is that the trade mark was registered in breach of s 3(1)(b), (c) or (d), the registration shall not be declared invalid if, in consequence of the use made of it, it has after registration acquired a distinctive character for the goods or services concerned. This in itself gives some support to the argument that, if a ground of invalidity is established there must be a declaration for invalidity. Section 47(5), like s 46, provides that where grounds for invalidity exist in respect of only some of the goods or services, the trade mark shall be declared invalid only as regards those goods or services; this again suggests that the word 'may' is to be understood as meaning 'shall'. As in the case of applications under s 46, applications under s 47 may be made by any person, there being no requirement that applicants be 'persons aggrieved', and subsection (3) further provides for a choice between the registrar and the court, with the same exceptions as under s 46(4). There is a special provision in subsection (4) that in the case of bad faith in the registration of a trade mark, the registrar himself may apply for a declaration of invalidity, but only to the court. Where a registration is declared invalid to any extent, subsection (6) provides that, to that extent, the registration shall be deemed never to have been made, although there is a saving for 'transactions past and closed', which are unaffected. This presumably means, for example, that a previous assignment or other transaction affecting the trade mark would not be regarded as void as between the parties.

10.10   Not much more needs to be said about the relevant transitional provisions in Sch 3. Paragraph 18(1)[1] provides that pending applications under ss 32 and 34 of the 1938 Act will be dealt with under that Act; otherwise, under subparagraph (2), s 47 applies to existing registered marks as if the provisions of the 1994 Act had been in force at all material times. This relates in particular to invalidity on the grounds for refusal under ss 3 and 5. The only exception under para 18(2) is that the relative ground specified in s 5(3), which is based on conflict with a trade mark registered or applied for in respect of different goods or services, cannot be relied upon in respect of an existing registered mark.

---

1   See also para 10.7.

ACQUIESCENCE

10.11 The 1994 Act contains a special provision regarding acquiescence, which is virtually identical to Article 9 of the Directive. It is, by its terms, limited to cases of acquiescence in the use of a registered trade mark in the UK. There is no provision for acquiescence in use of a trade mark which is not registered; in such a case the common law doctrine of acquiescence will still apply.[1] Under s 48, the acquiescence required is for a continuous period of five years, the proprietor of the earlier trade mark or right being aware of such use, which must mean awareness of the use for the whole five year period. It seems likely that the common law rule requiring reliance on the acquiescence will not apply as such, and that it will suffice for the purposes of s 48 that the proprietor is aware of the use for five years and does nothing about it. If, on the other hand, he makes a complaint but delays taking proceedings under s 47 until a five year period has passed, then so long as he has clearly reserved his rights he may be held not to have acquiesced within the meaning of s 48. The consequences of a finding of acquiescence, unless the registration in question was applied for in bad faith, are that the owner of the earlier trade mark or other right may not seek a declaration of invalidity under s 47, and that he may not oppose the use of the later trade mark for the goods or services for which it has been used for the requisite period. The last mentioned provision is unnecessary in so far as it relates to opposing use by infringement proceedings, because s 11(1) provides a defence so long as the registration cannot be invalidated. It is likely that the reference to opposing use includes opposing it by means of a passing off action. Although s 2(2) of the 1994 Act preserves the action for passing off, the wording of s 48(1)(b) seems unambiguous and at least arguably should prevail over s 2(2). Nevertheless the matter is not free from doubt.

---

1   See for example the decision of the Court of Appeal in *Habib Bank Ltd v Habib Bank AG Zurich* [1981] 2 All ER 650, [1982] RPC 1.

11 Certification marks

THE NEW PROVISIONS

11.1   Certification trade marks were introduced in to UK law as 'standardisation marks' under s 62 of the Trade Marks Act 1905 and continued, as certification trade marks, under s 37 of, and Sch 1 to, the 1938 Act. When the legislation made provision for the registration of service marks, certification marks were not extended to services. The new provisions, contained in s 50, and Sch 2, apply to both goods and services. A significant change is that the whole responsibility for all aspects of the registration and maintenance of certification marks is now given to the registrar, whereas under the 1938 Act matters such as the approval and alteration of the regulations governing use of certification marks were dealt with by the Department of Trade and Industry (formerly the Board of Trade). Section 50(1) defines a certification mark as 'a mark indicating that the goods or services in connection with which it is used are certified by the proprietor of the mark in respect of origin, material, mode of manufacture of goods or performance of services, quality, accuracy or other characteristics'. Apart from the extension to services, the definition is essentially the same as in the 1938 Act. Subsection (2) refers to Sch 2 which, in para 1, applies the provisions of the Act generally, subject only to the following provisions of the Schedule.

DIFFERENCES FROM OTHER TRADE MARKS

11.2   The kinds of signs which may qualify as certification marks are the same as those set out in the definition in s 1 of the Act, with the different requirement, in Sch 2, para 2, that they be capable of distinguishing goods or services which are certified from those which are not. Similarly to the 1938 provisions, Sch 2, para 4 prohibits registration of a certification mark if the proprietor carries on a business involving the supply of goods or services of the kind certified. Schedule 2, para 3 excludes from the absolute grounds for refusal the provisions of s 3(1)(c) in so far as they refer to signs or indications which may serve to designate the geographical origin of goods or services, but adds a provision that the proprietor is 'not entitled to prohibit the use of the signs or indications in accordance with honest practices in industrial or commercial matters (in particular, by a person who is entitled to use a geographical name)'. The purpose of this last part is not clear; it could be understood as referring to established use of such a name. An additional provision, which may be regarded as an absolute ground for refusal, is contained in Sch 2, para 5, which prohibits registration where the public is liable to be misled as to the character or significance of the mark, in particular if it is likely to be taken as something other than a certification mark. Accordingly the registrar may require inclusion in the mark of an indication that it is a certification mark, and this may involve amendment in the course of the registration procedure, notwithstanding s 39(2) of the Act. Another difference, in Sch 2, para 12, is that the registrar's consent must be given before any assignment or transmission can take effect.

THE REGULATIONS

11.3   The provisions governing the filing, approval and amendment of the regulations, which are to be open to public inspection and must indicate (among other things) who is authorised to use the mark and the characteristics to be certified, are contained in Sch 2, paras 6–11. Paragraph 7 prohibits registration unless the regulations comply with the requirements of para 6(2) (and any further requirements imposed by rules), and are not contrary to public policy or accepted principles of morality. Also, the applicant must be competent to certify the goods or services concerned. There are provisions for opposition, and for the making of observations, relating to these matters as well as to other grounds available under the Act. Regulations governing the use of an existing certification mark, registered under the 1938 Act, are to be treated after commencement as if filed under Sch 2, para 6 (see the transitional provisions in Sch 3, para 19); requests for the amendment of regulations, pending at commencement, will be dealt with under the 1938 Act provisions.

INFRINGEMENT

11.4   The provisions of the Act concerning infringement are generally applicable to certification marks. However, Sch 2, para 13 makes certain additions, which place an authorised user in the position of a licensee for the purposes of some provisions (eg ss 10(5), 19(2) and 89). Paragraph 14 requires any loss suffered, or likely to be suffered, by authorised users to be taken into account in infringement proceedings, and the court may give directions as to the holding of the proceeds of any pecuniary remedy on behalf of such users. By virtue of Sch 3, para 6(2) this only applies to infringements committed after commencement of the Act.

REVOCATION AND INVALIDITY

11.5   In addition to the grounds for revocation provided for in s 46, further possible grounds are contained in Sch 2, para 15. These are: that the proprietor has begun to carry on business supplying the goods or services; that the mark has been used by the proprietor in a manner likely to mislead the public within the meaning of para 5(1); that the proprietor has failed to observe, or to secure the observance of, the regulations governing the use of the mark; that an amendment of the regulations has been made so that they no longer comply with para 6(2) and any further conditions imposed by rules, or are contrary to public policy or to accepted principles of morality; or that the proprietor is no longer competent to certify the goods or services. With regard to the invalidity of registration Sch 2, para 16 adds a further ground, to those available under s 47, namely that the mark was registered in breach of paras 4, 5(1) or 7(1) of Sch 2.

12 Collective marks

THE NEW PROVISIONS

12.1   Collective marks have never previously been registrable in the UK. They differ from certification marks in that they are protected in the name of an association, the members of which carry on business supplying the goods or services concerned. The new provisions, which make such registration possible, are contained in s 49, with further detailed provisions, on similar lines to those for certification marks, set out in Sch 1. Section 49(1) defines a collective mark as 'a mark distinguishing the goods or services of members of the association which is the proprietor of the mark from those of other undertakings'. Subsection (2) refers to Sch 1, para 1, which applies the provisions of the Act generally to collective marks, subject to the following provisions of that Schedule.

DIFFERENCES FROM OTHER TRADE MARKS

12.2   The kinds of signs which may qualify as collective marks are the same as for ordinary trade marks, as set out in s 1 of the Act, but Sch 1, para 2 provides that the reference to 'distinguishing goods or services of one undertaking from those of other undertakings' is to be construed as a reference to distinguishing goods or services of members of the association which is the proprietor, from those of other undertakings. As with certification marks, Sch 1, para 3 excludes from the absolute grounds for refusal s 3(1)(c) in so far as it refers to signs or indications which may serve to designate the geographical origin of goods or services, however, it adds an identical provision to the effect that the proprietor is not entitled to prohibit the use of the signs or indications in accordance with honest practices in industrial or commercial matters (in particular, by a person who is entitled to use a geographical name). As in the case of certification marks, there is an additional absolute ground for refusal (contained in Sch 1, para 4) which prohibits registration where the public is liable to be misled as to the character or significance of the mark, in particular if it is likely to be taken as something other than a collective mark, and again the registrar may require inclusion in the mark of an indication that it is a collective mark, with amendment if necessary during the course of the registration procedure.

REGULATIONS

12.3   Like certification marks, collective marks must be subject to regulations governing use. The provisions regarding the filing, approval and amendment of the regulations, which are to be open to public inspection and must specify (among other things) the persons authorised to use the mark, the conditions of membership of the association and any conditions of use of the mark, are contained in Sch 1, paras 5–10. Paragraph 6 prohibits registration unless the regulations comply with the requirements of para 5(2) and any further requirements imposed by rules, and are not contrary to public policy or accepted principles of morality. There are provisions for opposition, and for the making of observations, relating to the matters set out in para 6, as well as to other grounds provided by the Act.

INFRINGEMENT

12.4   The provisions of the Act concerning infringement are generally applicable to collective marks, but Sch 1, para 11 makes identical additions, placing an authorised user in the position of a licensee, to those made for authorised users of certification marks (see para 11.4). Schedule 1, para 12 gives authorised users similar rights to take proceedings, to those provided for licensees by s 30 of the Act. Paragraph 12(6) contains provisions, corresponding to Sch 2, para 14, requiring any loss suffered or likely to be suffered, by authorised users to be taken into account in infringement proceedings, and for the giving of directions as to the holding of the proceeds of any pecuniary remedy on behalf of such users.

REVOCATION AND INVALIDITY

12.5   As with certification marks, there are further grounds for revocation, in addition to those available under s 46. They are contained in Sch 1, para 13, and are: that the manner in which the mark has been used by the proprietor has caused it to become liable to mislead the public in the manner referred to in para 4(1); that the proprietor has failed to observe, or secure the observance of, the regulations governing the use of the mark; that an amendment of the regulations has been made so that they no longer comply with para 5(2), and any further conditions imposed by rules, or are contrary to public policy or accepted principles of morality. With regard to grounds for invalidity of registration, para 14 adds a further ground in addition to those provided by s 47 of the Act, namely that the mark was registered in breach of Sch 1, paras 4(1) or 6(1).

13 Community trade marks and international matters

COMMUNITY TRADE MARKS

The Community Trade Mark Regulation

13.1   On 20 December 1993 the Community Trade Mark Regulation[1] was adopted by the Council. This will allow for the protection of trade marks in all the countries of the European Union by means of a single filing. Section 51 provides that for the purposes of the 1994 Act, and of regulations made under s 52, 'Community trade mark' has the same meaning as in Article 1(1) of the Regulation, that is—

> 'A trade mark for goods or services which is registered in accordance with the conditions contained in this Regulation and in the manner herein provided'.

The Community trade mark will have a unitary character and is to have equal effect throughout the Community. It is not expected that applications for the registration of Community trade marks will be received before 1996.

---

1   Defined in s 51 of the Act as 'Council Regulation (EC) No 40/94 of 20 December 1993 on the Community trade mark'.

Regulations under the 1994 Act

13.2   Section 52(1) of the Act gives the Secretary of State the power to make such provision by regulations as he considers appropriate (ie by statutory instrument under subsection (4)) in connection with the operation of the Community Trade Mark Regulation. This a general power, but subsections (2) and (3) give specific powers to make provision for particular matters.

13.3   Under subsection (2) provision may, in particular, be made with respect to: the making of applications for Community trade marks by way of the Patent Office; the procedures for determining a posteriori the invalidity, or liability to revocation, of the registration of a trade mark from which a Community trade mark derives seniority under Article 34 of the Regulation; the conversion of a Community trade mark, or an application for a Community trade mark, into an application for registration under the Act; and the designation of courts in the UK having jurisdiction over proceedings arising out of the Regulation (see Article 91 of the Regulation).

13.4   Subsection (3) is concerned with the application of certain provisions of the Act to Community trade marks. Under subsection (3)(a) regulations may be made applying, in relation to a Community trade mark, the provisions of s 21 (groundless threats), ss 89 to 91 (importation of infringing goods, material or articles) and ss 92, 93, 95 and 96 (offences). Under subsection (3)(b) provision may be made in relation to the list of professional representatives maintained under Article 89 of the Regulation, and persons on that list, corresponding to the provision made or capable of being made, under ss 84 to 88 of the Act (relating to the register of trade mark agents and registered trade mark agents).

INTERNATIONAL REGISTRATION UNDER THE MADRID PROTOCOL

The Madrid Protocol

13.5   The Madrid Protocol, which s 53 identifies as 'the Protocol relating to the Madrid Agreement concerning the International Registration of Marks,[1] adopted at Madrid on 27 June 1989', will enable applications to be made, through one filing, for the national registration of trade marks in a number of countries. The actual number will be determined by the number of countries which ratify the Madrid Protocol. The UK, which was one of four member states of the Community[2] that were not members of the original Madrid Agreement, intends to ratify the Madrid Protocol by 1 January 1995, although the Protocol is not expected to come into force until later that year. The system will, like the Madrid Agreement, operate through the International Bureau (of the World Intellectual Property Organisation). By virtue of s 53 of the Act 'international trade mark (UK)' means a trade mark entitled to protection in the UK under the Protocol.

---

1   Of 14 April 1894, as revised on a number of occasions.
2   The others being Denmark, Eire and Greece.

Provisions under the Act for giving effect to the Protocol

13.6   Section 54(1) empowers the Secretary of State by order (by statutory instrument under subsection (4)) to make such provision as he thinks fit for giving effect to the provisions of the Protocol in the UK. As in the case for regulations concerning the Community trade mark, the power is granted in very general terms, but subsections (2) and (3) deal with particular matters without prejudicing the general power.

13.7   Under subsection (2) provision may, in particular, be made with respect to: the making of applications for international registrations by way of the Patent Office as office of origin; the procedures to be followed where the basic UK application or registration fails or ceases to be in force; the procedures to be followed where the International Bureau requests the Patent Office for the extension of protection to the UK, and the effects of a successful request for such extension; the transformation of an application for an international registration, or an international registration, into a national application for registration; the communication of information to the Bureau; and the payment of fees and amounts prescribed in respect of applications, extensions of protection and renewal.

13.8   Under subsection (3), provision may be made by regulations (also by statutory instrument under subsection (4)), applying provisions of the Act to an international trade mark (UK). As with the Community trade mark, these provisions are s 21 (groundless threats), ss 89 to 91 (importation of infringing goods, material or articles) and ss 92, 93, 95 and 96 (offences).

THE PARIS CONVENTION

13.9   As already mentioned (see para 5.4), the 1994 Act contains several provisions which are concerned with the UK's obligations under the Paris Convention, identified in s 55(1) as 'the Paris Convention for the Protection of Industrial Property of 20 March 1883, as revised or amended from time to time'. For the purposes of the Act, s 55(1)(b) defines a 'Convention country' as a country, other than the UK, which is a party to the Paris Convention. Section 55(2) enables the Secretary of State, by statutory instrument under subsection (3), to make such amendments to the Act, and to rules made under the Act, which appear appropriate in consequence of any revision or amendment of the Paris Convention after the passing of the Act (21 July 1994). This does not enable any further changes to be made in the law to comply with any outstanding existing obligations under the Convention. But the Act does contain some provisions, in ss 56–60, implementing some of the UK's obligations under the Convention. Sections 57–59 have already been discussed (see paras 3.14 and 3.17). Sections 56 and 60 are considered below.

Protection of well-known trade marks

13.10 Section 56 of the Act contains an important new provision, in rather belated compliance with the obligations of the UK under Article 6bis of the Paris Convention, for the protection of any trade mark which is entitled to protection under the Convention as a well-known trade mark. References in the Act to such a trade mark are to a mark which is well known in the UK as being the mark of a person who is a national of, or is domiciled in, or has a real and effective industrial or commercial establishment in, a Convention country, whether or not that person carries on business, or has any goodwill, in the UK. References to the proprietor of such a mark are to be construed accordingly. There is no clear guidance as to what is 'well-known' for these purposes. But the mark must, it is suggested, be significantly better known than a mark having a 'reputation' for the purposes of ss 5(3) and 10(3).

13.11   Under s 56(2) the proprietor of a well-known trade mark, in the sense described above, is entitled to restrain by injunction the use in the UK of a trade mark which, or the essential part of which, is identical or similar to his mark, in relation to identical or similar goods or services, where the use is likely to cause confusion. The reference to 'identical or similar goods or services', although not actually explained in s 56, must clearly be a reference to goods or services for which the well-known mark is used (see Article 6bis itself). Although there is no mention of any remedy other than an injunction, it is considered that the court could, in appropriate cases, grant other remedies such as delivery up and destruction, or the obliteration of offending marks, where the purpose is to enhance the efficacy of injunctive relief.

13.12   There are two further matters that, under s 56, may affect the rights given to the proprietor of a well-known mark. Firstly, subsection (2) provides that the right is subject to s 48 (ie, acquiescence see para 10.11). This will only apply where the other mark is registered and, it would seem, is not liable to invalidation (in respect of the relevant goods or services) which has the effect that to the extent of the invalidation, the mark is deemed never to have been registered. Secondly, subsection (3) protects the continuation of any bona fide use of a trade mark begun before commencement of this provision.

Acts of agent or representative

13.13 Section 60 deals with a situation (which has arisen from time to time in the past and is often difficult to resolve because it has not been covered expressly in any agreement between the parties), in which a trade mark is registered by an agent or distributor for a foreign trader who owns the rights to the mark in his own country, and which is the subject of Article 6*septies* of the Paris Convention. Section 60 greatly clarifies the legal position in such situations and should frequently remove the need for litigation. Subsection (1) states that the provisions apply where an application for registration of a trade mark is made by a person who is an agent or representative of a person who is the proprietor of the mark in a Convention country. Subsection (2) states that the application shall be refused if the proprietor opposes it. If the application (not being opposed) is granted, subsection (3) entitles the foreign proprietor to apply for a declaration of the invalidity of the registration, or to apply for his name to be substituted as the proprietor. Notwithstanding the rights conferred by the Act in relation to a registered trade mark, subsection (4) entitles the foreign proprietor to restrain unauthorised use of the trade mark in the UK. The application of all these provisions is excluded by subsection (5) if, or to the extent that, the agent or representative justifies his action. Such justification might be in the form of an express agreement, or, in the case of subsection (4), would normally exist if the goods or services were in fact the genuine goods or services of the foreign proprietor. By subsection (6), an application under subsection (3), for a declaration of invalidity or rectification must be made within three years of the proprietor becoming aware of the registration. Furthermore, an injunction under subsection (4) is to be refused in respect of a use in which the proprietor has acquiesced for a continuous period of three years or more.

MISCELLANEOUS—STAMP DUTY

13.14 Section 61 makes special provision regarding stamp duty in respect of Community trade marks and international trade marks (UK). It provides that stamp duty shall not be chargeable on an instrument relating to any such trade mark, or an application for any such mark, by reason only of the fact that such a mark has legal effect in the UK. Presumably the liability of any such instrument to duty will depend upon what, if any, other subject matter is included.

14 Administrative and other supplementary provisions

GENERAL

14.1   Part III of the Act (ss 62 to 98) contains a number of provisions regarding the registry and administrative matters, including rule making powers and provisions relating to trade mark agents. Also included are provisions relating to the importation of infringing goods, material or articles (ss 89 to 91) and provisions concerned with certain criminal offences (ss 92 to 98). These latter two groups of sections are dealt with in Chapter 15.

THE REGISTRAR AND THE REGISTER

14.2   Section 62 provides that, as previously, the registrar is the Comptroller-General of Patents, Designs and Trade Marks. Section 63 continues the obligation on the registrar to maintain a register of trade marks ('the register'), and the expression 'registered trade mark' and other references to registration are, unless the context otherwise requires, references to registration in the register. Section 63(2) specifies what is to be entered in the register, in accordance with the Act, namely registered trade marks, prescribed particulars of registrable transactions (under s 25), and such other matters relating to registered trade marks as may be prescribed. Under subsection (3), the register is to be kept in such manner as may be prescribed by rules, and provision has to be made for public inspection and the supply of certified or uncertified copies, or extracts, of entries in the register.

14.3   Under Sch 3, para 2, on the commencement of the Act all existing registered trade marks will be transferred to the register kept under the 1994 Act and have effect as if registered thereunder, subject to the provisions of that Schedule. Existing marks registered as a series are similarly to be registered in the new register. All associations between registered mark cease to have effect. Under Sch 3, para 3 conditions of registration entered on the former register, in relation to an existing registered mark, cease to have effect, but pending proceedings under s 33 of the 1938 Act, for expunging or varying a condition, will be dealt with under that Act. However, in exercising the discretion which he has under s 33 of the 1938 Act, the registrar may well take into consideration the fact that the condition will cease to exist under the 1994 Act. On the other hand existing disclaimers or limitations on the former register are retained by Sch 3, para 3(2) and have effect as if entered on the register pursuant to s 13 of the Act.

14.4   Section 64 makes provision for the rectification or correction of the register, in respect of matters not affecting the validity of the registration of a trade mark. Any person having a sufficient interest may apply for the rectification of an error or omission in the register. As with applications for revocation or declarations of invalidity, the application may be to the registrar or the court, except where proceedings concerning the trade mark are pending in the court when the application must be made to the court, and subject to the registrar's right to refer the application to the court. Under subsection (3), the effect of rectification is that the error or omission shall be deemed never to have been made, except where the tribunal directs otherwise. Subsection (4) makes separate provision for requests by a proprietor or a licensee to enter any change in his name or address as recorded in the register. Under subsection (5), the registrar may remove from the register any matter appearing to him to have ceased to have effect. Procedures will be laid down by rules.

14.5   Amendment of the classification of goods or services is dealt with under s 65. Provision may be made by rules empowering the registrar to do what he considers necessary to implement any amended or substituted classification of goods or services and for the amendment of existing entries in the register, so as to accord with the new classification. Under Sch 3, para 12, the registrar may exercise the powers conferred by the rules to secure that any existing registered marks, which do not conform to the system prescribed under s 34, are brought into conformity with that system. Subsection (3) provides that any such power of amendment must not be exercised so as to extend the rights conferred by registration, except where it appears to the registrar that compliance with this requirement would involve undue complexity, and that any extension would not be substantial and would not adversely affect the rights of any person. By virtue of subsection (4), rules may empower the registrar to require a proprietor to file a proposal for amendment of the register, within such time as may be prescribed, and to cancel or refuse to renew the registration in question if the proprietor fails to do so. Under subsection (5), any proposal for amendment is to be advertised, and may be opposed.

POWERS AND DUTIES OF THE REGISTRAR

14.6   Section 66 empowers the registrar to require the use of such forms as he may direct. The forms, and any directions for their use, are to be published in the prescribed manner. Section 67 is concerned with the inspection of documents relating to applications for registration. After an application has been published, the registrar is required by subsection (1) to provide a person, on request, with such information and permit him to inspect such documents relating to the application, or any registered trade mark resulting from it, as may be specified. This is however subject to any prescribed restrictions. This move towards more openness in matters relating to trade mark registration is welcome, and it is hoped that there will not be any unnecessary restriction under the rules. Any request is to be made in the prescribed manner and is to be accompanied by any prescribed fee. Subsection (2) states that before the publication of an application for registration, documents or information constituting or relating to the application are not to be published by the registrar or communicated by him, to any person except in such cases and to such extent as may be prescribed or with the consent of the applicant. However, subsection (3) makes an exception in favour of a person who has been notified that an application for registration has been made and that the applicant will, if the application is granted, bring proceedings against him in respect of acts done after publication of the application. In such a case the person concerned may make a request under subsection (1), which shall apply accordingly. In practice, this exception may not assist a third party very much because if the applicant is careful only to mention the application, and does not indicate that proceedings will be brought if the application succeeds, it would seem that the exception does not apply.

COSTS

14.7   As before, the rules will make provisions relating to the award of costs. Under s 68, the rules may empower the registrar, in any proceedings before him under the Act, to award any party such costs as he may consider reasonable, and to direct how, and by what parties, they are to be paid. Under subsection (2), orders as to costs are enforceable in England and Wales or Northern Ireland in the same way as orders of the High Court, and in Scotland, in the same way as a decree for expenses granted by the Court of Session. By virtue of subsection (3), rules may empower the registrar to require any party to give security for costs (in the proceedings in question or on appeal) and make provision as to the consequences if security is not given.

EVIDENCE AND RELATED MATTERS

14.8   Provisions regarding evidence and other matters, such as the attendance and examination of witnesses and the discovery and production of documents, may be made by rules under s 69. The provisions may be as to the giving of evidence in proceedings before the registrar by affidavit or statutory declaration, as to the conferring on the registrar of the powers of an Official Referee of the Supreme Court as regards the examination of witnesses on oath and the discovery and production of documents, and applying, in relation to the attendance of witnesses, the rules applicable before an Official Referee. Where witnesses are to be cross-examined, the discovery and production of material documents may be very important, and it is to be expected that these matters will be provided for in the rules.

OTHER MATTERS

14.9   Section 70(1) excludes any warranty by the registrar as to the validity of any registration, and subsection (2) provides for the exclusion of any liability of the registrar in respect of official acts. These provisions are supplemented by subsection (3), which provides that no proceedings lie against an officer of the registrar in respect of any matter for which, by virtue of this section, the registrar is not liable. Section 71 makes provision for the Comptroller-General's annual report, under s 121 of the Patents Act 1977, to include a report on the execution of the Act, including the discharge of functions under the Madrid Protocol; the report is also to include an account of all money received and paid under or by virtue of the Act.

LEGAL PROCEEDINGS AND APPEALS

Legal proceedings

14.10 Section 72 continues the position under s 46 of the 1938 Act that in all legal proceedings relating to a registered trade mark (including rectification proceedings) the registration of a person as proprietor of a trade mark is prima facie evidence of the validity of the original registration, and of any subsequent assignment or transmission. Section 73 contains familiar provisions for the court to certify the validity of a registration where that validity had been contested in any proceedings before it. For the purpose of this provision validity must have been contested and there must be a finding by the court that the registration is valid. The effect of such a certificate is that if validity of the registration is again questioned in subsequent proceedings and the proprietor obtains a final order or judgment in his favour, he is entitled to his costs as between solicitor and client unless the court directs otherwise. The provision does not extend to the costs of a subsequent appeal in such proceedings. By virtue of Sch 3, para 21, a certificate of contested validity granted under s 47 of the 1938 Act shall have effect as if given under s 73(1) of the 1994 Act.

14.11   Section 74, again continuing previous practice, provides that the registrar is entitled to appear, and shall appear if directed by the court, in any proceedings before the court for revocation of a registration (s 46), a declaration of invalidity (s 47) or rectification (s 64). Under s 74(2) the registrar has the option, unless directed otherwise by the court, of submitting a signed written statement, giving particulars of any proceedings before him in relation to the matter in issue, the grounds for any decision by him affecting it, the practice of the Patent Office in like cases, or such other matters relevant to the issues and within his knowledge as registrar, as he thinks fit. Such a statement is deemed to form part of the evidence in the proceedings. Under s 74(3) anything authorised or required to be done under the section by the registrar may be done on his behalf by a duly authorised officer. Section 75 provides that, unless the context otherwise requires, 'the Court' in the 1994 Act means the High Court, in England, Wales, and Northern Ireland, and the Court of Session in Scotland.

Appeals from the registrar

14.12 Section 76(1) provides that an appeal lies from any decision of the registrar under the Act, except as otherwise expressly provided by rules. 'Decision' includes any act of the registrar in exercise of a discretion vested in him by or under the Act. This appears to extend the right of appeal to interlocutory decisions, as well as final decisions, which represents a change from the position under the 1938 Act. If so, then there will rarely, if ever, be any cases in which an application for judicial review would be necessary or appropriate. Judicial review may perhaps be appropriate in some cases in which a right of appeal may be excluded by rules. Under subsection (2), any appeal may be brought either to 'an appointed person' or to the court. This provision retains the alternative routes of appeal available under the 1938 Act, with the difference that the 'appointed person' is no longer appointed by the Department of Trade and Industry, but by the Lord Chancellor (who must consult with the Lord Advocate). Furthermore, the appointed person can hear appeals in opposition and other inter partes proceedings. This is another important change. Provisions governing the appointment and eligibility for appointment, and the holding and vacation of the office of the appointed person, are set out in s 77. By virtue of s 76(3), where an appeal is made to an appointed person, he may refer the appeal to the court if it appears to him that a point of general legal importance is involved, if the registrar requests referral, or if such a request is made by any party to the proceedings before the registrar in which the decision was made. However, the appointed person must give the appellant and any other party an opportunity to make representations as to whether the appeal should be referred to the court. Under subsections (4) and (5), if the appeal is not referred to the court, then the appointed person hears and determines the appeal, his decision being final, and the provisions of ss 68 and 69, relating to costs and security for costs, apply to the proceedings before an appointed person.

RULES, FEES AND HOURS OF BUSINESS

14.13   The general rule making powers of the Secretary of State are conferred by s 78. Rules, which are to be made by statutory instrument, may be made for the purposes of any provision of the Act authorising the making of rules with respect to any matter, and for prescribing anything authorised or required by any provision of the Act to be prescribed, as well as generally for regulating practice and procedure under the Act. Subsection (2) details a number of particular matters as to which provision may be made. These matters need no discussion here and do not affect the general scope of the powers conferred. Section 79 contains provision relating to such payment of fees, in respect of applications and registration and other matters under the Act, as may be prescribed. Provision may be made by rules as to the payment of a single fee in respect of two or more matters, and the circumstances (if any) in which a fee may be repaid or remitted. Section 80 makes provision for the registrar to give directions as to hours of business and business days. Business done on any day after the specified hours of business, or on a day which is not a business day, shall be deemed to have been done on the next business day. If the time for doing anything under the Act expires on a day which is not a business day, the time is extended to the next business day. Directions may make different provision for different classes of business; they must be published in the manner prescribed (under the rules). Attention should be drawn here to a possible danger where time is non-extendable, for example the time for opposing. It would seem that if the act is done outside business hours on the final day for doing the act, then it is necessarily out of time. Section 81 makes provisions regarding the publication of the Trade Marks Journal. This will be dealt with in rules and no further comment is needed.

TRADE MARK AGENTS

14.14   Sections 82 to 88 deal with matters concerning trade mark agents, including recognition of agents, the register of trade mark agents, the use of the description 'registered trade mark agent', mixed partnerships, privilege for communications and the power of the registrar to deal with certain agents. These provisions generally follow the corresponding provisions found in the Copyright, Designs and Patents Act 1988, ss 282–284. (See also ss 274–280 relating to patent agents, and also to mixed partnerships.) A significant new provision is s 86, which allows the use of the term 'trade mark attorney' by a registered trade mark agent, without an offence being committed under the legislation relating to solicitors. This is in line with provisions previously made permitting patent agents to use the term 'patent attorney'.

14.15   Section 82 states that, except as otherwise provided by rules, any act required or authorised to be done under the Act by or to a person may be done by or to a duly authorised agent. Authority may be given orally or in writing. Rules have already been made regarding the register of trade mark agents;[1] by virtue of Sch 3, para 22(1) they will continue in force for the purposes of s 83 unless varied or revoked by further rules under the 1994 Act. The use of the description 'registered trade mark agent' is regulated by s 84, which is in identical terms to the repealed provisions of the Copyright, Designs and Patents Act 1988, s 283(1)–(3), (6). Mixed partnerships are subject to rules made under s 85.[2] The provisions of s 87, relating to privilege for communications with registered trade mark agents, are identical to the previous provisions in s 284(1)–(3) of the 1988 Act. Section 88, which confers power on the Secretary of State to make rules authorising the registrar to refuse to recognise certain persons as agents in respect of any business under the Act, are for practical purposes, the same as the previous provisions (s 281 of the 1988 Act, and see rule 15(5) of the Trade Marks and Service Marks Rules 1986 (SI 1986/1319)). Although Sch 3, para 22(2) provides for the continuation of these rules, new rules are expected to cover this aspect afresh.

1   The Register of Trade Mark Agents Rules 1990 (SI 1990/1458) made under s 282 of the 1988 Act continued under the new law by virtue of Sch 3, para 22(1).
2   The corresponding provisions of the 1988 Act are ss 279 and 283(4), (5). The Registered Trade Mark Agents (Mixed Partnerships and Bodies Corporate) Rules 1994 (SI 1994/363) were made under s 283(4) and will continue under the new law by virtue of Sch 3, para 22(1). New rules may be made later in 1994.

15 Importation of infringing goods, material or articles and offences

GOODS TREATED AS PROHIBITED GOODS

15.1 Section 89, which is similar to previous provisions, enables a proprietor of a registered trade mark, or a licensee, to give notice in writing to the Commissioners of Customs and Excise, requesting that certain goods be treated as prohibited goods. The notice must state that he is the proprietor, or as the case may be, a licensee, of the registered trade mark and must further specify the time and place at which goods (which are, in relation to that trade mark, infringing goods) material or articles, are expected to arrive in the UK. The goods must either be from outside the European Economic Area, or be from within that Area but not having been entered for free circulation. Under subsection (2), when a notice is in force under this section, the importation of the goods otherwise than by a person for his private and domestic use is prohibited. A person is not liable, by reason of the prohibition, to any penalty other than forfeiture of the goods. Subsection (3) excludes from the operation of the section goods entered, or expected to be entered, for free circulation in respect of which the proprietor, or a licensee, is entitled to lodge an application under Article 3(1) of Council Regulation (EEC) No 3842/86 laying down measures to prohibit the release for free circulation of counterfeit goods. Section 90 gives power to the Commissioners of Customs and Excise to make regulations, by statutory instrument,[1] prescribing the form in which a notice is to be given under s 89, and requiring the furnishing of evidence and the compliance with such other conditions as may be specified. By virtue of subsection (2), such regulations may cover the payment of fees, the provision of security for any liability or expense which the Commissioners may incur, and the indemnification of the Commissioners in respect of such liability or expense. Section 91 concerns disclosure by the Commissioners of Customs and Excise, of information relating to infringing goods, material or articles obtained by them for the purposes of, or in connection with, the exercise of their functions in relation to imported goods. The Commissioners may authorise the disclosure of such information for the purpose of facilitating the exercise by any person of any function in connection with the investigation or prosecution of an offence under s 92 or under the Trade Descriptions Act 1968. This provision may prove useful in dealing with some problems involving counterfeit goods which are imported from abroad.

---

1 The existing regulations made under s 64A of the 1938 Act, the Trade Marks (Customs) Regulations 1970 (SI 1970/212) are not continued when the 1994 Act comes into force. It is understood that new regulations are in the course of preparation.

OFFENCES

Unauthorised use of trade mark

15.2 Section 92 is intended to strengthen the position of trade mark proprietors against counterfeiting and dealing in counterfeit goods, in particular to prevent counterfeiters and dealers from avoiding conviction by publishing 'disclaimers' indicating that goods bearing trade marks are counterfeit or copies and not genuine goods of the trade mark proprietor. The provision contained in the originally published Bill was far too broad, making almost any infringement of a trade mark, in respect of goods, a criminal offence. Section 92 now attempts to focus on what counterfeiting essentially is. In particular, counterfeiting usually involves the use of a mark which is identical to the brand owner's mark, or very similar to it, and more often than not it involves copying a well-known mark even if the goods are of a kind not dealt in by the proprietor of the trade mark. Accordingly, the commission of an offence under s 92 requires the use of a sign which is identical to, or likely to be mistaken for, a registered trade mark. By virtue of subsection (4), the goods in question must either be covered by a registration of the trade mark or, if they are not, it is necessary that the trade mark has a reputation in the UK and that use of the sign concerned takes, or would take, unfair advantage of, or is or would be detrimental to, the distinctive character or repute of the trade mark. This, it should be noted, follows the concept of dilution as seen in ss 5(3) and 10(3). Subject to the requirement of subsection (4), subsections (1), (2) and (3) set out the various acts which constitute an offence under this section, in particular, the application of the sign to goods or their packaging, dealing in goods bearing such sign, the possession, custody or control of such goods, similar acts in respect of packaging material, and the making or possessing of articles for making copies of an offending sign. In each case the act must be done by the alleged offender 'with a view to gain for himself or another, or with intent to cause loss to another, and without the consent of the proprietor'. This is a requirement which can be expected to be met in cases involving counterfeit goods. In the case of articles for making copies of the sign in question, subsection (3) further requires that the person concerned knew or had reason to believe that the article had been, or was to be, used to produce goods, or material for labelling or packaging goods, as a business paper in relation to goods, or for advertising goods. Again, this will normally present no difficulty. Subsection (5) provides a defence for a person charged with an offence under the section, that is, if he shows that he believed, on reasonable grounds, that the use of the sign in question was not an infringement of the registered trade mark. Ignorance of the registration would be no defence under this provision, because there would be no basis for a reasonable belief of non-infringement. The penalties provided by subsection (6) should be noted; conviction on indictment can result in an unlimited fine or imprisonment for up to 10 years, or both.

15.3   The duty of enforcing s 92 is placed on local weights and measures authorities, by s 93, which applies certain powers conferred on such authorities by the Trade Descriptions Act 1968. One problem that can arise is what should be done with goods, material or articles which are counterfeit or used for packaging or making counterfeit goods; such questions can occur not only when a person is convicted of an offence, but also when a defendant is acquitted although it is clear that the goods, material or articles are not the genuine goods, material or articles of the trade mark proprietor. Section 97 makes provision for the forfeiture of counterfeit goods that come into the possession of any person in connection with the investigation or prosecution of a relevant offence. Under subsection (8) a 'relevant offence' is an offence under s 92 or under the Trade Descriptions Act 1968, or any offence involving dishonesty or deception, which would cover, for example, conspiracy cases involving counterfeit goods. The court must be satisfied that a relevant offence has been committed in relation to the goods, material or articles concerned. Section 98 makes similar provisions for Scotland. There are provisions in both ss 97 and 98 for appeals, and for the destruction of forfeited goods, material or articles. There is also the possibility for the goods, material or articles to be released if the offending sign is erased, removed or obliterated.

Other offences

15.4   Section 94 is concerned with the falsification of the register and similar offences. Under subsection (1), it is an offence for a person to make, or cause to be made, a false entry in the register, knowing or having reason to believe that it is false. Under subsection (2), it is an offence for a person to make, or cause to be made, anything falsely purporting to be a copy of an entry in the register, or to produce or tender, or cause to be produced or tendered in evidence any such thing, knowing or having reason to believe that it is false. The penalties on conviction are set out in subsection (3).

15.5   Section 95 creates two offences, similar to those under s 60 of the 1938 Act, of falsely representing that a mark is a registered trade mark, and making a false representation as to the goods or services for which a trade mark is registered. In either case, it is necessary that the person concerned made the representation knowing or having reason to believe that it was false; this was not a requirement under the 1938 Act. Subsection (2) states that for the purposes of this section, the use in the UK of the word 'registered', or of any other word or symbol importing a reference (express or implied) to registration, is deemed to be a representation as to registration under the Act, unless it is shown that the reference is to registration elsewhere and that the trade mark is in fact so registered for the goods or services in question. This is in some respects less strict than s 60 of the 1938 Act, under which 'registered' normally meant registered in the UK and the exceptions were in practice difficult to satisfy. The penalty for an offence is specified in subsection (3).

Supplementary provisions relating to Scotland

15.6   Section 96 makes special provision regarding the period in which summary proceedings may be begun in Scotland for any offence under the Act. No special comment is necessary here.

16 Miscellaneous and general provisions

INTRODUCTION

16.1   Part IV of the Act (ss 99 to 110) contains a variety of miscellaneous provisions, some of which have already been referred to elsewhere in this guide. It is not necessary to deal with any of these at any length.

UNAUTHORISED USE OF ROYAL ARMS, ETC

16.2   Section 99 prohibits the unauthorised use by any person, in connection with any business, of the Royal arms (or arms so closely resembling the Royal arms as to be calculated to deceive) in such manner as to lead to the belief that he is duly authorised to so use the Royal arms. This is similar to the provision contained in s 61 of the 1938 Act. Also prohibited is the use, in connection with any business, without the authority of Her Majesty or of a member of the Royal family, of any device, emblem or title in such a manner as to be calculated to lead to the belief that the user is employed by, or supplies goods or services to, Her Majesty or that member of the Royal family. Under subsection (3), any contravention of subsection (1) or (2) is an offence punishable, on summary conviction, by a fine not exceeding level 2 on the standard scale. Additionally, subsection (4) provides for the grant of an injunction to restrain any such contravention, in proceedings brought by any person who is authorised to use the arms, device, emblem or title in question, or any person authorised by the Lord Chamberlain to take such proceedings. By subsection (5), any right of the proprietor of a trade mark containing any such arms, device, emblem or title, to use the trade mark, is unaffected.

BURDEN OF PROVING USE OF A TRADE MARK

16.3   Section 100, which has been mentioned in connection with revocation on grounds of non-use (ie under s 46, see para 10.4), provides that if, in any civil proceedings under the Act, a question arises as to the use to which a registered trade mark has been put, it is for the proprietor to show what use has been made of it. This corrects the position, which existed under the 1938 Act, that a person alleging non-use must prove a negative. This did not make much sense where the facts were within the knowledge of the proprietor. Section 100 also applies to use with the consent of the proprietor, and this is justifiable because the proprietor is better placed than any third party to know what his licensees are doing.

OFFENCES BY PARTNERSHIPS AND BODIES CORPORATE

16.4   Section 101(1) provides for a partnership to be prosecuted, for any offence under the Act alleged to have been committed by the partnership, in the name of the firm. But this does not affect the separate liability of any partners, under subsection

(4), to be proceeded against unless proved to have been ignorant of, or to have attempted to prevent the commission of, the offence. Subsection (2) applies certain procedural rules relating to companies, namely rules of court relating to the service of documents and some provisions relating to procedure on charge of an offence, for the purposes of proceedings against partnerships for offences under the Act. Subsection (3) provides for fines to be paid out of partnership assets. Subsection (5) relates to offences under the Act committed by a body corporate. If such an offence is proved to have been committed with the consent or connivance of a director, manager, secretary or other similar officer of the body, or someone purporting to act in any such capacity, then that person is also guilty of the offence and liable accordingly.

INTERPRETATION AND DEFINITIONS

16.5   Section 102 sets out details of certain expressions, used in the Act, adapted for the purpose of the application of the Act to Scotland. Section 103 contains several 'minor definitions', some of which are quite important. 'Business' is defined as including a trade or profession, and 'trade' as including any business or profession. 'Infringement proceedings', in relation to a registered trade mark, include proceedings under s 16 for delivery up (see para 8.5). 'Publish' means make available to the public, and 'publication' in relation to an application, refers to publication under s 38(1) and, in relation to registration, publication under s 40(4). 'Statutory provisions' includes provisions of subordinate legislation within the meaning of the Interpretation Act 1978. Already mentioned (see para 7.4) is s 103(2) which defines 'use' (or any particular description of use) of a trade mark, or of a sign identical with, similar to, or likely to be mistaken for a trade mark, to include any use (or that description of use) otherwise than by means of a graphic representation. Subsection (3) extends references to a Community instrument to any instrument amending or replacing that instrument. Section 104 is an 'index of defined expressions', and lists expressions which are defined by, or otherwise fall to be construed in accordance with, the provisions indicated. No specific analysis is required here.

OTHER GENERAL PROVISIONS

16.6   Section 105 introduces the transitional provisions set out in Sch 3. Many of these have already been mentioned elsewhere in this guide. Chapter 17 deals with them in more detail. Section 106(1) provides for the consequential amendments specified in Sch 4, and s 106(2) provides for the repeals which are specified in Sch 5. Section 107 contains special provisions as to the territorial waters of the UK, which are to be treated as part of the UK, and further applies the Act to certain things done in the UK sector of the continental shelf. Section 108(1) extends the Act to England, Wales, Scotland and Northern Ireland. Subsection (2) extends the Act to the Isle of Man, subject to any exceptions and modifications specified by Her Majesty by Order in Council. Section 109 is concerned with commencement. Under subsection (1) the provisions of the Act come into force on a day to be appointed by statutory instrument, and different days may be appointed for different provisions and different purposes. It has been announced that the main provisions will be brought into effect on 31 October 1994. These will not include the provisions relating to the

Community trade mark, or to the Madrid Protocol, although the Government has said that the latter will be brought into effect by 1 January 1995. Under subsection (2) the references to the commencement of this Act in Sch 3 and Sch 4 are to the commencement of the main provisions of Parts I and III of the Act and the consequential repeal of the 1938 Act. Section 110 simply sets out the title of the Act.

17 The transitional provisions

INTRODUCTION

17.1   Schedule 3 to the 1994 sets out transitional provisions, many of which have already been mentioned in the relevant earlier Chapters. However, some of them are of general application and require specific mention, and others do not really fall under any particular chapter heading. Even where mention has already been made, it may be helpful to summarise the relevant provisions, and to identify the Chapters in which they are discussed.

DEFINITIONS

17.2   Schedule 3, para 1 defines various expressions for the purposes of the Schedule. 'Existing registered mark' means a trade mark, certification mark or service mark registered under the 1938 Act immediately before commencement. The effect of this, in conjunction with para 10(1), is that a trade mark registered after commencement pursuant to an application made before commencement, and not converted under para 11, is an 'existing registered mark'. 'The old law' means the 1938 Act and any other enactment or rule of law applying to existing registered marks immediately before commencement. Applications are treated as pending on commencement if made, but not finally determined, before commencement; the date on which they were made shall be taken to be the date of filing under the 1938 Act.

EXISTING REGISTERED MARKS

17.3   These are dealt with in Sch 3, paras 2 and 3 (see para 14.3).

INFRINGEMENT AND RELATED MATTERS

17.4   Schedule 3, para 4 applies the rules for infringement to existing registered marks, but there are exceptions in favour of non-infringing use begun before commencement. These provisions are discussed at para 7.13. Schedule 3, para 5, mentioned at para 8.5 applies s 16 to infringing goods, material or articles generally, whenever made. Schedule 3, para 6(1), relates to remedies for licensees and authorised users (see paras 6.10 and 11.4).

OWNERSHIP OF AND TRANSACTIONS AFFECTING REGISTERED TRADE MARKS

17.5   Schedule 3, para 7 (see para 6.2) relates to co-ownership. Schedule 3, paras 8 (see para 6.13) and 9 (see paras 6.7 and 6.13) make provisions affecting licences and assignments.

PENDING APPLICATIONS, CLASSIFICATION AND PRIORITY

17.6   Schedule 3, paras 10 and 11 (see para 5.12) deal with pending applications and their conversion for the purposes of being dealt with under the new law. Schedule 3, para 12 (see para 14.5) deals with re-classification of old registrations and Sch 3, paras 13 and 14 make transitional provisions affecting priority (see paras 5.4 and 5.6).

DURATION AND RENEWAL, AND ALTERATION

17.7   Schedule 3, paras 15 and 16 respectively make provisions regarding duration and renewal, and pending applications for alteration (see Chapter 9).

REVOCATION FOR NON-USE AND RECTIFICATION

17.8   Schedule 3, para 17 (see para 10.7) relates to pending applications for removal, on grounds of non-use, and applications under the new law in respect of existing registered marks. Schedule 3, para 18 is concerned with pending applications for rectification and with the applicability of the new law to existing registered marks (see paras 10.8, 10.10).

OTHER TRANSITIONAL PROVISIONS

17.9   Schedule 3, para 19 (see para 11.3) deals with the continued effect of regulations governing the use of certification marks registered under the 1938 Act. Schedule 3, para 20 makes provision for treating the register of Sheffield marks as part of the new register. Schedule 3, para 21 (see para 14.10) preserves the effect of certificates of contested validity given under the 1938 Act. Schedule 3, para 22 contains provisions (see para 14.15) relating to trade mark agents and the register of trade mark agents, and the continuing of rules made under the Copyright, Designs and Patents Act 1988 affecting these matters.

Appendix 1

Trade Marks Act 1994

Trade Marks Act 1994

(1994 c 26)

ARRANGEMENT OF SECTIONS

PART I

REGISTERED TRADE MARKS

Introductory

PART II

COMMUNITY TRADE MARKS AND INTERNATIONAL MATTERS

Community trade marks

PART IV

MISCELLANEOUS AND GENERAL PROVISIONS

Miscellaneous

Interpretation

Other general provisions

SCHEDULES:

Schedule 1—Collective marks

Schedule 2—Certification marks

Schedule 3—Transitional provisions

Schedule 4—Consequential amendments

Schedule 5—Repeals and revocations

An Act to make new provision for registered trade marks, implementing Council Directive No 89/104/ EEC of 21st December 1988 to approximate the laws of the Member States relating to trade marks; to make provision in connection with Council Regulation (EC) No 40/94 of 20th December 1993 on the Community trade mark; to give effect to the Madrid Protocol Relating to the International Registration of Marks of 27th June 1989, and to certain provisions of the Paris Convention for the Protection of Industrial Property of 20th March 1883, as revised and amended; and for connected purposes.

[21 July 1994]

Parliamentary debates.

House of Lords:

2nd Reading 6 December 1993: 550 HL Official Report (5th series) col 749.

Committee Stage 13–20 January 1994.

Report 24 February 1994: 552 HL Official Report (5th series) col 728.

3rd Reading 14 March 1994: 553 HL Official Report (5th series) col 69.

Commons' Amendments 15 July 1994: 556 HL Official Report (5th series) col 2105.

House of Commons:

2nd Reading 18 April 1994: 241 HC Official Report (6th series) col 658.

Committee 17 May 1994: HC Official Report, SC B (Trade Marks Bill).

Remaining Stages 20 June 1994: 245 HC Official Report (6th series) col 78.

PART I

REGISTERED TRADE MARKS

Introductory

1   Trade marks

(1)   In this Act a "trade mark" means any sign capable of being represented graphically which is capable of distinguishing goods or services of one undertaking from those of other undertakings.

A trade mark may, in particular, consist of words (including personal names), designs, letters, numerals or the shape of goods or their packaging.

(2)   References in this Act to a trade mark include, unless the context otherwise requires, references to a collective mark (see section 49) or certification mark (see section 50).

References   See Chapter 2.

---

2   Registered trade marks

(1)   A registered trade mark is a property right obtained by the registration of the trade mark under this Act and the proprietor of a registered trade mark has the rights and remedies provided by this Act.

(2)   No proceedings lie to prevent or recover damages for the infringement of an unregistered trade mark as such; but nothing in this Act affects the law relating to passing off.

Definitions   For "trade mark", see s 1; for "registered trade mark" and as to "registration", see s 63(1).
References   See paras 1.8, 6.1.

Grounds for refusal of registration

3   Absolute grounds for refusal of registration

(1)   The following shall not be registered—
- (a)   signs which do not satisfy the requirements of section 1(1),
- (b)   trade marks which are devoid of any distinctive character,
- (c)   trade marks which consist exclusively of signs or indications which may serve, in trade, to designate the kind, quality, quantity, intended purpose, value, geographical origin, the time of production of goods or of rendering of services, or other characteristics of goods or services,
- (d)   trade marks which consist exclusively of signs or indications which have become customary in the current language or in the *bona fide* and established practices of the trade:

Provided that, a trade mark shall not be refused registration by virtue of paragraph (b), (c) or (d) above if, before the date of application for registration, it has in fact acquired a distinctive character as a result of the use made of it.

(2)   A sign shall not be registered as a trade mark if it consists exclusively of—
- (a)   the shape which results from the nature of the goods themselves,
- (b)   the shape of goods which is necessary to obtain a technical result, or
- (c)   the shape which gives substantial value to the goods.

(3)   A trade mark shall not be registered if it is—
- (a)   contrary to public policy or to accepted principles of morality, or
- (b)   of such a nature as to deceive the public (for instance as to the nature, quality or geographical origin of the goods or service).

(4)   A trade mark shall not be registered if or to the extent that its use is prohibited in the United Kingdom by any enactment or rule of law or by any provision of Community law.

(5)   A trade mark shall not be registered in the cases specified, or referred to, in section 4 (specially protected emblems).

(6)   A trade mark shall not be registered if or to the extent that the application is made in bad faith.

Definitions   For "trade mark", see s 1; as to "the date of application for registration", see s 33(2); as to "registered" and "registration", see s 63(1); for "trade" and as to "use" in relation to a trade mark, see s 103(1), (2).
References   See Chapter 3.

---

4   Specially protected emblems

(1)   A trade mark which consists of or contains—
- (a)   the Royal arms, or any of the principal armorial bearings of the Royal arms, or any insignia or device so nearly resembling the Royal arms or any such armorial bearing as to be likely to be mistaken for them or it,

(b)   a representation of the Royal crown or any of the Royal flags,

(c)   a representation of Her Majesty or any member of the Royal family, or any colourable imitation thereof, or

(d)   words, letters or devices likely to lead persons to think that the applicant either has or recently has had Royal patronage or authorisation,

shall not be registered unless it appears to the registrar that consent has been given by or on behalf of Her Majesty or, as the case may be, the relevant member of the Royal family.

(2)   A trade mark which consists of or contains a representation of—

(a)   the national flag of the United Kingdom (commonly known as the Union Jack), or

(b)   the flag of England, Wales, Scotland, Northern Ireland or the Isle of Man,

shall not be registered if it appears to the registrar that the use of the trade mark would be misleading or grossly offensive.

Provision may be made by rules identifying the flags to which paragraph (b) applies.

(3)   A trade mark shall not be registered in the cases specified in—

section 57 (national emblems, &c of Convention countries), or

section 58 (emblems, &c of certain international organisations).

(4)   Provision may be made by rules prohibiting in such cases as may be prescribed the registration of a trade mark which consists of or contains—

(a)   arms to which a person is entitled by virtue of a grant of arms by the Crown, or

(b)   insignia so nearly resembling such arms as to be likely to be mistaken for them,

unless it appears to the registrar that consent has been given by or on behalf of that person.

Where such a mark is registered, nothing in this Act shall be construed as authorising its use in any way contrary to the laws of arms.

Definitions   For "trade mark", see s 1; for "the registrar", see s 62; as to "registered" and "registration", see s 63(1); as to "use" in relation to a trade mark, see s 103(2).
References   See paras 3.14–3.18.

---

5   Relative grounds for refusal of registration

(1)   A trade mark shall not be registered if it is identical with an earlier trade mark and the goods or services for which the trade mark is applied for are identical with the goods or services for which the earlier trade mark is protected.

(2)   A trade mark shall not be registered if because—

(a)   it is identical with an earlier trade mark and is to be registered for goods or services similar to those for which the earlier trade mark is protected, or

(b)   it is similar to an earlier trade mark and is to be registered for goods or services identical with or similar to those for which the earlier trade mark is protected,

there exists a likelihood of confusion on the part of the public, which includes the likelihood of association with the earlier trade mark.

(3) A trade mark which—
  (a) is identical with or similar to an earlier trade mark, and
  (b) is to be registered for goods or services which are not similar to those for which the earlier trade mark is protected,

shall not be registered if, or to the extent that, the earlier trade mark has a reputation in the United Kingdom (or, in the case of a Community trade mark, in the European Community) and the use of the later mark without due cause would take unfair advantage of, or be detrimental to, the distinctive character or the repute of the earlier trade mark.

(4) A trade mark shall not be registered if, or to the extent that, its use in the United Kingdom is liable to be prevented—
  (a) by virtue of any rule of law (in particular, the law of passing off) protecting an unregistered trade mark or other sign used in the course of trade, or
  (b) by virtue of an earlier right other than those referred to in subsections (1) to (3) or paragraph (a) above, in particular by virtue of the law of copyright, design right or registered designs.

A person thus entitled to prevent the use of a trade mark is referred to in this Act as the proprietor of an "earlier right" in relation to the trade mark.

(5) Nothing in this section prevents the registration of a trade mark where the proprietor of the earlier trade mark or other earlier right consents to the registration.

Definitions   For "trade mark", see s 1; for "earlier trade mark", see s 6; for "Community trade mark", see s 51; as to "registered" and "registration", see s 63(1); for "trade", see s 103(1); as to "use", see s 103(2). Note as to "earlier right" sub-s (4) above.
References   See Chapter 4.

---

6   Meaning of "earlier trade mark"

(1) In this Act an "earlier trade mark" means—
  (a) a registered trade mark, international trade mark (UK) or Community trade mark which has a date of application for registration earlier than that of the trade mark in question, taking account (where appropriate) of the priorities claimed in respect of the trade marks,
  (b) a Community trade mark which has a valid claim to seniority from an earlier registered trade mark or international trade mark (UK), or
  (c) a trade mark which, at the date of application for registration of the trade mark in question or (where appropriate) of the priority claimed in respect of the application, was entitled to protection under the Paris Convention as a well known trade mark.

(2) References in this Act to an earlier trade mark include a trade mark in respect of which an application for registration has been made and which, if registered, would be an earlier trade mark by virtue of subsection 1(a) or (b), subject to its being so registered.

(3) A trade mark within subsection (1)(a) or (b) whose registration expires shall continue to be taken into account in determining the registrability of a later mark for a period of one year after the expiry unless the registrar is satisfied that there was no *bona fide* use of the mark during the two years immediately preceding the expiry.

Definitions   For "trade mark", see s 1; as to "the date of application for registration", see s 33(2); for "Community trade mark", see s 51; for "international trade mark (UK)", see s 53; for "the Paris Convention", see s 55(1)(a); as to "well known trade mark entitled to protection under the Paris Convention", see s 56; for "the registrar", see s 62; for "registered trade mark" and as to "registered" and "registration", see s 63(1); as to "use" in relation to a trade mark, see s 103(2).
References   See Chapter 4.

7   Raising of relative grounds in case of honest concurrent use

(1)   This section applies where on an application for the registration of a trade mark it appears to the registrar—

  (a)   that there is an earlier trade mark in relation to which the conditions set out in section 5(1), (2) or (3) obtain, or

  (b)   that there is an earlier right in relation to which the condition set out in section 5(4) is satisfied,

but the applicant shows to the satisfaction of the registrar that there has been honest concurrent use of the trade mark for which registration is sought.

(2)   In that case the registrar shall not refuse the application by reason of the earlier trade mark or other earlier right unless objection on that ground is raised in opposition proceedings by the proprietor of that earlier trade mark or other earlier right.

(3)   For the purposes of this section "honest concurrent use" means such use in the United Kingdom, by the applicant or with his consent, as would formerly have amounted to honest concurrent use for the purposes of section 12(2) of the Trade Marks Act 1938.

(4)   Nothing in this section affects—

  (a)   the refusal of registration on the grounds mentioned in section 3 (absolute grounds for refusal), or

  (b)   the making of an application for a declaration of invalidity under section 47(2) (application on relative grounds where no consent to registration).

(5)   This section does not apply when there is an order in force under section 8 below.

Definitions   For "trade mark", see s 1; for "earlier right", see s 5(4); for "earlier trade mark", see s 6; for "the registrar", see s 62; as to "registration", see s 63(1); as to "use" in relation to a trade mark, see s 103(2). Note as to "honest concurrent use", sub-s (3) above.
References   See para 4.7.

8   Power to require that relative grounds be raised in opposition proceedings

(1)   The Secretary of State may by order provide that in any case a trade mark shall not be refused registration on a ground mentioned in section 5 (relative grounds for refusal) unless objection on that ground is raised in opposition proceedings by the proprietor of the earlier trade mark or other earlier right.

(2)   The order may make such consequential provision as appears to the Secretary of State appropriate—

    (a) with respect to the carrying out by the registrar of searches of earlier trade marks, and

    (b) as to the persons by whom an application for a declaration of invalidity may be made on the grounds specified in section 47(2) (relative grounds).

(3)   An order making such provision as is mentioned in subsection (2)(a) may direct that so much of section 37 (examination of application) as requires a search to be carried out shall cease to have effect.

(4)   An order making such provision as is mentioned in subsection (2)(b) may provide that so much of section 47(3) as provides that any person may make an application for a declaration of invalidity shall have effect subject to the provisions of the order.

(5)   An order under this section shall be made by statutory instrument, and no order shall be made unless a draft of it has been laid before and approved by a resolution of each House of Parliament.

No such draft of an order making such provision as is mentioned in subsection (1) shall be laid before Parliament until after the end of the period of ten years beginning with the day on which applications for Community trade marks may first be filed in pursuance of the Community Trade Mark Regulation.

(6)   An order under this section may contain such transitional provisions as appear to the Secretary of State to be appropriate.

Definitions   For "trade mark", see s 1; for "earlier right", see s 5(4); for "earlier trade mark", see s 6; for "Community trade mark" and "Community Trade Mark Regulation", see s 51; for "the registrar", see s 62; as to "registration", see s 63(1).
References   See paras 1.19, 4.1, 4.7.

Effects of registered trade mark

9   Rights conferred by registered trade mark

(1)   The proprietor of a registered trade mark has exclusive rights in the trade mark which are infringed by use of the trade mark in the United Kingdom without his consent.

The acts amounting to infringement, if done without the consent of the proprietor, are specified in section 10.

(2)   References in this Act to the infringement of a registered trade mark are to any such infringement of the rights of the proprietor.

(3)   The rights of the proprietor have effect from the date of registration (which in accordance with section 40(3) is the date of filing of the application for registration):

Provided that—

    (a) no infringement proceedings may be begun before the date on which the trade mark is in fact registered; and

    (b) no offence under section 92 (unauthorised use of trade mark, &c in relation to goods) is committed by anything done before the date of publication of the registration.

Definitions   For "trade mark", see s 1; as to "the date of filing of an application for registration", see s 33(1); for "registered trade mark" and as to "registered" and "registration", see s 63(1); for "infringement proceedings" and "publication" and as to "use" in relation to a trade mark, see s 103(1), (2).
References   See Chapter 7.

10   Infringement of registered trade mark

(1)   A person infringes a registered trade mark if he uses in the course of trade a sign which is identical with the trade mark in relation to goods or services which are identical with those for which it is registered.

(2)   A person infringes a registered trade mark if he uses in the course of trade a sign where because—

    (a)   the sign is identical with the trade mark and is used in relation to goods or services similar to those for which the trade mark is registered, or

    (b)   the sign is similar to the trade mark and is used in relation to goods or services identical with or similar to those for which the trade mark is registered,

there exists a likelihood of confusion on the part of the public, which includes the likelihood of association with the trade mark.

(3)   A person infringes a registered trade mark if he uses in the course of trade a sign which—

    (a)   is identical with or similar to the trade mark, and

    (b)   is used in relation to goods or services which are not similar to those for which the trade mark is registered,

where the trade mark has a reputation in the United Kingdom and the use of the sign, being without due cause, takes unfair advantage of, or is detrimental to, the distinctive character or the repute of the trade mark.

(4)   For the purposes of this section a person uses a sign if, in particular, he—

    (a)   affixes it to goods or the packaging thereof;

    (b)   offers or exposes goods for sale, puts them on the market or stocks them for those purposes under the sign, or offers or supplies services under the sign;

    (c)   imports or exports goods under the sign; or

    (d)   uses the sign on business papers or in advertising.

(5)   A person who applies a registered trade mark to material intended to be used for labelling or packaging goods, as a business paper, or for advertising goods or services, shall be treated as a party to any use of the material which infringes the registered trade mark if when he applied the mark he knew or had reason to believe that the application of the mark was not duly authorised by the proprietor or a licensee.

(6)   Nothing in the preceding provisions of this section shall be construed as preventing the use of a registered trade mark by any person for the purpose of identifying goods or services as those of the proprietor or a licensee.

But any such use otherwise than in accordance with honest practices in industrial or commercial matters shall be treated as infringing the registered trade mark if the use without due cause takes unfair advantage of, or is detrimental to, the distinctive character or repute of the trade mark.

Definitions   For "trade mark", see s 1; for "registered trade mark" and as to "registered", see s 63(1); for "business" and "trade", see s 103(1); as to "use", see s 103(2) (and note sub-s (4) above).
References   See Chapter 7.

11   Limits on effect of registered trade mark

(1)   A registered trade mark is not infringed by the use of another registered trade mark in relation to goods or services for which the latter is registered (but see section 47(6) (effect of declaration of invalidity of registration)).

(2)   A registered trade mark is not infringed by—
    (a)   the use by a person of his own name or address,
    (b)   the use of indications concerning the kind, quality, quantity, intended purpose, value, geographical origin, the time of production of goods or of rendering of services, or other characteristics of goods or services, or
    (c)   the use of the trade mark where it is necessary to indicate the intended purpose of a product or service (in particular, as accessories or spare parts),

provided the use is in accordance with honest practices in industrial or commercial matters.

(3)   A registered trade mark is not infringed by the use in the course of trade in a particular locality of an earlier right which applies only in that locality.

For this purpose an "earlier right" means an unregistered trade mark or other sign continuously used in relation to goods or services by a person or a predecessor in title of his from a date prior to whichever is the earlier of—
    (a)   the use of the first-mentioned trade mark in relation to those goods or services by the proprietor or a predecessor in title of his, or
    (b)   the registration of the first-mentioned trade mark in respect of those goods or services in the name of the proprietor or a predecessor in title of his;

and an earlier right shall be regarded as applying in a locality if, or to the extent that, its use in that locality is protected by virtue of any rule of law (in particular, the law of passing off).

Definitions   For "trade mark", see s 1; for "registered trade mark" and as to "registered" and "registration", see s 63(1); for "trade", see s 103(1); as to "use", see s 103(2).
References   See paras 7.8–7.10.

12   Exhaustion of rights conferred by registered trade mark

(1)   A registered trade mark is not infringed by the use of the trade mark in relation to goods which have been put on the market in the European Economic Area under that trade mark by the proprietor or with his consent.

(2)   Subsection (1) does not apply where there exist legitimate reasons for the proprietor to oppose further dealings in the goods (in particular, where the condition of the goods has been changed or impaired after they have been put on the market).

Definitions   For "trade mark", see s 1; for "registered trade mark", see s 63(1); as to "use" in relation to a trade mark, see s 103(2).
References   See para 7.11.

13   Registration subject to disclaimer or limitation

(1)   An applicant for registration of a trade mark, or the proprietor of a registered trade mark, may—

(a)   disclaim any right to the exclusive use of any specified element of the trade mark, or

(b)   agree that the rights conferred by the registration shall be subject to a specified territorial or other limitation;

and where the registration of a trade mark is subject to a disclaimer or limitation, the rights conferred by section 9 (rights conferred by registered trade mark) are restricted accordingly.

(2)   Provision shall be made by rules as to the publication and entry in the register of a disclaimer or limitation.

Definitions   For "trade mark", see s 1; for "the register" and "registered trade mark" and as to "registration", see s 63(1); for "publication", see s 103(1); as to "use", see s 103(2).
References   See para 7.12.

Infringement proceedings

14   Action for infringement

(1)   An infringement of a registered trade mark is actionable by the proprietor of the trade mark.

(2)   In an action for infringement all such relief by way of damages, injunctions, accounts or otherwise is available to him as is available in respect of the infringement of any other property right.

Definitions   For "trade mark", see s 1; for "infringement", see ss 9(1), (2), 10; for "registered trade mark", see s 63(1).
References   See para 8.1.

15   Order for erasure, &c of offending sign

(1)   Where a person is found to have infringed a registered trade mark, the court may make an order requiring him—

(a)   to cause the offending sign to be erased, removed or obliterated from any infringing goods, material or articles in his possession, custody or control, or

(b)   if it is not reasonably practicable for the offending sign to be erased, removed or obliterated, to secure the destruction of the infringing goods, material or articles in question.

(2)   If an order under subsection (1) is not complied with, or it appears to the court likely that such an order would not be complied with, the court may order that the infringing goods, material or articles be delivered to such person as the court may direct for erasure, removal or obliteration of the sign, or for destruction, as the case may be.

Definitions   For "infringing articles", "infringing goods" and "infringing material", see s 17; for "registered trade mark", see s 63(1); for "the court", see s 75.
References   See para 8.4.

16   Order for delivery up of infringing goods, material or articles

(1)   The proprietor of a registered trade mark may apply to the court for an order for the delivery up to him, or such other person as the court may direct, of any infringing goods, material or articles which a person has in his possession, custody or control in the course of a business.

(2)   An application shall not be made after the end of the period specified in section 18 (period after which remedy of delivery up not available); and no order shall be made unless the court also makes, or it appears to the court that there are grounds for making, an order under section 19 (order as to disposal of infringing goods, &c).

(3)   A person to whom any infringing goods, material or articles are delivered up in pursuance of an order under this section shall, if an order under section 19 is not made, retain them pending the making of an order, or the decision not to make an order, under that section.

(4)   Nothing in this section affects any other power of the court.

Definitions   For "infringing articles", "infringing goods" and "infringing material", see s 17; for "registered trade mark", see s 63(1); for "the court", see s 75; for "business", see s 103(1).
References   See paras 8.5, 8.7.

17   Meaning of "infringing goods, material or articles"

(1)   In this Act the expressions "infringing goods", "infringing material" and "infringing articles" shall be construed as follows.

(2)   Goods are "infringing goods", in relation to a registered trade mark, if they or their packaging bear a sign identical or similar to that mark and—
    (a)   the application of the sign to the goods or their packaging was an infringement of the registered trade mark, or
    (b)   the goods are proposed to be imported into the United Kingdom and the application of the sign in the United Kingdom to them or their packaging would be an infringement of the registered trade mark, or
    (c)   the sign has otherwise been used in relation to the goods in such a way as to infringe the registered trade mark.

(3)   Nothing in subsection (2) shall be construed as affecting the importation of goods which may lawfully be imported into the United Kingdom by virtue of an enforceable Community right.

(4)   Material is "infringing material", in relation to a registered trade mark if it bears a sign identical or similar to that mark and either—
    (a)   it is used for labelling or packaging goods, as a business paper, or for advertising goods or services, in such a way as to infringe the registered trade mark, or
    (b)   it is intended to be so used and such use would infringe the registered trade mark.

(5)   "Infringing articles", in relation to a registered trade mark, means articles—
    (a)   which are specifically designed or adapted for making copies of a sign identical or similar to that mark, and
    (b)   which a person has in his possession, custody or control, knowing or having reason to believe that they have been or are to be used to produce infringing goods or material.

Definitions   For "infringement", see ss 9(1), (2), 10; for "registered trade mark", see s 63(1); for "business", see s 103(1); as to "use", see s 103(2).
References   See paras 8.2, 8.3.

18   Period after which remedy of delivery up not available

(1)   An application for an order under section 16 (order for delivery up of infringing goods, material or articles) may not be made after the end of the period of six years from—

    (a)   in the case of infringing goods, the date on which the trade mark was applied to the goods or their packaging,

    (b)   in the case of infringing material, the date on which the trade mark was applied to the material, or

    (c)   in the case of infringing articles, the date on which they were made,

except as mentioned in the following provisions.

(2)   If during the whole or part of that period the proprietor of the registered trade mark—

    (a)   is under a disability, or

    (b)   is prevented by fraud or concealment from discovering the facts entitling him to apply for an order,

an application may be made at any time before the end of the period of six years from the date on which he ceased to be under a disability or, as the case may be, could with reasonable diligence have discovered those facts.

(3)   In subsection (2) "disability"—

    (a)   in England and Wales, has the same meaning as in the Limitation Act 1980;

    (b)   in Scotland, means legal disability within the meaning of the Prescription and Limitation (Scotland) Act 1973;

    (c)   in Northern Ireland, has the same meaning as in the Limitation (Northern Ireland) Order 1989.

Definitions   For "trade mark", see s 1; for "infringing articles", "infringing goods" and "infringing material", see s 17; for "registered trade mark", see s 63(1).
References   See para 8.7.

19   Order as to disposal of infringing goods, material or articles

(1)   Where infringing goods, material or articles have been delivered up in pursuance of an order under section 16, an application may be made to the court—

    (a)   for an order that they be destroyed or forfeited to such person as the court may think fit, or

    (b)   for a decision that no such order should be made.

(2)   In considering what order (if any) should be made, the court shall consider whether other remedies available in an action for infringement of the registered trade mark would be adequate to compensate the proprietor and any licensee and protect their interests.

(3)   Provision shall be made by rules of court as to the service of notice on persons having an interest in the goods, material or articles, and any such person is entitled—

(a) to appear in proceedings for an order under this section, whether or not he was served with notice, and

(b) to appeal against any order made, whether or not he appeared;

and an order shall not take effect until the end of the period within which notice of an appeal may be given or, if before the end of that period notice of appeal is duly given, until the final determination or abandonment of the proceedings on the appeal.

(4) Where there is more than one person interested in the goods, material or articles, the court shall make such order as it thinks just.

(5) If the court decides that no order should be made under this section, the person in whose possession, custody or control the goods, material or articles were before being delivered up is entitled to their return.

(6) References in this section to a person having an interest in goods, material or articles include any person in whose favour an order could be made under this section or under section 114, 204 or 231 of the Copyright, Designs and Patents Act 1988 (which make similar provision in relation to infringement of copyright, rights in performances and design right).

Definitions For "trade mark", see s 1; for "infringement", see ss 9(1), (2), 10; for "infringing articles", "infringing goods" and "infringing material", see s 17; for "registered trade mark", see s 63(1); for "the court", see s 75. Note as to "person having an interest in goods, material or articles", sub-s (6) above.
References See paras 8.6–8.8.

20 Jurisdiction of sheriff court or county court in Northern Ireland

Proceedings for an order under section 16 (order for delivery up of infringing goods, material or articles) or section 19 (order as to disposal of infringing goods, &c) may be brought—

(a) in the sheriff court in Scotland, or

(b) in a county court in Northern Ireland.

This does not affect the jurisdiction of the Court of Session or the High Court in Northern Ireland.

References See para 8.6.

21 Remedy for groundless threats of infringement proceedings

(1) Where a person threatens another with proceedings for infringement of a registered trade mark other than—

(a) the application of the mark to goods or their packaging,

(b) the importation of goods to which, or to the packaging of which, the mark has been applied, or

(c) the supply of services under the mark,

any person aggrieved may bring proceedings for relief under this section.

(2) The relief which may be applied for is any of the following—

(a) a declaration that the threats are unjustifiable,

(b) an injunction against the continuance of the threats,

(c) damages in respect of any loss he has sustained by the threats;

and the plaintiff is entitled to such relief unless the defendant shows that the acts in respect of which proceedings were threatened constitute (or if done would constitute) an infringement of the registered trade mark concerned.

(3) If that is shown by the defendant, the plaintiff is nevertheless entitled to relief if he shows that the registration of the trade mark is invalid or liable to be revoked in a relevant respect.

(4) The mere notification that a trade mark is registered, or that an application for registration has been made, does not constitute a threat of proceedings for the purposes of this section.

Definitions For "trade mark", see s 1; for "infringement", see ss 9(1), (2), 10; for "registered trade mark" and as to "registered" and "registration", see s 63(1); for "infringement proceedings", see s 103(1).
References See para 8.9.

Registered trade mark as object of property

22 Nature of registered trade mark

A registered trade mark is personal property (in Scotland, incorporeal moveable property).

References See para 6.1.

23 Co-ownership of registered trade mark

(1) Where a registered trade mark is granted to two or more persons jointly, each of them is entitled, subject to any agreement to the contrary, to an equal undivided share in the registered trade mark.

(2) The following provisions apply where two or more persons are co-proprietors of a registered trade mark, by virtue of subsection (1) or otherwise.

(3) Subject to any agreement to the contrary, each co-proprietor is entitled, by himself or his agents, to do for his own benefit and without the consent of or the need to account to the other or others, any act which would otherwise amount to an infringement of the registered trade mark.

(4) One co-proprietor may not without the consent of the other or others—
    (a) grant a licence to use the registered trade mark, or
    (b) assign or charge his share in the registered trade mark (or, in Scotland, cause or permit security to be granted over it).

(5) Infringement proceedings may be brought by any co-proprietor, but he may not, without the leave of the court, proceed with the action unless the other, or each of the others, is either joined as a plaintiff or added as a defendant.

A co-proprietor who is thus added as a defendant shall not be made liable for any costs in the action unless he takes part in the proceedings.

Nothing in this subsection affects the granting of interlocutory relief on the application of a single co-proprietor.

(6) Nothing in this section affects the mutual rights and obligations of trustees or personal representatives, or their rights and obligations as such.

Definitions   For "infringement", see ss 9(1), (2), 10; for "registered trade mark", see s 63(1); for "the court", see s 75; and for "infringement proceedings", see s 103(1).
References   See Chapter 6.

24   Assignment, &c of registered trade mark

(1)   A registered trade mark is transmissible by assignment, testamentary disposition or operation of law in the same way as other personal or moveable property.

It is so transmissible either in connection with the goodwill of a business or independently.

(2)   An assignment or other transmission of a registered trade mark may be partial, that is, limited so as to apply—

(a)   in relation to some but not all of the goods or services for which the trade mark is registered, or

(b)   in relation to use of the trade mark in a particular manner or a particular locality.

(3)   An assignment of a registered trade mark, or an assent relating to a registered trade mark, is not effective unless it is in writing signed by or on behalf of the assignor or, as the case may be, a personal representative.

Except in Scotland, this requirement may be satisfied in a case where the assignor or personal representative is a body corporate by the affixing of its seal.

(4)   The above provisions apply to assignment by way of security as in relation to any other assignment.

(5)   A registered trade mark may be the subject of a charge (in Scotland, security) in the same way as other personal or moveable property.

(6)   Nothing in this Act shall be construed as affecting the assignment or other transmission of an unregistered trade mark as part of the goodwill of a business.

Definitions   For "trade mark", see s 1; for "registered trade mark" and as to "registered", see s 63(1); for "business", see s 103(1).
References   See Chapter 6.

25   Registration of transactions affecting registered trade mark

(1)   On application being made to the registrar by—

(a)   a person claiming to be entitled to an interest in or under a registered trade mark by virtue of a registrable transaction, or

(b)   any other person claiming to be affected by such a transaction,

the prescribed particulars of the transaction shall be entered in the register.

(2)   The following are registrable transactions—

(a)   an assignment of a registered trade mark or any right in it;

(b)   the grant of a licence under a registered trade mark;

(c)   the granting of any security interest (whether fixed or floating) over a registered trade mark or any right in or under it;

(d)   the making by personal representatives of an assent in relation to a registered trade mark or any right in or under it;

(e) an order of a court or other competent authority transferring a registered trade mark or any right in or under it.

(3)   Until an application has been made for registration of the prescribed particulars of a registrable transaction—

(a) the transaction is ineffective as against a person acquiring a conflicting interest in or under the registered trade mark in ignorance of it, and

(b) a person claiming to be a licensee by virtue of the transaction does not have the protection of section 30 or 31 (rights and remedies of licensee in relation to infringement).

(4)   Where a person becomes the proprietor or a licensee of a registered trade mark by virtue of a registrable transaction, then unless—

(a) an application for registration of the prescribed particulars of the transaction is made before the end of the period of six months beginning with its date, or

(b) the court is satisfied that it was not practicable for such an application to be made before the end of that period and that an application was made as soon as practicable thereafter,

he is not entitled to damages or an account of profits in respect of any infringement of the registered trade mark occurring after the date of the transaction and before the prescribed particulars of the transaction are registered.

(5)   Provision may be made by rules as to—

(a) the amendment of registered particulars relating to a licence so as to reflect any alteration of the terms of the licence, and

(b) the removal of such particulars from the register—

(i) where it appears from the registered particulars that the licence was granted for a fixed period and that period has expired, or

(ii) where no such period is indicated and, after such period as may be prescribed, the registrar has notified the parties of his intention to remove the particulars from the register.

(6)   Provision may also be made by rules as to the amendment or removal from the register of particulars relating to a security interest on the application of, or with the consent of, the person entitled to the benefit of that interest.

Definitions   For "infringement", see ss 9(1), (2), 10; for "the registrar", see s 62; for "the register", "registered trade mark" and as to "registered" and "registration", see s 63(1); for "the court", see s 75. Note as to "registrable transactions" sub-s (2) above.
References   See Chapter 6.

---

26   Trusts and equities

(1)   No notice of any trust (express, implied or constructive) shall be entered in the register; and the registrar shall not be affected by any such notice.

(2)   Subject to the provisions of this Act, equities (in Scotland, rights) in respect of a registered trade mark may be enforced in like manner as in respect of other personal or moveable property.

Definitions   For "the registrar", see s 62; for "the register" and "registered trade mark" see s 63(1).
References   See Chapter 6.

27 Application for registration of trade mark as an object of property

(1)   The provisions of sections 22 to 26 (which relate to a registered trade mark as an object of property) apply, with the necessary modifications, in relation to an application for the registration of a trade mark as in relation to a registered trade mark.

(2)   In section 23 (co-ownership of registered trade mark) as it applies in relation to an application for registration the reference in subsection (1) to the granting of the registration shall be construed as a reference to the making of the application.

(3)   In section 25 (registration of transactions affecting registered trade marks) as it applies in relation to a transaction affecting an application for the registration of a trade mark, the references to the entry of particulars in the register, and to the making of an application to register particulars, shall be construed as references to the giving of notice to the registrar of those particulars.

Definitions   For "trade mark", see s 1; for "the registrar", see s 62; for "the register", "registered trade mark" and as to "registration", see s 63(1), 6.3, 6.4.
References   See paras 6.1, 6.3, 6.4.

Licensing

28 Licensing of registered trade mark

(1)   A licence to use a registered trade mark may be general or limited.

A limited licence may, in particular, apply—
   (a)   in relation to some but not all of the goods or services for which the trade mark is registered, or
   (b)   in relation to use of the trade mark in a particular manner or a particular locality.

(2)   A licence is not effective unless it is in writing signed by or on behalf of the grantor.

Except in Scotland, this requirement may be satisfied in a case where the grantor is a body corporate by the affixing of its seal.

(3)   Unless the licence provides otherwise, it is binding on a successor in title to the grantor's interest.

References in this Act to doing anything with, or without, the consent of the proprietor of a registered trade mark shall be construed accordingly.

(4)   Where the licence so provides, a sub-licence may be granted by the licensee; and references in this Act to a licence or licensee include a sub-licence or sub-licensee.

Definitions   For "trade mark", see s 1; for "registered trade mark" and as to "registered", see s 63(1); as to "use" in relation to a trade mark, see s 103(2). Note as to "consent of the proprietor of a registered trade mark", see sub-s (3) above, and as to "licence" and "licensee", sub-s (4) above.
References   See Chapter 6.

29 Exclusive licenses

(1)   In this Act an "exclusive licence" means a licence (whether general or limited) authorising the licensee to the exclusion of all other persons, including the

person granting the licence, to use a registered trade mark in the manner authorised by the licence.

The expression "exclusive licensee" shall be construed accordingly.

(2) An exclusive licensee has the same rights against a successor in title who is bound by the licence as he has against the person granting the licence.

Definitions   For "registered trade mark", see s 63(1); as to "use" in relation to a trade mark, see s 103(2).
References   See Chapter 6.

30   General provisions as to rights of licensees in case of infringement

(1) This section has effect with respect to the rights of a licensee in relation to infringement of a registered trade mark.

The provisions of this section do not apply where or to the extent that, by virtue of section 31(1) below (exclusive licensee having rights and remedies of assignee), the licensee has a right to bring proceedings in his own name.

(2) A licensee is entitled, unless his licence, or any licence through which his interest is derived, provides otherwise, to call on the proprietor of the registered trade mark to take infringement proceedings in respect of any matter which affects his interests.

(3) If the proprietor—
    (a)   refuses to do so, or
    (b)   fails to do so within two months after being called upon,

the licensee may bring the proceedings in his own name as if he were the proprietor.

(4) Where infringement proceedings are brought by a licensee by virtue of this section, the licensee may not, without the leave of the court, proceed with the action unless the proprietor is either joined as a plaintiff or added as a defendant.

This does not affect the granting of interlocutory relief on an application by a licensee alone.

(5) A proprietor who is added as a defendant as mentioned in subsection (4) shall not be made liable for any costs in the action unless he takes part in the proceedings.

(6) In infringement proceedings brought by the proprietor of a registered trade mark any loss suffered or likely to be suffered by licensees shall be taken into account; and the court may give such directions as it thinks fit as to the extent to which the plaintiff is to hold the proceeds of any pecuniary remedy on behalf of licensees.

(7) The provisions of this section apply in relation to an exclusive licensee if or to the extent that he has, by virtue of section 31(1), the rights and remedies of an assignee as if he were the proprietor of the registered trade mark.

Definitions   For "infringement", see ss 9(1), (2), 10; as to "licence" and "licensee", see s 28(4); for "exclusive licensee", see s 29(1); for "registered trade mark", see s 63(1); for "the court", see s 75; for "infringement proceedings", see s 103(1).
References   See Chapter 6.

31   Exclusive licensee having rights and remedies of assignee

(1) An exclusive licence may provide that the licensee shall have, to such extent as may be provided by the licence, the same rights and remedies in respect of matters occurring after the grant of the licence as if the licence had been an assignment.

Where or to the extent that such provision is made, the licensee is entitled, subject to the provisions of the licence and to the following provisions of this section, to bring infringement proceedings, against any person other than the proprietor, in his own name.

(2)   Any such rights and remedies of an exclusive licensee are concurrent with those of the proprietor of the registered trade mark; and references to the proprietor of a registered trade mark in the provisions of this Act relating to infringement shall be construed accordingly.

(3)   In an action brought by an exclusive licensee by virtue of this section a defendant may avail himself of any defence which would have been available to him if the action had been brought by the proprietor of the registered trade mark.

(4)   Where proceedings for infringement of a registered trade mark brought by the proprietor or an exclusive licensee relate wholly or partly to an infringement in respect of which they have concurrent rights of action, the proprietor or, as the case may be, the exclusive licensee may not, without the leave of the court, proceed with the action unless the other is either joined as a plaintiff or added as a defendant.

This does not affect the granting of interlocutory relief on an application by a proprietor or exclusive licensee alone.

(5)   A person who is added as a defendant as mentioned in subsection (4) shall not be made liable for any costs in the action unless he takes part in the proceedings.

(6)   Where an action for infringement of a registered trade mark is brought which relates wholly or partly to an infringement in respect of which the proprietor and an exclusive licensee have or had concurrent rights of action—

    (a)   the court shall in assessing damages take into account—

        (i)   the terms of the licence, and

        (ii) any pecuniary remedy already awarded or available to either of them in respect of the infringement;

    (b)   no account of profits shall be directed if an award of damages has been made, or an account of profits has been directed, in favour of the other of them in respect of the infringement; and

    (c)   the court shall if an account 6f profits is directed apportion the profits between them as the court considers just, subject to any agreement between them.

The provisions of this subsection apply whether or not the proprietor and the exclusive licensee are both parties to the action; and if they are not both parties the court may give such directions as it thinks fit as to the extent to which the party to the proceedings is to hold the proceeds of any pecuniary remedy on behalf of the other.

(7)   The proprietor of a registered trade mark shall notify any exclusive licensee who has a concurrent right of action before applying for an order under section 16 (order for delivery up); and the court may on the application of the licensee make such order under that section as it thinks fit having regard to the terms of the licence.

(8)   The provisions of subsections (4) to (7) above have effect subject to any agreement to the contrary between the exclusive licensee and the proprietor.

Definitions   For "infringement", see ss 9(1), (2), 10; for "exclusive licence" and "exclusive licensee", see s 29(1); for "registered trade mark", see s 63(1); for "the court", see s 75; for "infringement proceedings", see s 103(1).
References   See Chapter 6.

Application for registered trade mark

32 Application for registration

(1)   An application for registration of a trade mark shall be made to the registrar.

(2)   The application shall contain—
    (a)   a request for registration of a trade mark,
    (b)   the name and address of the applicant,
    (c)   a statement of the goods or services in relation to which it is sought to register the trade mark, and
    (d)   a representation of the trade mark.

(3)   The application shall state that the trade mark is being used, by the applicant or with his consent, in relation to those goods or services, or that he has a *bona fide* intention that it should be so used.

(4)   The application shall be subject to the payment of the application fee and such class fees as may be appropriate.

Definitions   For "trade mark", see s 1; for "the registrar", see s 62; as to "registration", see s 63(1); as to "use" in relation to a trade mark, see s 103(2).
References   See para 5.1.

33 Date of filing

(1)   The date of filing of an application for registration of a trade mark is the date on which documents containing everything required by section 32(2) are furnished to the registrar by the applicant.

If the documents are furnished on different days, the date of filing is the last of those days.

(2)   References in this Act to the date of application for registration are to the date of filing of the application.

Definitions   For "trade mark", see s 1; for "the registrar", see s 62; as to "registration", see s 63(1).
Note as to "the date of application for registration", sub-s (2) above.
References   See para 5.2.

34 Classification of trade marks

(1)   Goods and services shall be classified for the purposes of the registration of trade marks according to a prescribed system of classification.

(2)   Any question arising as to the class within which any goods or services fall shall be determined by the registrar, whose decision shall be final.

Definitions   For "trade mark", see s 1; for "the registrar", see s 62; as to "registration", see s 63(1).
References   See para 5.3.

Priority

35 Claim to priority of Convention application

(1)   A person who has duly filed an application for protection of a trade mark in a

Convention country (a "Convention application"), or his successor in title, has a right to priority, for the purposes of registering the same trade mark under this Act for some or all of the same goods or services, for a period of six months from the date of filing of the first such application.

(2)   If the application for registration under this Act is made within that six-month period—

    (a)   the relevant date for the purposes of establishing which rights take precedence shall be the date of filing of the first Convention application, and

    (b)   the registrability of the trade mark shall not be affected by any use of the mark in the United Kingdom in the period between that date and the date of the application under this Act.

(3)   Any filing which in a Convention country is equivalent to a regular national filing, under its domestic legislation or an international agreement, shall be treated as giving rise to the right of priority.

A "regular national filing" means a filing which is adequate to establish the date on which the application was filed in that country, whatever may be the subsequent fate of the application.

(4)   A subsequent application concerning the same subject as the first Convention application, filed in the same Convention country, shall be considered the first Convention application (of which the filing date is the starting date of the period of priority), if at the time of the subsequent application—

    (a)   the previous application has been withdrawn, abandoned or refused, without having been laid open to public inspection and without leaving any rights outstanding, and

    (b)   it has not yet served as a basis for claiming a right of priority.

The previous application may not thereafter serve as a basis for claiming a right of priority.

(5)   Provision may be made by rules as to the manner of claiming a right to priority on the basis of a Convention application.

(6)   A right to priority arising as a result of a Convention application may be assigned or otherwise transmitted, either with the application or independently.

The reference in subsection (1) to the applicant's "successor in title" shall be construed accordingly.

Definitions   For "trade mark", see s 1; for "date of filing", see s 33(1); for "date of registration", see s 33(2); for "Convention country", see s 55(1)(b); as to "registering" and "registration", see s 63(1); as to "use" in relation to a trade mark, see s 103(2). Note as to "Convention application", sub-s (1) above, and as to "regular national filing", sub-s (3) above.
References   See paras 5.4–5.6.

36   Claim to priority from other relevant overseas application

(1)   Her Majesty may by Order in Council make provision for conferring on a person who has duly filed an application for protection of a trade mark in—

    (a)   any of the Channel Islands or a colony, or

    (b)   a country or territory in relation to which Her Majesty's Government in the United Kingdom have entered into a treaty, convention, arrangement or engagement for the reciprocal protection of trade marks,

a right to priority, for the purpose of registering the same trade mark under this Act for some or all of the same goods or services, for a specified period from the date of filing of that application.

(2)   An Order in Council under this section may make provision corresponding to that made by section 35 in relation to Convention countries or such other provision as appears to Her Majesty to be appropriate.

(3)   A statutory instrument containing an Order in Council under this section shall be subject to annulment in pursuance of a resolution of either House of Parliament.

Definitions   For "trade mark", see s 1; as to the "date of filing" of an application, see s 33(1); for "Convention country", see s 55(1)(b); as to "registering", see s 63(1).
References   See paras 5.4–5.6.

Registration procedure

37   Examination of application

(1)   The registrar shall examine whether an application for registration of a trade mark satisfies the requirements of this Act (including any requirements imposed by rules).

(2)   For that purpose he shall carry out a search, to such extent as he considers necessary, of earlier trade marks.

(3)   If it appears to the registrar that the requirements for registration are not met, he shall inform the applicant and give him an opportunity, within such period as the registrar may specify, to make representations or to amend the application.

(4)   If the applicant fails to satisfy the registrar that those requirements are met, or to amend the application so as to meet them, or fails to respond before the end of the specified period, the registrar shall refuse to accept the application.

(5)   If it appears to the registrar that the requirements for registration are met, he shall accept the application.

Definitions   For "trade mark", see s 1; for "earlier trade mark", see s 6; for "the registrar", see s 62; as to "registration", see s 63(1).
References   See para 5.7.

38   Publication, opposition proceedings and observations

(1)   When an application for registration has been accepted, the registrar shall cause the application to be published in the prescribed manner.

(2)   Any person may, within the prescribed time from the date of the publication of the application, give notice to the registrar of opposition to the registration.

The notice shall be given in writing in the prescribed manner, and shall include a statement of the grounds of opposition.

(3)   Where an application has been published, any person may, at any time before

the registration of the trade mark, make observations in writing to the registrar as to whether the trade mark should be registered; and the registrar shall inform the applicant of any such observations.

A person who makes observations does not thereby become a party to the proceedings on the application.

Definitions For "trade mark", see s 1; for "the registrar", see s 62; as to "registered" and "registration", see s 63(1); for "publish", see s 103(1).
References See para 5.8.

39 Withdrawal, restriction or amendment of application

(1) The applicant may at any time withdraw his application or restrict the goods or services covered by the application.

If the application has been published, the withdrawal or restriction shall also be published.

(2) In other respects, an application may be amended, at the request of the applicant, only by correcting—
  (a) the name or address of the applicant,
  (b) errors of wording or of copying, or
  (c) obvious mistakes,

and then only where the correction does not substantially affect the identity of the trade mark or extend the goods or services covered by the application.

(3) Provision shall be made by rules for the publication of any amendment which affects the representation of the trade mark, or the goods or services covered by the application, and for the making of objections by any person claiming to be affected by it.

Definitions For "trade mark", see s 1; for "publish" and references to "publication", see s 103(1).
References See para 5.9.

40 Registration

(1) Where an application has been accepted and—
  (a) no notice of opposition is given within the period referred to in section 38(2), or—
  (b) all opposition proceedings are withdrawn or decided in favour of the applicant,

the registrar shall register the trade mark, unless it appears to him having regard to matters coming to his notice since he accepted the application that it was accepted in error.

(2) A trade mark shall not be registered unless any fee prescribed for the registration is paid within the prescribed period.

If the fee is not paid within that period, the application shall be deemed to be withdrawn.

(3) A trade mark when registered shall be registered as of the date of filing of the application for registration; and that date shall be deemed for the purposes of this Act to be the date of registration.

(4)   On the registration of a trade mark the registrar shall publish the registration in the prescribed manner and issue to the applicant a certificate of registration.

Definitions   For "trade mark", see s 1; as to the "date of filing", see s 33(1); for "the registrar", see s 62; as to "register", "registered" and "registration", see s 63(1); for "publish", see s 103(1). Note as to the "date of registration", sub-s (3) above.
References   See para 5.11.

---

41   Registration: supplementary provisions

(1)   Provision may be made by rules as to—
    (a)   the division of an application for the registration of a trade mark into several applications;
    (b)   the merging of separate applications or registrations;
    (c)   the registration of a series of trade marks.

(2)   A series of trade marks means a number of trade marks which resemble each other as to their material particulars and differ only as to matters of a non-distinctive character not substantially affecting the identity of the trade mark.

(3)   Rules under this section may include provision as to—
    (a)   the circumstances in which, and conditions subject to which, division, merger or registration of a series is permitted, and
    (b)   the purposes for which an application to which the rules apply is to be treated as a single application and those for which it is to be treated as a number of separate applications.

Definitions   For "trade mark", see s 1; as to "registration", see s 63(1).
References   See para 5.10.

Duration, renewal and alteration of registered trade mark

42   Duration of registration

(1)   A trade mark shall be registered for a period of ten years from the date of registration.

(2)   Registration may be renewed in accordance with section 43 for further periods of ten years.

Definitions   For "trade mark", see s 1; as to the "date of registration", see s 40(3); as to "registered" and "registration"*, see s 63(1).
References   See para 9.1.

---

43   Renewal of registration

(1)   The registration of a trade mark may be renewed at the request of the proprietor, subject to payment of a renewal fee.

(2)   Provision shall be made by rules for the registrar to inform the proprietor of a registered trade mark, before the expiry of the registration, of the date of expiry and the manner in which the registration may be renewed.

(3)   A request for renewal must be made, and the renewal fee paid, before the expiry of the registration.

Failing this, the request may be made and the fee paid within such further period (of not less than six months) as may be prescribed, in which case an additional renewal fee must also be paid within that period.

(4)   Renewal shall take effect from the expiry of the previous registration.

(5)   If the registration is not renewed in accordance with the above provisions, the registrar shall remove the trade mark from the register.

Provision may be made by rules for the restoration of the registration of a trade mark which has been removed from the register, subject to such conditions (if any) as may be prescribed.

(6)   The renewal or restoration of the registration of a trade mark shall be published in the prescribed manner.

Definitions   For "trade mark", see s 1; for "the registrar", see s 62; for "the register", "registered trade mark" and as to "registration", see s 63(1); for "publish", see s 103(1).
References   See para 9.2.

44   Alteration of registered trade mark

(1)   A registered trade mark shall not be altered in the register, during the period of registration or on renewal.

(2)   Nevertheless, the registrar may, at the request of the proprietor, allow the alteration of a registered trade mark where the mark includes the proprietor's name or address and the alteration is limited to alteration of that name or address and does not substantially affect the identity of the mark.

(3)   Provision shall be made by rules for the publication of any such alteration and the making of objections by any person claiming to be affected by it.

Definitions   For "trade mark", see s 1; for "the registrar", see s 62; for "the register", "registered trade mark" and as to "registration", see s 63(1); as to "publication", see s 103(1).
References   See para 9.3.

Surrender, revocation and invalidity

45   Surrender of registered trade mark

(1)   A registered trade mark may be surrendered by the proprietor in respect of some or all of the goods or services for which it is registered.

(2)   Provision may be made by rules—
    (a)   as to the manner and effect of a surrender, and
    (b)   for protecting the interests of other persons having a right in the registered trade mark.

Definitions   For "registered trade mark" and as to "registered", see s 63(1).
References   See para 10.1.

46   Revocation of registration

(1)   The registration of a trade mark may be revoked on any of the following grounds—
    (a)   that within the period of five years following the date of completion of the registration procedure it has not been put to genuine use in the United Kingdom, by the proprietor or with his consent, in relation to

the goods or services for which it is registered, and there are no proper reasons for non-use;

(b)   that such use has been suspended for an uninterrupted period of five years, and there are no proper reasons for non-use;

(c)   that, in consequence of acts or inactivity of the proprietor, it has become the common name in the trade for a product or service for which it is registered;

(d)   that in consequence of the use made of it by the proprietor or with his consent in relation to the goods or services for which it is registered, it is liable to mislead the public, particularly as to the nature, quality or geographical origin of those goods or services.

(2)   For the purposes of subsection (1) use of a trade mark includes use in a form differing in elements which do not alter the distinctive character of the mark in the form in which it was registered, and use in the United Kingdom includes affixing the trade mark to goods or to the packaging of goods in the United Kingdom solely for export purposes.

(3)   The registration of a trade mark shall not be revoked on the ground mentioned in subsection (1)(a) or (b) if such use as is referred to in that paragraph is commenced or resumed after the expiry of the five year period and before the application for revocation is made:

Provided that, any such commencement or resumption of use after the expiry of the five year period but within the period of three months before the making of the application shall be disregarded unless preparations for the commencement or resumption began before the proprietor became aware that the application might be made.

(4)   An application for revocation may be made by any person, and may be made either to the registrar or to the court, except that—

(a)   if proceedings concerning the trade mark in question are pending in the court, the application must be made to the court; and

(b)   if in any other case the application is made to the registrar, he may at any stage of the proceedings refer the application to the court.

(5)   Where grounds for revocation exist in respect of only some of the goods or services for which the trade mark is registered, revocation shall relate to those goods or services only.

(6)   Where the registration of a trade mark is revoked to any extent, the rights of the proprietor shall be deemed to have ceased to that extent as from—

(a)   the date of the application for revocation, or

(b)   if the registrar or court is satisfied that the grounds for revocation existed at an earlier date, that date.

Definitions   For "trade mark", see s 1; for "the registrar", see s 62; as to "registered" and "registration", see s 63(1); for "the court", see s 75; for "trade", see s 103(1); as to "use" in relation to a trade mark, see s 103(2) (and note sub-s (2) above).
References   See paras 10.2–10.8.

47   Grounds for invalidity of registration

(1)   The registration of a trade mark may be declared invalid on the ground that the trade mark was registered in breach of section 3 or any of the provisions referred to in that section (absolute grounds for refusal of registration).

Where the trade mark was registered in breach of subsection (1)(b), (c) or (d) of that section, it shall not be declared invalid if, in consequence of the use which has been made of it, it has after registration acquired a distinctive character in relation to the goods or services for which it is registered.

(2)   The registration of a trade mark may be declared invalid on the ground—

    (a)   that there is an earlier trade mark in relation to which the conditions set out in section 5(1), (2) or (3) obtain, or

    (b)   that there is an earlier right in relation to which the condition set out in section 5(4) is satisfied,

unless the proprietor of that earlier trade mark or other earlier right has consented to the registration.

(3)   An application for a declaration of invalidity may be made by any person, and may be made either to the registrar or to the court, except that—

    (a)   if proceedings concerning the trade mark in question are pending in the court, the application must be made to the court; and

    (b)   if in any other case the application is made to the registrar, he may at any stage of the proceedings refer the application to the court.

(4)   In the case of bad faith in the registration of a trade mark, the registrar himself may apply to the court for a declaration of the invalidity of the registration.

(5)   Where the grounds of invalidity exist in respect of only some of the goods or services for which the trade mark is registered, the trade mark shall be declared invalid as regards those goods or services only.

(6)   Where the registration of a trade mark is declared invalid to any extent, the registration shall to that extent be deemed never to have been made:

Provided that this shall not affect transactions past and closed.

Definitions   For "trade mark", see s 1; for "earlier right", see s 5(4); for "earlier trade mark", see s 6; for "the registrar", see s 62; as to "registered" and "registration", see s 63(1); for "the court", see s 75; as to "use" in relation to a trade mark, see s 103(2).
References   See paras 10.9, 10.10.

48   Effect of acquiescence

(1)   Where the proprietor of an earlier trade mark or other earlier right has acquiesced for a continuous period of five years in the use of a registered trade mark in the United Kingdom, being aware of that use, there shall cease to be any entitlement on the basis of that earlier trade mark or other right—

    (a)   to apply for a declaration that the registration of the later trade mark is invalid, or

    (b)   to oppose the use of the later trade mark in relation to the goods or services in relation to which it has been so used,

unless the registration of the later trade mark was applied for in bad faith.

(2)   Where subsection (1) applies, the proprietor of the later trade mark is not entitled to oppose the use of the earlier trade mark or, as the case may be, the exploitation of the earlier right, notwithstanding that the earlier trade mark or right may no longer be invoked against his later trade mark.

Definitions   For "trade mark", see s 1; for "earlier right", see s 5(4); for "earlier trade mark", see s 6; for "registered trade mark" and as to "registration", see s 63(1); as to "use" in relation to a trade mark, see s 103(2).
References   See para 10.11.

Collective marks

49 Collective marks

(1) A collective mark is a mark distinguishing the goods or services of members of the association which is the proprietor of the mark from those of other undertakings.

(2) The provisions of this Act apply to collective marks subject to the provisions of Schedule 1.

References   See Chapter 12.

Certification marks

50 Certification marks

(1) A certification mark is a mark indicating that the goods or services in connection with which it is used are certified by the proprietor of the mark in respect of origin, material, mode of manufacture of goods or performance of services, quality, accuracy or other characteristics.

(2) The provisions of this Act apply to certification marks subject to the provisions of Schedule 2.

References   See Chapter 11.

PART II

COMMUNITY TRADE MARKS AND INTERNATIONAL MATTERS

Community trade marks

51 Meaning of "Community trade mark"

In this Act—
> "Community trade mark" has the meaning given by Article 1(1) of the Community Trade Mark Regulation; and
> "the Community Trade Mark Regulation" means Council Regulation (EC) No 40/94 of 20th December 1993 on the Community trade mark.

References   See paras 13.1–13.4.

52 Power to make provision in connection with Community Trade Mark Regulation

(1) The Secretary of State may by regulations make such provision as he considers appropriate in connection with the operation of the Community Trade Mark Regulation.

(2) Provision may, in particular, be made with respect to—
> (a) the making of applications for Community trade marks by way of the Patent Office;

(b) the procedures for determining *a posteriori* the invalidity, or liability to revocation, of the registration of a trade mark from which a Community trade mark claims seniority;

(c) the conversion of a Community trade mark, or an application for a Community trade mark, into an application for registration under this Act;

(d) the designation of courts in the United Kingdom having jurisdiction over proceedings arising out of the Community Trade Mark Regulation.

(3) Without prejudice to the generality of subsection (1), provision may be made by regulations under this section—

(a) applying in relation to a Community trade mark the provisions of—
    (i) section 21 (remedy for groundless threats of infringement proceedings);
    (ii) sections 89 to 91 (importation of infringing goods, material or articles); and
    (iii) sections 92, 93, 95 and 96 (offences); and

(b) making in relation to the list of professional representatives maintained in pursuance of Article 89 of the Community Trade Mark Regulation, and persons on that list, provision corresponding to that made by, or capable of being made under, sections 84 to 88 in relation to the register of trade mark agents and registered trade mark agents.

(4) Regulations under this section shall be made by statutory instrument which shall be subject to annulment in pursuance of a resolution of either House of Parliament.

Definitions   For "trade mark", see s 1; for "Community trade mark" and "Community Trade Mark Regulation", see s 51; for "the register" and as to "registration", see s 63(1); for "registered trade mark agent", see s 83(1).
References   See paras 13.2–13.4.

The Madrid Protocol: international registration

53   The Madrid Protocol

In this Act—
    "the Madrid Protocol" means the Protocol relating to the Madrid Agreement concerning the International Registration of Marks, adopted at Madrid on 27th June 1989;
    "the International Bureau" has the meaning given by Article 2(1) of that Protocol; and
    "international trade mark (UK)" means a trade mark which is entitled to protection in the United Kingdom under that Protocol.

References   See paras 13.5–13.8.

---

54   Power to make provision giving effect to Madrid Protocol

(1) The Secretary of State may by order make such provision as he thinks fit for giving effect in the United Kingdom to the provisions of the Madrid Protocol.

(2)   Provision may, in particular, be made with respect to—

    (a)   the making of applications for international registrations by way of the Patent Office as office of origin;

    (b)   the procedures to be followed where the basic United Kingdom application or registration fails or ceases to be in force;

    (c)   the procedures to be followed where the Patent Office receives from the International Bureau a request for extension of protection to the United Kingdom;

    (d)   the effects of a successful request for extension of protection to the United Kingdom;

    (e)   the transformation of an application for an international registration, or an international registration, into a national application for registration;

    (f)   the communication of information to the International Bureau;

    (g)   the payment of fees and amounts prescribed in respect of applications for international registrations, extensions of protection and renewals.

(3)   Without prejudice to the generality of subsection (1), provision may be made by regulations under this section applying in relation to an international trade mark (UK) the provisions of—

    (a)   section 21 (remedy for groundless threats of infringement proceedings);

    (b)   sections 89 to 91 (importation of infringing goods, material or articles); and

    (c)   sections 92, 93, 95 and 96 (offences).

(4)   An order under this section shall be made by statutory instrument which shall be subject to annulment in pursuance of a resolution of either House of Parliament.

Definitions   For "the Madrid Protocol", "the International Bureau" and "international trade mark (UK)", see s 53.
References   See paras 13.6–13.8.

The Paris Convention: supplementary provisions

55   The Paris Convention

(1)   In this Act—

    (a)   "the Paris Convention" means the Paris Convention for the Protection of Industrial Property of March 20th 1883, as revised or amended from time to time, and

    (b)   a "Convention country" means a country, other than the United Kingdom, which is a party to that Convention.

(2)   The Secretary of State may by order make such amendments of this Act, and rules made under this Act, as appear to him appropriate in consequence of any revision or amendment of the Paris Convention after the passing of this Act.

(3)   Any such order shall be made by statutory instrument which shall be subject to annulment in pursuance of a resolution of either House of Parliament.

References   See para 13.9.

56   Protection of well-known trade marks: Article 6*bis*

(1)   References in this Act to a trade mark which is entitled to protection under the Paris Convention as a well known trade mark are to a mark which is well-known in the United Kingdom as being the mark of a person who—

(a) is a national of a Convention country, or

(b) is domiciled in, or has a real and effective industrial or commercial establishment in, a Convention country,

whether or not that person carries on business, or has any goodwill, in the United Kingdom.

References to the proprietor of such a mark shall be construed accordingly.

(2) The proprietor of a trade mark which is entitled to protection under the Paris Convention as a well known trade mark is entitled to restrain by injunction the use in the United Kingdom of a trade mark which, or the essential part of which, is identical or similar to his mark, in relation to identical or similar goods or services, where the use is likely to cause confusion.

This right is subject to section 48 (effect of acquiescence by proprietor of earlier trade mark).

(3) Nothing in subsection (2) affects the continuation of any *bona fide* use of a trade mark begun before the commencement of this section.

Definitions   For "trade mark", see s 1, and for "the Paris Convention" and a "Convention country", see s 55(1); for "business", see s 103(1); as to "use" in relation to a trade mark, see s 103(2).
References   See paras 13.10–13.12.

57   National emblems, &c of Convention countries: Article 6*ter*

(1)   A trade mark which consists of or contains the flag of a Convention country shall not be registered without the authorisation of the competent authorities of that country, unless it appears to the registrar that use of the flag in the manner proposed is permitted without such authorisation.

(2)   A trade mark which consists of or contains the armorial bearings or any other state emblem of a Convention country which is protected under the Paris Convention shall not be registered without the authorisation of the competent authorities of that country.

(3)   A trade mark which consists of or contains an official sign or hallmark adopted by a Convention country and indicating control and warranty shall not, where the sign or hallmark is protected under the Paris Convention, be registered in relation to goods or services of the same, or a similar kind, as those in relation to which it indicates control and warranty, without the authorisation of the competent authorities of the country concerned.

(4)   The provisions of this section as to national flags and other state emblems, and official signs or hallmarks, apply equally to anything which from a heraldic point of view imitates any such flag or other emblem, or sign or hallmark.

(5)   Nothing in this section prevents the registration of a trade mark on the application of a national of a country who is authorised to make use of a state emblem, or official sign or hallmark, of that country, notwithstanding that it is similar to that of another country.

(6)   Where by virtue of this section the authorisation of the competent authorities of a Convention country is or would be required for the registration of a trade mark, those authorities are entitled to restrain by injunction any use of the mark in the United Kingdom without their authorisation.

Definitions   For "trade mark", see s 1; for "the Paris Convention" and a "Convention country", see s 55(1);
for "the registrar", see s 62; and as to "registered" and "registration", see s 63(1); as to "use" in relation to a trade
mark, see s 103(2).
References   See paras 3.14, 3.17.

58   Emblems, &c of certain international organisations: Article 6*ter*

(1)   This section applies to—

    (a)   the armorial bearings, flags or other emblems, and

    (b)   the abbreviations and names,

of international intergovernmental organisations of which one or more Convention countries are members.

(2)   A trade mark which consists of or contains any such emblem, abbreviation or name which is protected under the Paris Convention shall not be registered without the authorisation of the international organisation concerned, unless it appears to the registrar that the use of the emblem, abbreviation or name in the manner proposed—

    (a)   is not such as to suggest to the public that a connection exists between the organisation and the trade mark, or

    (b)   is not likely to mislead the public as to the existence of a connection between the user and the organisation.

(3)   The provisions of this section as to emblems of an international organisation apply equally to anything which from a heraldic point of view imitates any such emblem.

(4)   Where by virtue of this section the authorisation of an international organisation is or would be required for the registration of a trade mark, that organisation is entitled to restrain by injunction any use of the mark in the United Kingdom without its authorisation.

(5)   Nothing in this section affects the rights of a person whose *bona fide* use of the trade mark in question began before 4th January 1962 (when the relevant provisions of the Paris Convention entered into force in relation to the United Kingdom).

Definitions   For "trade mark", see s 1; for "the Paris Convention" and a "Convention country", see s 55(1);
for "the registrar", see s 62; as to "registered" and "registration", see s 63(1); as to "use" in relation to a trade
mark, see s 103(2).
References   See paras 3.14, 3.17.

59   Notification under Article 6*ter* of the Convention

(1)   For the purposes of section 57 state emblems of a Convention country (other than the national flag), and official signs or hallmarks, shall be regarded as protected under the Paris Convention only if, or to the extent that—

    (a)   the country in question has notified the United Kingdom in accordance with Article 6*ter*(3) of the Convention that it desires to protect that emblem, sign or hallmark,

    (b)   the notification remains in force, and

    (c)   the United Kingdom has not objected to it in accordance with Article 6*ter*(4) or any such objection has been withdrawn.

(2)   For the purposes of section 58 the emblems, abbreviations and names of an international organisation shall be regarded as protected under the Paris Convention only if, or to the extent that—

(a) the organisation in question has notified the United Kingdom in accordance with Article 6*ter*(3) of the Convention that it desires to protect that emblem, abbreviation or name,

(b) the notification remains in force, and

(c) the United Kingdom has not objected to it in accordance with Article 6*ter*(4) or any such objection has been withdrawn.

(3)   Notification under Article 6*ter*(3) of the Paris Convention shall have effect only in relation to applications for registration made more than two months after the receipt of the notification.

(4)   The registrar shall keep and make available for public inspection by any person, at all reasonable hours and free of charge, a list of—

(a) the state emblems and official signs or hallmarks, and

(b) the emblems, abbreviations and names of international organisations,

which are for the time being protected under the Paris Convention by virtue of notification under Article 6*ter*(3).

Definitions   For "the Paris Convention" and "Convention country", see s 55(1); for "the registrar", see s 62.
References   See para 3.11.

---

60   Acts of agent or representative: Article 6*septies*

(1)   The following provisions apply where an application for registration of a trade mark is made by a person who is an agent or representative of a person who is the proprietor of the mark in a Convention country.

(2)   If the proprietor opposes the application, registration shall be refused.

(3)   If the application (not being so opposed) is granted, the proprietor may—

(a) apply for a declaration of the invalidity of the registration, or

(b) apply for the rectification of the register so as to substitute his name as the proprietor of the registered trade mark.

(4)   The proprietor may (notwithstanding the rights conferred by this Act in relation to a registered trade mark) by injunction restrain any use of the trade mark in the United Kingdom which is not authorised by him.

(5)   Subsections (2), (3) and (4) do not apply if, or to the extent that, the agent or representative justifies his action.

(6)   An application under subsection (3)(a) or (b) must be made within three years of the proprietor becoming aware of the registration; and no injunction shall be granted under subsection (4) in respect of a use in which the proprietor has acquiesced for a continuous period of three years or more.

Definitions   For "trade mark", see s 1; for "Convention country", see s 55(1)(b); for "registered trade mark" and as to "registration", see s 62(1); for "the register", see s 63(1); as to "use" in relation to a trade mark, see s 103(2).
References   See para 13.13.

Miscellaneous

61   Stamp duty

Stamp duty shall not be chargeable on an instrument relating to a Community trade mark or an international trade mark (UK), or an application for any such mark, by reason only of the fact that such a mark has legal effect in the United Kingdom.

Definitions For "Community trade mark", see s 51, and; for "international trade mark (UK)", see s 53.
References See para 13.14.

PART III
ADMINISTRATIVE AND OTHER SUPPLEMENTARY PROVISIONS

The registrar

62 The registrar

In this Act "the registrar" means the Comptroller-General of Patents, Designs and Trade Marks.

References See para 14.2.

The register

63 The register

(1) The registrar shall maintain a register of trade marks.

References in this Act to "the register" are to that register; and references to registration (in particular, in the expression "registered trade mark") are, unless the context otherwise requires, to registration in that register.

(2) There shall be entered in the register in accordance with this Act—
    (a) registered trade marks,
    (b) such particulars as may be prescribed of registrable transactions affecting a registered trade mark, and
    (c) such other matters relating to registered trade marks as may be prescribed.

(3) The register shall be kept in such manner as may be prescribed, and provision shall in particular be made for—
    (a) public inspection of the register, and
    (b) the supply of certified or uncertified copies, or extracts, of entries in the register.

Definitions For "trade mark", see s 1; as to "registrable transaction", see s 25(2); for "the registrar", see s 62. Note as to "the register" and references to "registration", sub-s (1) above.
References See para 14.2.

64 Rectification or correction of the register

(1) Any person having a sufficient interest may apply for the rectification of an error or omission in the register:

Provided that an application for rectification may not be made in respect of a matter affecting the validity of the registration of a trade mark.

(2) An application for rectification may be made either to the registrar or to the court, except that—
    (a) if proceedings concerning the trade mark in question are pending in the court, the application must be made to the court; and
    (b) if in any other case the application is made to the registrar, he may at any stage of the proceedings refer the application to the court.

(3) Except where the registrar or the court directs otherwise the effect of rectification of the register is that the error or omission in question shall be deemed never to have been made.

(4) The registrar may, on request made in the prescribed manner by the proprietor of a registered trade mark, or a licensee, enter any change in his name or address as recorded in the register.

(5) The registrar may remove from the register matter appearing to him to have ceased to have effect.

Definitions   For "trade mark", see s 1; for "the registrar", see s 62; for "the register", "registered trade mark" and as to references to "registration", see s 63(1); for "the court", see s 75.
References   See para 14.4.

65   Adaptation of entries to new classification

(1) Provision may be made by rules empowering the registrar to do such things as he considers necessary to implement any amended or substituted classification of goods or services for the purposes of the registration of trade marks.

(2) Provision may in particular be made for the amendment of existing entries on the register so as to accord with the new classification.

(3) Any such power of amendment shall not be exercised so as to extend the rights conferred by the registration, except where it appears to the registrar that compliance with this requirement would involve undue complexity and that any extension would not be substantial and would not adversely affect the rights of any person.

(4) The rules may empower the registrar—
    (a) to require the proprietor of a registered trade mark, within such time as may be prescribed, to file a proposal for amendment of the register, and
    (b) to cancel or refuse to renew the registration of the trade mark in the event of his failing to do so.

(5) Any such proposal shall be advertised, and may be opposed, in such manner as may be prescribed.

Definitions   For "trade mark", see s 1; for "the registrar", see s 62; for "the register", "registered trade mark" and as to references to "registration", see s 63(1).
References   See para 14.5.

Powers and duties of the registrar

66   Power to require use of forms

(1) The registrar may require the use of such forms as he may direct for any purpose relating to the registration of a trade mark or any other proceeding before him under this Act.

(2) The forms, and any directions of the registrar with respect to their use, shall be published in the prescribed manner.

Definitions   For "trade mark", see s 1; for "the registrar", see s 62; and as to references to "registration", see s 63(1); as to "publish", see s 103(1).
References   See para 14.6.

67   Information about applications and registered trade marks

(1)   After publication of an application for registration of a trade mark, the registrar shall on request provide a person with such information and permit him to inspect such documents relating to the application, or to any registered trade mark resulting from it, as may be specified in the request, subject, however, to any prescribed restrictions.

Any request must be made in the prescribed manner and be accompanied by the appropriate fee (if any).

(2)   Before publication of an application for registration of a trade mark, documents or information constituting or relating to the application shall not be published by the registrar or communicated by him to any person except—

    (a)   in such cases and to such extent as may be prescribed, or

    (b)   with the consent of the applicant;

but subject as follows.

(3)   Where a person has been notified that an application for registration of a trade mark has been made, and that the applicant will if the application is granted bring proceedings against him in respect of acts done after publication of the application, he may make a request under subsection (1) notwithstanding that the application has not been published and that subsection shall apply accordingly.

Definitions   For "trade mark", see s 1; for "the registrar", see s 62; for "registered trade mark" and as to references to "registration", see s 63(1); as to "publication", see s 103(1).
References   See para 14.6.

68   Costs and security for costs

(1)   Provision may be made by rules empowering the registrar, in any proceedings before him under this Act—

    (a)   to award any party such costs as he may consider reasonable, and

    (b)   to direct how and by what parties they are to be paid.

(2)   Any such order of the registrar may be enforced—

    (a)   in England and Wales or Northern Ireland, in the same way as an order of the High Court;

    (b)   in Scotland, in the same way as a decree for expenses granted by the Court of Session.

(3)   Provision may be made by rules empowering the registrar, in such cases as may be prescribed, to require a party to proceedings before him to give security for costs, in relation to those proceedings or to proceedings on appeal, and as to the consequences if security is not given.

References   See para 14.7.

69   Evidence before registrar

Provision may be made by rules—

    (a)   as to the giving of evidence in proceedings before the registrar under this Act by affidavit or statutory declaration;

    (b)   conferring on the registrar the powers of an official referee of the Supreme Court as regards the examination of witnesses on oath and the discovery and production of documents; and

  (c) applying in relation to the attendance of witnesses in proceedings before the registrar the rules applicable to the attendance of witnesses before such a referee.

References See para 14.8.

70 Exclusion of liability in respect of official acts

(1) The registrar shall not be taken to warrant the validity of the registration of a trade mark under this Act or under any treaty, convention, arrangement or engagement to which the United Kingdom is a party.

(2) The registrar is not subject to any liability by reason of, or in connection with, any examination required or authorised by this Act, or any such treaty, convention, arrangement or engagement, or any report or other proceedings consequent on such examination.

(3) No proceedings lie against an officer of the registrar in respect of any matter for which, by virtue of this section, the registrar is not liable.

Definitions For "trade mark", see s 1; for "the registrar", see s 62; as to references to "registration", see s 63(1).
References See para 14.9.

71 Registrar's annual report

(1) The Comptroller-General of Patents, Designs and Trade Marks shall in his annual report under section 121 of the Patents Act 1977, include a report on the execution of this Act, including the discharge of his functions under the Madrid Protocol.

(2) The report shall include an account of all money received and paid by him under or by virtue of this Act.

References See para 14.9.

Legal proceedings and appeals

72 Registration to be *prima facie* evidence of validity

In all legal proceedings relating to a registered trade mark (including proceedings for rectification of the register) the registration of a person as proprietor of a trade mark shall be prima facie evidence of the validity of the original registration and of any subsequent assignment or other transmission of it.

Definitions For "trade mark", see s 1; for "the register", "registered trade mark" and as to "registration", see s 63(1).
References See para 14.10.

73 Certificate of validity of contested registration

(1) If in proceedings before the court the validity of the registration of a trade mark is contested and it is found by the court that the trade mark is validly registered, the court may give a certificate to that effect.

(2) If the court gives such a certificate and in subsequent proceedings—
  (a) the validity of the registration is again questioned, and

(b)   the proprietor obtains a final order or judgment in his favour,

he is entitled to his costs as between solicitor and client unless the court directs otherwise.

This subsection does not extend to the costs of an appeal in any such proceedings.

Definitions   For "trade mark", see s 1; as to "registered" and "registration", see s 63(1); for "the court", see s 75.
References   See para 14.10.

74   Registrar's appearance in proceedings involving the register

(1)   In proceedings before the court involving an application for—
    (a)   the revocation of the registration of a trade mark,
    (b)   a declaration of the invalidity of the registration of a trade mark, or
    (c)   the rectification of the register,

the registrar is entitled to appear and be heard, and shall appear if so directed by the court.

(2)   Unless otherwise directed by the court, the registrar may instead of appearing submit to the court a statement in writing signed by him, giving particulars of—
    (a)   any proceedings before him in relation to the matter in issue,
    (b)   the grounds of any decision given by him affecting it,
    (c)   the practice of the Patent Office in like cases, or
    (d)   such matters relevant to the issues and within his knowledge as registrar as he thinks fit;

and the statement shall be deemed to form part of the evidence in the proceedings.

(3)   Anything which the registrar is or may be authorised or required to do under this section may be done on his behalf by a duly authorised officer.

Definitions   For "trade mark", see s 1; for "the registrar", see s 62; for "the register" and as to "registration", see s 63(1); for "the court", see s 75.
References   See para 14.11.

75   The court

In this Act, unless the context otherwise requires, "the court" means—
    (a)   in England and Wales and Northern Ireland, the High Court, and
    (b)   in Scotland, the Court of Session.

References   See para 14.11.

76   Appeals from the registrar

(1)   An appeal lies from any decision of the registrar under this Act, except as otherwise expressly provided by rules.

For this purpose "decision" includes any act of the registrar in exercise of a discretion vested in him by or under this Act.

(2)   Any such appeal may be brought either to an appointed person or to the court.

(3)   Where an appeal is made to an appointed person, he may refer the appeal to the court if—

    (a) it appears to him that a point of general legal importance is involved,

    (b) the registrar requests that it be so referred, or

    (c) such a request is made by any party to the proceedings before the registrar in which the decision appealed against was made.

Before doing so the appointed person shall give the appellant and any other party to the appeal an opportunity to make representations as to whether the appeal should be referred to the court.

(4)   Where an appeal is made to an appointed person and he does not refer it to the court, he shall hear and determine the appeal and his decision shall be final.

(5)   The provisions of sections 68 and 69 (costs and security for costs; evidence) apply in relation to proceedings before an appointed person as in relation to proceedings before the registrar.

Definitions   For "the registrar", see s 62; for "appointed person", see s 77; for "the court", see s 75. Note as to "decision", sub-s (1) above.
References   See para 14.12.

77   Persons appointed to hear and determine appeals

(1)   For the purposes of section 76 an "appointed person" means a person appointed by the Lord Chancellor to hear and decide appeals under this Act.

(2)   A person is not eligible for such appointment unless—

    (a) he has a 7 year general qualification, within the meaning of section 71 of the Courts and Legal Services Act 1990;

    (b) he is an advocate or solicitor in Scotland of at least 7 years' standing;

    (c) he is a member of the Bar of Northern Ireland or solicitor of the Supreme Court of Northern Ireland of at least 7 years' standing; or

    (d) he has held judicial office.

(3)   An appointed person shall hold and vacate office in accordance with his terms of appointment, subject to the following provisions—

    (a) there shall be paid to him such remuneration (whether by way of salary or fees), and such allowances, as the Secretary of State with the approval of the Treasury may determine;

    (b) he may resign his office by notice in writing to the Lord Chancellor;

    (c) the Lord Chancellor may by notice in writing remove him from office if—

        (i) he has become bankrupt or made an arrangement with his creditors or, in Scotland, his estate has been sequestrated or he has executed a trust deed for his creditors or entered into a composition contract, or

        (ii) he is incapacitated by physical or mental illness,

    or if he is in the opinion of the Lord Chancellor otherwise unable or unfit to perform his duties as an appointed person.

(4)   The Lord Chancellor shall consult the Lord Advocate before exercising his powers under this section.

References   See para 14.12.

Rules, fees, hours of business, &c

78 Power of Secretary of State to make rules

(1) The Secretary of State may make rules—
- (a) for the purposes of any provision of this Act authorising the making of rules with respect to any matter, and
- (b) for prescribing anything authorised or required by any provision of this Act to be prescribed,

and generally for regulating practice and procedure under this Act.

(2) Provision may, in particular, be made—
- (a) as to the manner of filing of applications and other documents;
- (b) requiring and regulating the translation of documents and the filing and authentication of any translation;
- (c) as to the service of documents;
- (d) authorising the rectification of irregularities of procedure;
- (e) prescribing time limits for anything required to be done in connection with any proceeding under this Act;
- (f) providing for the extension of any time limit so prescribed, or specified by the registrar, whether or not it has already expired.

(3) Rules under this Act shall be made by statutory instrument which shall be subject to annulment in pursuance of a resolution of either House of Parliament.

References   See para 14.13.

79 Fees

(1) There shall be paid in respect of applications and registration and other matters under this Act such fees as may be prescribed.

(2) Provision may be made by rules as to—
- (a) the payment of a single fee in respect of two or more matters, and
- (b) the circumstances (if any) in which a fee may be repaid or remitted.

References   See para 14.13.

80 Hours of business and business days

(1) The registrar may give directions specifying the hours of business of the Patent Office for the purpose of the transaction by the public of business under this Act, and the days which are business days for that purpose.

(2) Business done on any day after the specified hours of business, or on a day which is not a business day, shall be deemed to have been done on the next business day; and where the time for doing anything under this Act expires on a day which is not a business day, that time shall be extended to the next business day.

(3) Directions under this section may make different provision for different classes of business and shall be published in the prescribed manner.

Definitions   For "the register", see s 62; as to "business" and "published", see s 103(1).
References   See para 14.13.

81 The trade marks journal

Provision shall be made by rules for the publication by the registrar of a journal containing particulars of any application for the registration of a trade mark (including a representation of the mark) and such other information relating to trade marks as the registrar thinks fit.

Definitions For "trade mark", see s 1; for "the registrar", see s 62; as to "registration", see s 63(1); as to "publication", see s 103(1).
References See para 14.13.

Trade mark agents, &c

82 Recognition of agents

Except as otherwise provided by rules, any act required or authorised by this Act to be done by or to a person in connection with the registration of a trade mark, or any procedure relating to a registered trade mark, may be done by or to an agent authorised by that person orally or in writing.

Definitions For "trade mark", see s 1; for "registered trade mark" and as to "registration", see s 63(1).
References See paras 14.14–14.15.

83 The register of trade mark agents

(1)   The Secretary of State may make rules requiring the keeping of a register of persons who act as agent for others for the purpose of applying for or obtaining the registration of trade marks; and in this Act a "registered trade mark agent" means a person whose name is entered in the register kept under this section.

(2)   The rules may contain such provision as the Secretary of State thinks fit regulating the registration of persons, and may in particular—
    (a)   require the payment of such fees as may be prescribed, and
    (b)   authorise in prescribed cases the erasure from the register of the name of any person registered in it, or the suspension of a person's registration.

(3)   The rules may delegate the keeping of the register to another person, and may confer on that person—
    (a)   power to make regulations—
        (i)   with respect to the payment of fees, in the cases and subject to the limits prescribed by the rules, and
        (ii)   with respect to any other matter which could be regulated by the rules, and
    (b)   such other functions, including disciplinary functions, as may be prescribed by the rules.

Definitions For "trade mark", see s 1; as to "registration" in relation to trade marks, see s 63(1). Note as to "registered trade mark agent", sub-s (1) above.
References See paras 14.14–14.15.

84 Unregistered persons not to be described as registered trade mark agents

(1)   An individual who is not a registered trade mark agent shall not—
    (a)   carry on a business (otherwise than in partnership) under any name or other description which contains the words "registered trade mark agent"; or

(b) in the course of a business otherwise describe or hold himself out, or permit himself to be described or held out, as a registered trade mark agent.

(2) A partnership shall not—
(a) carry on a business under any name or other description which contains the words "registered trade mark agent"; or
(b) in the course of a business otherwise describe or hold itself out, or permit itself to be described or held out, as a firm of registered trade mark agents,

unless all the partners are registered trade mark agents or the partnership satisfies such conditions as may be prescribed for the purposes of this section.

(3) A body corporate shall not—
(a) carry on a business (otherwise than in partnership) under any name or other description which contains the words "registered trade mark agent"; or
(b) in the course of a business otherwise describe or hold itself out, or permit itself to be described or held out, as a registered trade mark agent,

unless all the directors of the body corporate are registered trade mark agents or the body satisfies such conditions as may be prescribed for the purposes of this section.

(4) A person who contravenes this section commits an offence and is liable on summary conviction to a fine not exceeding level 5 on the standard scale; and proceedings for such an offence may be begun at any time within a year from the date of the offence.

Definitions For "registered trade mark agent", see s 83(1); for "business" and "director", see s 103(1).
References See paras 14.14–14.15.

85 Power to prescribe conditions, &c for mixed partnerships and bodies corporate

(1) The Secretary of State may make rules prescribing the conditions to be satisfied for the purposes of section 84 (persons entitled to be described as registered trade mark agents)—
(a) in relation to a partnership where not all the partners are qualified persons, or
(b) in relation to a body corporate where not all the directors are qualified persons,

and imposing requirements to be complied with by such partnerships or bodies corporate.

(2) The rules may, in particular—
(a) prescribe conditions as to the number or proportion of partners or directors who must be qualified persons;
(b) impose requirements as to—
  (i) the identification of qualified and unqualified persons in professional advertisements, circulars or letters issued by or with the consent of the partnership or body corporate and which relate to its business, and

(ii) the manner in which a partnership or body corporate is to organise its affairs so as to secure that qualified persons exercise a sufficient degree of control over the activities of unqualified persons.

(3) Contravention of a requirement imposed by the rules is an offence for which a person is liable on summary conviction to a fine not exceeding level 5 on the standard scale.

(4) In this section "qualified person" means a registered trade mark agent.

Definitions For "registered trade mark agent", see s 83(1); for "business" and "director", see s 103(1).
References See paras 14.14–14.15.

86 Use of the term "trade mark attorney"

(1) No offence is committed under the enactments restricting the use of certain expressions in reference to persons not qualified to act as solicitors by the use of the term "trade mark attorney" in reference to a registered trade mark agent.

(2) The enactments referred to in subsection (1) are section 21 of the Solicitors Act 1974, section 31 of the Solicitors (Scotland) Act 1980 and Article 22 of the Solicitors (Northern Ireland) Order 1976.

References See paras 14.14–14.15.

87 Privilege for communications with registered trade mark agents

(1) This section applies to communications as to any matter relating to the protection of any design or trade mark, or as to any matter involving passing off.

(2) Any such communication—
  (a) between a person and his trade mark agent, or
  (b) for the purpose of obtaining, or in response to a request for, information which a person is seeking for the purpose of instructing his trade mark agent,

is privileged from, or in Scotland protected against, disclosure in legal proceedings in the same way as a communication between a person and his solicitor or, as the case may be, a communication for the purpose of obtaining, or in response to a request for, information which a person is seeking for the purpose of instructing his solicitor.

(3) In subsection (2) "trade mark agent" means—
  (a) a registered trade mark agent, or
  (b) a partnership entitled to describe itself as a firm of registered trade mark agents, or
  (c) a body corporate entitled to describe itself as a registered trade mark agent.

Definitions For "trade mark", see s 1; for "registered trade mark agent", see s 83(1).
References See paras 14.14–14.15.

88 Power of registrar to refuse to deal with certain agents

(1) The Secretary of State may make rules authorising the registrar to refuse to recognise as agent in respect of any business under this Act—

(a) a person who has been convicted of an offence under section 84 (unregistered persons describing themselves as registered trade mark agents);

(b) an individual whose name has been erased from and not restored to, or who is suspended from, the register of trade mark agents on the ground of misconduct;

(c) a person who is found by the Secretary of State to have been guilty of such conduct as would, in the case of an individual registered in the register of trade mark agents, render him liable to have his name erased from the register on the ground of misconduct;

(d) a partnership or body corporate of which one of the partners or directors is a person whom the registrar could refuse to recognise under paragraph (a), (b) or (c) above.

(2)   The rules may contain such incidental and supplementary provisions as appear to the Secretary of State to be appropriate and may, in particular, prescribe circumstances in which a person is or is not to be taken to have been guilty of misconduct.

Definitions   For "the registrar", see s 62; for "director", see s 103(1).
References   See paras 14.14–14.15.

Importation of infringing goods, material or articles

89   Infringing goods, material or articles may be treated as prohibited goods

(1)   The proprietor of a registered trade mark, or a licensee, may give notice in writing to the Commissioners of Customs and Excise—

(a) that he is the proprietor or, as the case may be, a licensee of the registered trade mark,

(b) that, at a time and place specified in the notice, goods which are, in relation to that registered trade mark, infringing goods, material or articles are expected to arrive in the United Kingdom—

    (i)   from outside the European Economic Area, or

    (ii)   from within that Area but not having been entered for free circulation, and

(c) that he requests the Commissioners to treat them as prohibited goods.

(2)   When a notice is in force under this section the importation of the goods to which the notice relates, otherwise than by a person for his private and domestic use, is prohibited; but a person is not by reason of the prohibition liable to any penalty other than forfeiture of the goods.

(3)   This section does not apply to goods entered, or expected to be entered, for free circulation in respect of which the proprietor of the registered trade mark, or a licensee, is entitled to lodge an application under Article 3(1) of Council Regulation (EEC) No 3842/86 laying down measures to prohibit the release for free circulation of counterfeit goods.

Definitions   For "infringing goods", "infringing material" and "infringing articles", see s 17; for "registered trade mark", see s 63(1).
References   See para 15.1.

90   Power of Commissioners of Customs and Excise to make regulations

(1)   The Commissioners of Customs and Excise may make regulations prescribing the form in which notice is to be given under section 89 and requiring a person giving notice—

   (a)   to furnish the Commissioners with such evidence as may be specified in the regulations, either on giving notice or when the goods are imported, or at both those times, and

   (b)   to comply with such other conditions as may be specified in the regulations.

(2)   The regulations may, in particular, require a person giving such a notice—

   (a)   to pay such fees in respect of the notice as may be specified by the regulations;

   (b)   to give such security as may be so specified in respect of any liability or expense which the Commissioners may incur in consequence of the notice by reason of the detention of any goods or anything done to goods detained;

   (c)   to indemnify the Commissioners against any such liability or expense, whether security has been given or not.

(3)   The regulations may make different provision as respects different classes of case to which they apply and may include such incidental and supplementary provisions as the Commissioners consider expedient.

(4)   Regulations under this section shall be made by statutory instrument which shall be subject to annulment in pursuance of a resolution of either House of Parliament.

(5)   Section 17 of the Customs and Excise Management Act 1979 (general provisions as to Commissioners' receipts) applies to fees paid in pursuance of regulations under this section as to receipts under the enactments relating to customs and excise.

References   See para 15.1.

---

91   Power of Commissioners of Customs and Excise to disclose information

Where information relating to infringing goods, material or articles has been obtained by the Commissioners of Customs and Excise for the purposes of, or in connection with, the exercise of their functions in relation to imported goods, the Commissioners may authorise the disclosure of that information for the purpose of facilitating the exercise by any person of any function in connection with the investigation or prosecution of an offence under section 92 below (unauthorised use of trade mark, &c in relation to goods) or under the Trade Descriptions Act 1968.

References   See para 15.1.

Offences

92   Unauthorised use of trade mark, &c in relation to goods

(1)   A person commits an offence who with a view to gain for himself or another, or with intent to cause loss to another, and without the consent of the proprietor—

    (a)   applies to goods or their packaging a sign identical to, or likely to be mistaken for, a registered trade mark, or

    (b)   sells or lets for hire, offers or exposes for sale or hire or distributes goods which bear, or the packaging of which bears, such a sign, or

    (c)   has in his possession, custody or control in the course of a business any such goods with a view to the doing of anything, by himself or another, which would be an offence under paragraph (b).

(2)   A person commits an offence who with a view to gain for himself or another, or with intent to cause loss to another, and without the consent of the proprietor—

    (a)   applies a sign identical to, or likely to be mistaken for, a registered trade mark to material intended to be used—

        (i)   for labelling or packaging goods,

        (ii) as a business paper in relation to goods, or

        (iii) for advertising goods, or

    (b)   uses in the course of a business material bearing such a sign for labelling or packaging goods, as a business paper in relation to goods, or for advertising goods, or

    (c)   has in his possession, custody or control in the course of a business any such material with a view to the doing of anything, by himself or another, which would be an offence under paragraph (b).

(3)   A person commits an offence who with a view to gain for himself or another, or with intent to cause loss to another, and without the consent of the proprietor—

    (a)   makes an article specifically designed or adapted for making copies of a sign identical to, or likely to be mistaken for, a registered trade mark, or

    (b)   has such an article in his possession, custody or control in the course of a business,

knowing or having reason to believe that it has been, or is to be, used to produce goods, or material for labelling or packaging goods, as a business paper in relation to goods, or for advertising goods.

(4)   A person does not commit an offence under this section unless—

    (a)   the goods are goods in respect of which the trade mark is registered, or

    (b)   the trade mark has a reputation in the United Kingdom and the use of the sign takes or would take unfair advantage of, or is or would be detrimental to, the distinctive character or the repute of the trade mark.

(5)   It is a defence for a person charged with an offence under this section to show that he believed on reasonable grounds that the use of the sign in the manner in which it was used, or was to be used, was not an infringement of the registered trade mark.

(6)   A person guilty of an offence under this section is liable—

    (a)   on summary conviction to imprisonment for a term not exceeding six months or a fine not exceeding the statutory maximum, or both;

    (b)   on conviction on indictment to a fine or imprisonment for a term not exceeding ten years, or both.

Definitions   For "trade mark", see s 1; for "infringement", see ss 9(1), (2), 10; for "registered trade mark" and as to "registered", see s 63(1); for "business" and as to "use", see s 103(1), (2).
References   See paras 15.2, 15.3.

93 Enforcement function of local weights and measures authority

(1)   It is the duty of every local weights and measures authority to enforce within their area the provisions of section 92 (unauthorised use of trade mark, &c in relation to goods).

(2)   The following provisions of the Trade Descriptions Act 1968 apply in relation to the enforcement of that section as in relation to the enforcement of that Act—

> section 27 (power to make test purchases),
> section 28 (power to enter premises and inspect and seize goods and documents),
> section 29 (obstruction of authorised officers), and
> section 33 (compensation for loss, &c of goods seized).

(3)   Subsection (1) above does not apply in relation to the enforcement of section 92 in Northern Ireland, but it is the duty of the Department of Economic Development to enforce that section in Northern Ireland.

For that purpose the provisions of the Trade Descriptions Act 1968 specified in subsection (2) apply as if for the references to a local weights and measures authority and any officer of such an authority there were substituted references to that Department and any of its officers.

(4)   Any enactment which authorises the disclosure of information for the purpose of facilitating the enforcement of the Trade Descriptions Act 1968 shall apply as if section 92 above were contained in that Act and as if the functions of any person in relation to the enforcement of that section were functions under that Act.

(5)   Nothing in this section shall be construed as authorising a local weights and measures authority to bring proceedings in Scotland for an offence.

References   See para 15.3.

---

94 Falsification of register, &c

(1)   It is an offence for a person to make, or cause to be made, a false entry in the register of trade marks, knowing or having reason to believe that it is false.

(2)   It is an offence for a person—
  (a) to make or cause to be made anything falsely purporting to be a copy of an entry in the register, or
  (b) to produce or tender or cause to be produced or tendered in evidence any such thing,

knowing or having reason to believe that it is false.

(3)   A person guilty of an offence under this section is liable—
  (a) on conviction on indictment, to imprisonment for a term not exceeding two years or a fine, or both;
  (b) on summary conviction, to imprisonment for a term not exceeding six months or a fine not exceeding the statutory maximum, or both.

Definitions   For "trade mark", see s 1; for "the register", see s 63(1).
References   See para 15.4.

95   Falsely representing trade mark as registered

(1)   It is an offence for a person—

    (a)   falsely to represent that a mark is a registered trade mark, or

    (b)   to make a false representation as to the goods or services for which a trade mark is registered

knowing or having reason to believe that the representation is false.

(2)   For the purposes of this section, the use in the United Kingdom in relation to a trade mark—

    (a)   of the word "registered", or

    (b)   of any other word or symbol importing a reference (express or implied) to registration,

shall be deemed to be a representation as to registration under this Act unless it is shown that the reference is to registration elsewhere than in the United Kingdom and that the trade mark is in fact so registered for the goods or services in question.

(3)   A person guilty of an offence under this section is liable on summary conviction to a fine not exceeding level 3 on the standard scale.

Definitions   For "trade mark", see s 1; for "the register", "registered trade mark" and as to "registered" and "registration", see s 63(1); as to "use" in relation to a trade mark, see s 103(2).
References   See para 15.5.

96   Supplementary provisions as to summary proceedings in Scotland

(1)   Notwithstanding anything in section 331 of the Criminal Procedure (Scotland) Act 1975, summary proceedings in Scotland for an offence under this Act may be begun at any time within six months after the date on which evidence sufficient in the Lord Advocate's opinion to justify the proceedings came to his knowledge.

For this purpose a certificate of the Lord Advocate as to the date on which such evidence came to his knowledge is conclusive evidence.

(2)   For the purposes of subsection (1) and of any other provision of this Act as to the time within which summary proceedings for an offence may be brought, proceedings in Scotland shall be deemed to be begun on the date on which a warrant to apprehend or to cite the accused is granted, if such warrant is executed without undue delay.

References   See para 15.6.

Forfeiture of counterfeit goods, &c

97   Forfeiture: England and Wales or Northern Ireland

(1)   In England and Wales or Northern Ireland where there has come into the possession of any person in connection with the investigation or prosecution of a relevant offence—

    (a)   goods which, or the packaging of which, bears a sign identical to or likely to be mistaken for a registered trade mark,

    (b)   material bearing such a sign and intended to be used for labelling or packaging goods, as a business paper in relation to goods, or for advertising goods, or

(c) articles specifically designed or adapted for making copies of such a sign,

that person may apply under this section for an order for the forfeiture of the goods, material or articles.

(2) An application under this section may be made—
    (a) where proceedings have been brought in any court for a relevant offence relating to some or all of the goods, material or articles, to that court;
    (b) where no application for the forfeiture of the goods, material or articles has been made under paragraph (a), by way of complaint to a magistrates' court.

(3) On an application under this section the court shall make an order for the forfeiture of any goods, material or articles only if it is satisfied that a relevant offence has been committed in relation to the goods, material or articles.

(4) A court may infer for the purposes of this section that such an offence has been committed in relation to any goods, material or articles if it is satisfied that such an offence has been committed in relation to goods, material or articles which are representative of them (whether by reason of being of the same design or part of the same consignment or batch or otherwise).

(5) Any person aggrieved by an order made under this section by a magistrates' court, or by a decision of such a court not to make such an order, may appeal against that order or decision—
    (a) in England and Wales, to the Crown Court;
    (b) in Northern Ireland, to the county court;

and an order so made may contain such provision as appears to the court to be appropriate for delaying the coming into force of the order pending the making and determination of any appeal (including any application under section 111 of the Magistrates' Courts Act 1980 or Article 146 of the Magistrates' Courts (Northern Ireland) Order 1981 (statement of case)).

(6) Subject to subsection (7), where any goods, material or articles are forfeited under this section they shall be destroyed in accordance with such directions as the court may give.

(7) On making an order under this section the court may, if it considers it appropriate to do so, direct that the goods, material or articles to which the order relates shall (instead of being destroyed) be released, to such person as the court may specify, on condition that that person—
    (a) causes the offending sign to be erased, removed or obliterated and
    (b) complies with any order to pay costs which has been made against him in the proceedings for the order for forfeiture.

(8) For the purposes of this section a "relevant offence" means an offence under section 92 above (unauthorised use of trade mark, &c in relation to goods) or under the Trade Descriptions Act 1968 or any offence involving dishonesty or deception.

Definitions   For "registered trade mark", see s 59(1); for "the court", see s 75; and as to "use", see s 103(2).
References   See para 15.3.

98   Forfeiture: Scotland

(1)   In Scotland the court may make an order for the forfeiture of any—
   (a)   goods which bear, or the packaging of which bears, a sign identical to or likely to be mistaken for a registered trade mark,
   (b)   material bearing such a sign and intended to be used for labelling or packaging goods, as a business paper in relation to goods, or for advertising goods, or
   (c)   articles specifically designed or adapted for making copies of such a sign.

(2)   An order under this section may be made—
   (a)   on an application by the procurator-fiscal made in the manner specified in section 310 of the Criminal Procedure (Scotland) Act 1975, or
   (b)   where a person is convicted of a relevant offence, in addition to any other penalty which the court may impose.

(3)   On an application under subsection (2)(a), the court shall make an order for the forfeiture of any goods, material or articles only if it is satisfied that a relevant offence has been committed in relation to the goods, material or articles.

(4)   The court may infer for the purposes of this section that such an offence has been committed in relation to any goods, material or articles if it is satisfied that such an offence has been committed in relation to goods, material or articles which are representative of them (whether by reason of being of the same design or part of the same consignment or batch or otherwise).

(5)   The procurator-fiscal making the application under subsection (2)(a) shall serve on any person appearing to him to be the owner of, or otherwise to have an interest in, the goods, material or articles to which the application relates a copy of the application, together with a notice giving him the opportunity to appear at the hearing of the application to show cause why the goods, material or articles should not be forfeited.

(6)   Service under subsection (5) shall be carried out, and such service may be proved, in the manner specified for citation of an accused in summary proceedings under the Criminal Procedure (Scotland) Act 1975.

(7)   Any person upon whom notice is served under subsection (5) and any other person claiming to be the owner of, or otherwise to have an interest in, goods, material or articles to which an application under this section relates shall be entitled to appear at the hearing of the application to show cause why the goods, material or articles should not be forfeited.

(8)   The court shall not make an order following an application under subsection (2)(a)—
   (a)   if any person on whom notice is served under subsection (5) does not appear, unless service of the notice on that person is proved; or
   (b)   if no notice under subsection (5) has been served, unless the court is satisfied that in the circumstances it was reasonable not to serve such notice.

(9)   Where an order for the forfeiture of any goods, material or articles is made following an application under subsection (2)(a), any person who appeared, or was entitled to appear, to show cause why goods, material or articles should not be forfeited may, within 21 days of the making of the order, appeal to the High Court by Bill of Suspension; and section 452(4)(a) to (e) of the Criminal Procedure (Scotland)

Act 1975 shall apply to an appeal under this subsection as it applies to a stated case under Part II of that Act.

(10) An order following an application under subsection (2)(a) shall not take effect—

    (a) until the end of the period of 21 days beginning with the day after the day on which the order is made; or

    (b) if an appeal is made under subsection (9) above within that period, until the appeal is determined or abandoned.

(11) An order under subsection (2)(b) shall not take effect—

    (a) until the end of the period within which an appeal against the order could be brought under the Criminal Procedure (Scotland) Act 1975; or

    (b) if an appeal is made within that period, until the appeal is determined or abandoned.

(12) Subject to subsection (13), goods, material or articles forfeited under this section shall be destroyed in accordance with such directions as the court may give.

(13) On making an order under this section the court may if it considers it appropriate to do so, direct that the goods, material or articles to which the order relates shall (instead of being destroyed) be released, to such person as the court may specify, on condition that that person causes the offending sign to be erased, removed or obliterated.

(14) For the purposes of this section—

    "relevant offence" means an offence under section 92 (unauthorised use of trade mark, &c in relation to goods) or under the Trade Descriptions Act 1968 or any offence involving dishonesty or deception,

    "the court" means—

        (a) in relation to an order made on an application under subsection (2)(a), the sheriff, and

        (b) in relation to an order made under subsection (2)(b), the court which imposed the penalty.

Definitions   For "registered trade mark", see s 63(1).
References   See para 15.3.

PART IV
MISCELLANEOUS AND GENERAL PROVISIONS

Miscellaneous

99   Unauthorised use of Royal arms, &c

(1) A person shall not without the authority of Her Majesty use in connection with any business the Royal arms (or arms so closely resembling the Royal arms as to be calculated to deceive) in such manner as to be calculated to lead to the belief that he is duly authorised to use the Royal arms.

(2) A person shall not without the authority of Her Majesty or of a member of the Royal family use in connection with any business any device, emblem or title in such a manner as to be calculated to lead to the belief that he is employed by, or supplies goods or services to, Her Majesty or that member of the Royal family.

(3) A person who contravenes subsection (1) commits an offence and is liable on summary conviction to a fine not exceeding level 2 on the standard scale.

(4)   Contravention of subsection (1) or (2) may be restrained by injunction in proceedings brought by—

    (a)   any person who is authorised to use the arms, device, emblem or title in question, or

    (b)   any person authorised by the Lord Chamberlain to take such proceedings.

(5)   Nothing in this section affects any right of the proprietor of a trade mark containing any such arms, device, emblem or title to use that trade mark.

Definitions   For "trade mark", see s 1; for "business", see s 103(1).
References   See para 16.2.

100   Burden of proving use of trade mark

If in any civil proceedings under this Act a question arises as to the use to which a registered trade mark has been put, it is for the proprietor to show what use has been made of it.

Definitions   For "registered trade mark", see s 63(1); as to "use" in relation to a trade mark, see s 103(2).
References   See paras 10.4, 16.3.

101   Offences committed by partnerships and bodies corporate

(1)   Proceedings for an offence under this Act alleged to have been committed by a partnership shall be brought against the partnership in the name of the firm and not in that of the partners; but without prejudice to any liability of the partners under subsection (4) below.

(2)   The following provisions apply for the purposes of such proceedings as in relation to a body corporate—

    (a)   any rules of court relating to the service of documents;

    (b)   in England and Wales or Northern Ireland, Schedule 3 to the Magistrates' Courts Act 1980 or Schedule 4 to the Magistrates' Courts (Northern Ireland) Order 1981 (procedure on charge of offence).

(3)   A fine imposed on a partnership on its conviction in such proceedings shall be paid out of the partnership assets.

(4)   Where a partnership is guilty of an offence under this Act, every partner, other than a partner who is proved to have been ignorant of or to have attempted to prevent the commission of the offence, is also guilty of the offence and liable to be proceeded against and punished accordingly.

(5)   Where an offence under this Act committed by a body corporate is proved to have been committed with the consent or connivance of a director, manager, secretary or other similar officer of the body, or a person purporting to act in any such capacity, he as well as the body corporate is guilty of the offence and liable to be proceeded against and punished accordingly.

References   See para 16.4.

Interpretation

102   Adaptation of expressions for Scotland

In the application of this Act to Scotland—

    "account of profits" means accounting and payment of profits;

"accounts" means count, reckoning and payment;

"assignment" means assignation;

"costs" means expenses;

"declaration" means declarator;

"defendant" means defender;

"delivery up" means delivery;

"injunction" means interdict;

"interlocutory relief" means interim remedy; and

"plaintiff" means pursuer.

References   See para 16.5.

103   Minor definitions

(1)   In this Act—

"business" includes a trade or profession;

"director", in relation to a body corporate whose affairs are managed by its members, means any member of the body;

"infringement proceedings", in relation to a registered trade mark, includes proceedings under section 16 (order for delivery up of infringing goods, &c);

"publish" means make available to the public, and references to publication—

  (a)   in relation to an application for registration, are to publication under section 38(1), and

  (b)   in relation to registration, are to publication under section 40(4);

"statutory provisions" includes provisions of subordinate legislation within the meaning of the Interpretation Act 1978;

"trade" includes any business or profession.

(2)   References in this Act to use (or any particular description of use) of a trade mark, or of a sign identical with, similar to, or likely to be mistaken for a trade mark, include use (or that description of use) otherwise than by means of a graphic representation.

(3)   References in this Act to a Community instrument include references to any instrument amending or replacing that instrument.

Definitions   For "trade mark", see s 1; for "registered trade mark" and as to "registration", see s 63(1).
References   See paras 7.4, 16.5.

104   Index of defined expressions

In this Act the expressions listed below are defined by or otherwise fall to be construed in accordance with the provisions indicated—

collective mark	section 49(1)
commencement (of this Act)	section 109(2)
Community trade mark	section 51
Community Trade Mark Regulation	section 51
Convention country	section 55(1)(b)
costs (in Scotland)	section 102
the court	section 75
date of application	section 33(2)
date of filing	section 33(1)
date of registration	section 40(3)
defendant (in Scotland)	section 102
delivery up (in Scotland)	section 102
director	section 103(1)
earlier right	section 5(4)
earlier trade mark	section 6
exclusive licence and licensee	section 29(1)
infringement (of registered trade mark)	sections 9(1) and (2) and 10
infringement proceedings	section 103(1)
infringing articles	section 17
infringing goods	section 17
infringing material	section 17
injunction (in Scotland)	section 102
interlocutory relief (in Scotland)	section 102
the International Bureau	section 53
international trade mark (UK)	section 53
Madrid Protocol	section 53
Paris Convention	section 55(1)(a)
plaintiff (in Scotland)	section 102
prescribed	section 78(1)(b)
protected under the Paris Convention	
—well-known trade marks	section 56(1)
—state emblems and official signs or hallmarks	section 57(1)
—emblems, &c of international organisations	section 58(2)
publish and references to publication	section 103(1)
register, registered (and related expressions)	section 63(1)
registered trade mark agent	section 83(1)
registrable transaction	section 25(2)
the registrar	section 62
rules	section 78
statutory provisions	section 103(1)
trade	section 103(1)
trade mark	
—generally	section 1(1)
—includes collective mark or certification mark	section 1(2)
United Kingdom (references include Isle of Man)	section 108(2)
use (of trade mark or sign)	section 103(2)
well-known trade mark (under Paris Convention)	section 56(1)

References   See para 16.15.

Other general provisions

105 Transitional provisions

The provisions of Schedule 3 have effect with respect to transitional matters, including the treatment of marks registered under the Trade Marks Act 1938, and applications for registration and other proceedings pending under that Act, on the commencement of this Act.

References   See para 16.6.

106 Consequential amendments and repeals

(1)   The enactments specified in Schedule 4 are amended in accordance with that Schedule, the amendments being consequential on the provisions of this Act.

(2)   The enactments specified in Schedule 5 are repealed to the extent specified.

References   See para 16.6.

107 Territorial waters and the continental shelf

(1)   For the purposes of this Act the territorial waters of the United Kingdom shall be treated as part of the United Kingdom.

(2)   This Act applies to things done in the United Kingdom sector of the continental shelf on a structure or vessel which is present there for purposes directly connected with the exploration of the sea bed or subsoil or the exploitation of their natural resources as it applies to things done in the United Kingdom.

(3)   The United Kingdom sector of the continental shelf means the areas designated by order under section 1(7) of the Continental Shelf Act 1964.

References   See para 16.6.

108 Extent

(1)   This Act extends to England and Wales, Scotland and Northern Ireland.

(2)   This Act also extends to the Isle of Man, subject to such exceptions and modifications as Her Majesty may specify by Order in Council; and subject to any such Order references in this Act to the United Kingdom shall be construed as including the Isle of Man.

References   See para 16.6.

109 Commencement

(1)   The provisions of this Act come into force on such day as the Secretary of State may appoint by order made by statutory instrument.

Different days may be appointed for different provisions and different purposes.

(2)   The references to the commencement of this Act in Schedules 3 and 4 (transitional provisions and consequential amendments) are to the commencement of the main substantive provisions of Parts I and III of this Act and the consequential repeal of the Trade Marks Act 1938.

Provision may be made by order under this section identifying the date of that commencement.

References   See para 16.6.

110 Short title

This Act may be cited as the Trade Marks Act 1994.

References   See para 16.6.

SCHEDULES

SCHEDULE 1

Section 49

COLLECTIVE MARKS

General

1.   The provisions of this Act apply to collective marks subject to the following provisions.

Signs of which a collective mark may consist

2.   In relation to a collective mark the reference in section 1(1) (signs of which a trade mark may consist) to distinguishing goods or services of one undertaking from those of other undertakings shall be construed as a reference to distinguishing goods or services of members of the association which is the proprietor of the mark from those of other undertakings.

Indication of geographical origin

3.—(1)   Notwithstanding section 3(1)(c), a collective mark may be registered which consists of signs or indications which may serve, in trade, to designate the geographical origin of the goods or services.

(2)   However, the proprietor of such a mark is not entitled to prohibit the use of the signs or indications in accordance with honest practices in industrial or commercial matters (in particular, by a person who is entitled to use a geographical name).

Mark not to be misleading as to character or significance

4.—(1)   A collective mark shall not be registered if the public is liable to be misled as regards the character or significance of the mark, in particular if it is likely to be taken to be something other than a collective mark.

(2)   The registrar may accordingly require that a mark in respect of which application is made for registration include some indication that it is a collective mark.

Notwithstanding section 39(2), an application may be amended so as to comply with any such requirement.

Regulations governing use of collective mark

5.—(1)   An applicant for registration of a collective mark must file with the registrar regulations governing the use of the mark.

(2)   The regulations must specify the persons authorised to use the mark, the conditions of membership of the association and, where they exist, the conditions of use of the mark, including any sanctions against misuse.

Further requirements with which the regulations have to comply may be imposed by rules.

Approval of regulations by registrar

6.—(1) A collective mark shall not be registered unless the regulations governing the use of the mark—

(a) comply with paragraph 5(2) and any further requirements imposed by rules, and

(b) are not contrary to public policy or to accepted principles of morality.

(2) Before the end of the prescribed period after the date of the application for registration of a collective mark, the applicant must file the regulations with the registrar and pay the prescribed fee.

If he does not do so, the application shall be deemed to be withdrawn.

7.—(1) The registrar shall consider whether the requirements mentioned in paragraph 6(1) are met.

(2) If it appears to the registrar that those requirements are not met, he shall inform the applicant and give him an opportunity, within such period as the registrar may specify, to make representations or to file amended regulations.

(3) If the applicant fails to satisfy the registrar that those requirements are met, or to file regulations amended so as to meet them, or fails to respond before the end of the specified period, the registrar shall refuse the application.

(4) If it appears to the registrar that those requirements, and the other requirements for registration, are met, he shall accept the application and shall proceed in accordance with section 38 (publication, opposition proceedings and observations).

8. The regulations shall be published and notice of opposition may be given, and observations may be made, relating to the matters mentioned in paragraph 6(1).

This is in addition to any other grounds on which the application may be opposed or observations made.

Regulations to be open to inspection

9. The regulations governing the use of a registered collective mark shall be open to public inspection in the same way as the register.

Amendment of regulations

10.—(1) An amendment of the regulations governing the use of a registered collective mark is not effective unless and until the amended regulations are filed with the registrar and accepted by him.

(2) Before accepting any amended regulations the registrar may in any case where it appears to him expedient to do so cause them to be published.

(3) If he does so, notice of opposition may be given, and observations may be made, relating to the matters mentioned in paragraph 6(1).

Infringement: rights of authorised users

11. The following provisions apply in relation to an authorised user of a registered collective mark as in relation to a licensee of a trade mark—

(a) section 10(5) (definition of infringement: unauthorised application of mark to certain material);

(b) section 19(2) (order as to disposal of infringing goods, material or articles: adequacy of other remedies);

(c) section 89 (prohibition of importation of infringing goods, material or articles: request to Commissioners of Customs and Excise).

12.—(1) The following provisions (which correspond to the provisions of section 30 (general provisions as to rights of licensees in case of infringement)) have effect as regards the rights of an authorised user in relation to infringement of a registered collective mark.

(2)   An authorised user is entitled, subject to any agreement to the contrary between him and the proprietor, to call on the proprietor to take infringement proceedings in respect of any matter which affects his interests.

(3)   If the proprietor—
    (a)   refuses to do so, or
    (b)   fails to do so within two months after being called upon,
the authorised user may bring the proceedings in his own name as if he were the proprietor.

(4)   Where infringement proceedings are brought by virtue of this paragraph, the authorised user may not, without the leave of the court, proceed with the action unless the proprietor is either joined as a plaintiff or added as a defendant.

This does not affect the granting of interlocutory relief on an application by an authorised user alone.

(5)   A proprietor who is added as a defendant as mentioned in sub-paragraph (4) shall not be made liable for any costs in the action unless he takes part in the proceedings.

(6)   In infringement proceedings brought by the proprietor of a registered collective mark any loss suffered or likely to be suffered by authorised users shall be taken into account; and the court may give such directions as it thinks fit as to the extent to which the plaintiff is to hold the proceeds of any pecuniary remedy on behalf of such users.

Grounds for revocation of registration

13.   Apart from the grounds of revocation provided for in section 46, the registration of a collective mark may be revoked on the ground—
    (a)   that the manner in which the mark has been used by the proprietor has caused it to become liable to mislead the public in the manner referred to in paragraph 4(1), or
    (b)   that the proprietor has failed to observe, or to secure the observance of, the regulations governing the use of the mark, or
    (c)   that an amendment of the regulations has been made so that the regulations—
        (i)   no longer comply with paragraph 5(2) and any further conditions imposed by rules, or
        (ii)   are contrary to public policy or to accepted principles of morality.

Grounds for invalidity of registration

14.   Apart from the grounds of invalidity provided for in section 47, the registration of a collective mark may be declared invalid on the ground that the mark was registered in breach of the provisions of paragraph 4(1) or 6(1).

Definitions   For "trade mark", see s 1; for "infringement", see ss 9(1), (2), 10; as to "the date of application for registration", see s 33(2); for "collective mark", see s 49(1); for "the registrar", see s 62; for "the register" and as to "registered" and "registration", see s 63(1); for "the court", see s 75; for "publish", "trade" and "infringement proceedings", see s 103(1); as to "use" in relation to collective marks, see s 103(2), which applies to such marks by virtue of para 1 above.
References   See Chapter 12.

SCHEDULE 2

Section 50

CERTIFICATION MARKS

General

1.   The provisions of this Act apply to certification marks subject to the following provisions.

Signs of which a certification mark may consist

2.   In relation to a certification mark the reference in section 1(1) (signs of which a trade mark may consist) to distinguishing goods or services of one undertaking from those of other undertakings shall be construed as a reference to distinguishing goods or services which are certified from those which are not.

Indication of geographical origin

3.—(1)   Notwithstanding section 3(1)(c), a certification mark may be registered which consists of signs or indications which may serve, in trade, to designate the geographical origin of the goods or services.

(2)   However, the proprietor of such a mark is not entitled to prohibit the use of the signs or indications in accordance with honest practices in industrial or commercial matters (in particular, by a person who is entitled to use a geographical name).

Nature of proprietor's business

4.   A certification mark shall not be registered if the proprietor carries on a business involving the supply of goods or services of the kind certified.

Mark not to be misleading as to character or significance

5.—(1)   A certification mark shall not be registered if the public is liable to be misled as regards the character or significance of the mark, in particular if it is likely to be taken to be something other than a certification mark.

(2)   The registrar may accordingly require that a mark in respect of which application is made for registration include some indication that it is a certification mark.

Notwithstanding section 39(2), an application may be amended so as to comply with any such requirement.

Regulations governing use of certification mark

6.—(1)   An applicant for registration of a certification mark must file with the registrar regulations governing the use of the mark.

(2)   The regulations must indicate who is authorised to use the mark, the characteristics to be certified by the mark, how the certifying body is to test those characteristics and to supervise the use of the mark, the fees (if any) to be paid in connection with the operation of the mark and the procedures for resolving disputes.

Further requirements with which the regulations have to comply may be imposed by rules.

Approval of regulations, &c

7.—(1)   A certification mark shall not be registered unless—
    (a)   the regulations governing the use of the mark—
        (i)   comply with paragraph 6(2) and any further requirements imposed by rules, and
        (ii)   are not contrary to public policy or to accepted principles of morality, and
    (b)   the applicant is competent to certify the goods or services for which the mark is to be registered.

(2)   Before the end of the prescribed period after the date of the application for registration of a certification mark, the applicant must file the regulations with the registrar and pay the prescribed fee.

If he does not do so, the application shall be deemed to be withdrawn.

8.—(1)   The registrar shall consider whether the requirements mentioned in paragraph 7(1) are met.

(2) If it appears to the registrar that those requirements are not met, he shall inform the applicant and give him an opportunity, within such period as the registrar may specify, to make representations or to file amended regulations.

(3) If the applicant fails to satisfy the registrar that those requirements are met, or to file regulations amended so as to meet them, or fails to respond before the end of the specified period, the registrar shall refuse the application.

(4) If it appears to the registrar that those requirements, and the other requirements for registration, are met, he shall accept the application and shall proceed in accordance with section 38 (publication, opposition proceedings and observations).

9. The regulations shall be published and notice of opposition may be given, and observations may be made, relating to the matters mentioned in paragraph 7(1).

This is in addition to any other grounds on which the application may be opposed or observations made.

Regulations to be open to inspection

10. The regulations governing the use of a registered certification mark shall be open to public inspection in the same way as the register.

Amendment of regulations

11.—(1) An amendment of the regulations governing the use of a registered certification mark is not effective unless and until the amended regulations are filed with the registrar and accepted by him.

(2) Before accepting any amended regulations the registrar may in any case where it appears to him expedient to do so cause them to be published.

(3) If he does so, notice of opposition may be given, and observations may be made, relating to the matters mentioned in paragraph 7(1).

Consent to assignment of registered certification mark

12. The assignment or other transmission of a registered certification mark is not effective without the consent of the registrar.

Infringement: rights of authorised users

13. The following provisions apply in relation to an authorised user of a registered certification mark as in relation to a licensee of a trade mark—
  (a) section 10(5) (definition of infringement: unauthorised application of mark to certain material);
  (b) section 19(2) (order as to disposal of infringing goods, material or articles: adequacy of other remedies);
  (c) section 89 (prohibition of importation of infringing goods, material or articles: request to Commissioners of Customs and Excise).

14. In infringement proceedings brought by the proprietor of a registered certification mark any loss suffered or likely to be suffered by authorised users shall be taken into account; and the court may give such directions as it thinks fit as to the extent to which the plaintiff is to hold the proceeds of any pecuniary remedy on behalf of such users.

Grounds for revocation of registration

15. Apart from the grounds of revocation provided for in section 46, the registration of a certification mark may be revoked on the ground—
  (a) that the proprietor has begun to carry on such a business as is mentioned in paragraph 4,
  (b) that the manner in which the mark has been used by the proprietor has caused it to become liable to mislead the public in the manner referred to in paragraph 5(1),

(c) that the proprietor has failed to observe, or to secure the observance of, the regulations governing the use of the mark,

(d) that an amendment of the regulations has been made so that the regulations—

(i) no longer comply with paragraph 6(2) and any further conditions imposed by rules, or

(ii) are contrary to public policy or to accepted principles of morality, or

(e) that the proprietor is no longer competent to certify the goods or services for which the mark is registered.

Grounds for invalidity of registration

16. Apart from the grounds of invalidity provided for in section 47, the registration of a certification mark may be declared invalid on the ground that the mark was registered in breach of the provisions of paragraph 4, 5(1) or 7(1).

Definitions   For "trade mark", see s 1; as to "the date of application for registration", see s 33(2); for "certification mark", see s 50(1); for "the registrar", see s 62; for "the register" and as to "registered" and "registration", see s 63(1); for "the court", see s 75; for "business", "infringement proceedings", "publish" and "trade", see s 103(1); as to "use" in relation to certification marks, see s 103(2), which applies to such marks by virtue of para 1 above.
References   See Chapter 11.

SCHEDULE 3

Section 105

TRANSITIONAL PROVISIONS

Introductory

1.—(1) In this Schedule—

"existing registered mark" means a trade mark, certification trade mark or service mark registered under the 1938 Act immediately before the commencement of this Act;

"the 1938 Act" means the Trade Marks Act 1938; and

"the old law" means that Act and any other enactment or rule of law applying to existing registered marks immediately before the commencement of this Act.

(2) For the purposes of this Schedule—

(a) an application shall be treated as pending on the commencement of this Act if it was made but not finally determined before commencement, and

(b) the date on which it was made shall be taken to be the date of filing under the 1938 Act.

Definitions   For definitions, see note to para 22 below.
References   See para 17.2.

Existing registered marks

2.—(1) Existing registered marks (whether registered in Part A or B of the register kept under the 1938 Act) shall be transferred on the commencement of this Act to the register kept under this Act and have effect, subject to the provisions of this Schedule, as if registered under this Act.

(2) Existing registered marks registered as a series under section 21(2) of the 1938 Act shall be similarly registered in the new register.

Provision may be made by rules for putting such entries in the same form as is required for entries under this Act.

(3) In any other case notes indicating that existing registered marks are associated with other marks shall cease to have effect on the commencement of this Act.

Definitions For definitions, see note to para 22 below.
References See para 14.3.

3.—(1) A condition entered on the former register in relation to an existing registered mark immediately before the commencement of this Act shall cease to have effect on commencement.

Proceedings under section 33 of the 1938 Act (application to expunge or vary registration for breach of condition) which are pending on the commencement of this Act shall be dealt with under the old law and any necessary alteration made to the new register.

(2) A disclaimer or limitation entered on the former register in relation to an existing registered mark immediately before the commencement of this Act shall be transferred to the new register and have effect as if entered on the register in pursuance of section 13 of this Act.

Definitions For definitions, see note to para 22 below.
References See para 14.3.

Effects of registration: infringement

4.—(1) Sections 9 to 12 of this Act (effects of registration) apply in relation to an existing registered mark as from the commencement of this Act and section 14 of this Act (action for infringement) applies in relation to infringement of an existing registered mark committed after the commencement of this Act, subject to sub-paragraph (2) below.

The old law continues to apply in relation to infringements committed before commencement.

(2) It is not an infringement of—
   (a) an existing registered mark, or
   (b) a registered trade mark of which the distinctive elements are the same or substantially the same as those of an existing registered mark and which is registered for the same goods or services,

to continue after commencement any use which did not amount to infringement of the existing registered mark under the old law.

Definitions For definitions, see note to para 22 below.
References See paras 7.13, 7.14.

Infringing goods, material or articles

5. Section 16 of this Act (order for delivery up of infringing goods, material or articles) applies to infringing goods, material or articles whether made before or after the commencement of this Act.

Definitions For definitions, see note to para 22 below.
References See paras 8.6, 17.4.

Rights and remedies of licensee or authorised user

6.—(1) Section 30 (general provisions as to rights of licensees in case of infringement) of this Act applies to licences granted before the commencement of this Act, but only in relation to infringements committed after commencement.

(2) Paragraph 14 of Schedule 2 of this Act (court to take into account loss suffered by authorised users, &c) applies only in relation to infringements committed after commencement.

Definitions For definitions, see note to para 22 below.
References See paras 6.10, 11.4, 17.4.

Co-ownership of registered mark

7.   The provisions of section 23 of this Act (co-ownership of registered mark) apply as from the commencement of this Act to an existing registered mark of which two or more persons were immediately before commencement registered as joint proprietors.

But so long as the relations between the joint proprietors remain such as are described in section 63 of the 1938 Act (joint ownership) there shall be taken to be an agreement to exclude the operation of subsections (1) and (3) of section 23 of this Act (ownership in undivided shares and right of co-proprietor to make separate use of the mark).

Definitions For definitions, see note to para 22 below.
References See paras 6.2, 17.5.

Assignment, &c of registered mark

8.—(1)   Section 24 of this Act (assignment or other transmission of registered mark) applies to transactions and events occurring after the commencement of this Act in relation to an existing registered mark; and the old law continues to apply in relation to transactions and events occurring before commencement.

(2)   Existing entries under section 25 of the 1938 Act (registration of assignments and transmissions) shall be transferred on the commencement of this Act to the register kept under this Act and have effect as if made under section 25 of this Act.

Provision may be made by rules for putting such entries in the same form as is required for entries made under this Act.

(3)   An application for registration under section 25 of the 1938 Act which is pending before the registrar on the commencement of this Act shall be treated as an application for registration under section 25 of this Act and shall proceed accordingly.

The registrar may require the applicant to amend his application so as to conform with the requirements of this Act.

(4)   An application for registration under section 25 of the 1938 Act which has been determined by the registrar but not finally determined before the commencement of this Act shall be dealt with under the old law; and sub-paragraph (2) above shall apply in relation to any resulting entry in the register.

(5)   Where before the commencement of this Act a person has become entitled by assignment or transmission to an existing registered mark but has not registered his title, any application for registration after commencement shall be made under section 25 of this Act.

(6)   In cases to which sub-paragraph (3) or (5) applies section 25(3) of the 1938 Act continues to apply (and section 25(3) and (4) of this Act do not apply) as regards the consequences of failing to register.

Definitions For definitions, see note to para 22 below.
References See paras 6.13, 17.5.

Licensing of registered mark

9.—(1)   Sections 28 and 29(2) of this Act (licensing of registered trade mark; rights of exclusive licensee against grantor's successor in title) apply only in relation to licences granted after the commencement of this Act; and the old law continues to apply in relation to licences granted before commencement.

(2)   Existing entries under section 28 of the 1938 Act (registered users) shall be transferred on the commencement of this Act to the register kept under this Act and have effect as if made under section 25 of this Act.

Provision may be made by rules for putting such entries in the same form as is required for entries made under this Act.

(3)   An application for registration as a registered user which is pending before the registrar on the commencement of this Act shall be treated as an application for registration of a licence under section 25(1) of this Act and shall proceed accordingly.

The registrar may require the applicant to amend his application so as to conform with the requirements of this Act.

(4)   An application for registration as a registered user which has been determined by the registrar but not finally determined before the commencement of this Act shall be dealt with under the old law; and sub-paragraph (2) above shall apply in relation to any resulting entry in the register.

(5)   Any proceedings pending on the commencement of this Act under section 28(8) or (10) of the 1938 Act (variation or cancellation of registration of registered user) shall be dealt with under the old law and any necessary alteration made to the new register.

Definitions   For definitions, see note to para 22 below.
References   See paras 6.7, 6.13, 17.5.

Pending applications for registration

10.—(1)   An application for registration of a mark under the 1938 Act which is pending on the commencement of this Act shall be dealt with under the old law, subject as mentioned below, and if registered the mark shall be treated for the purposes of this Schedule as an existing registered mark.

(2)   The power of the Secretary of State under section 78 of this Act to make rules regulating practice and procedure, and as to the matters mentioned in subsection (2) of that section, is exercisable in relation to such an application; and different provision may be made for such applications from that made for other applications.

(3)   Section 23 of the 1938 Act (provisions as to associated trade marks) shall be disregarded in dealing after the commencement of this Act with an application for registration.

Definitions   For definitions, see note to para 22 below
References   See paras 5.12, 17.6.

Conversion of pending application

11.—(1)   In the case of a pending application for registration which has not been advertised under section 18 of the 1938 Act before the commencement of this Act, the applicant may give notice to the registrar claiming to have the registrability of the mark determined in accordance with the provisions of this Act.

(2)   The notice must be in the prescribed form, be accompanied by the appropriate fee and be given no later than six months after the commencement of this Act.

(3)   Notice duly given is irrevocable and has the effect that the application shall be treated as if made immediately after the commencement of this Act.

Definitions   For definitions, see note to para 22 below.
References   See paras 5.12, 17.6.

Trade marks registered according to old classification

12.   The registrar may exercise the powers conferred by rules under section 65 of this Act (adaptation of entries to new classification) to secure that any existing registered marks which do not conform to the system of classification prescribed under section 34 of this Act are brought into conformity with that system.

This applies, in particular, to existing registered marks classified according to the pre-1938 classification set out in Schedule 3 to the Trade Marks Rules 1986.

Definitions   For definitions, see note to para 22 below.
References   See paras 14.5, 17.6.

Claim to priority from overseas application

13.   Section 35 of this Act (claim to priority of Convention application) applies to an application for registration under this Act made after the commencement of this Act notwithstanding that the Convention application was made before commencement.

Definitions   For definitions, see note to para 22 below.
References   See paras 5.4, 5.12, 17.6.

14.—(1)   Where before the commencement of this Act a person has duly filed an application for protection of a trade mark in a relevant country within the meaning of section 39A of the 1938 Act which is not a Convention country (a "relevant overseas application"), he, or his successor in title, has a right to priority, for the purposes of registering the same trade mark under this Act for some or all of the same goods or services, for a period of six months from the date of filing of the relevant overseas application.

(2)   If the application for registration under this Act is made within that six-month period—

(a)   the relevant date for the purposes of establishing which rights take precedence shall be the date of filing of the relevant overseas application, and

(b)   the registrability of the trade mark shall not be affected by any use of the mark in the United Kingdom in the period between that date and the date of the application under this Act.

(3)   Any filing which in a relevant country is equivalent to a regular national filing, under its domestic legislation or an international agreement, shall be treated as giving rise to the right of priority.

A "regular national filing" means a filing which is adequate to establish the date on which the application was filed in that country, whatever may be the subsequent fate of the application.

(4)   A subsequent application concerning the same subject as the relevant overseas application, filed in the same country, shall be considered the relevant overseas application (of which the filing date is the starting date of the period of priority), if at the time of the subsequent application—

(a)   the previous application has been withdrawn, abandoned or refused, without having been laid open to public inspection and without leaving any rights outstanding, and

(b)   it has not yet served as a basis for claiming a right of priority.

The previous application may not thereafter serve as a basis for claiming a right of priority.

(5)   Provision may be made by rules as to the manner of claiming a right to priority on the basis of a relevant overseas application.

(6)   A right to priority arising as a result of a relevant overseas application may be assigned or otherwise transmitted, either with the application or independently.

The reference in sub-paragraph (1) to the applicant's "successor in title" shall be construed accordingly.

(7) Nothing in this paragraph affects proceedings on an application for registration under the 1938 Act made before the commencement of this Act (see paragraph 10 above).

Definitions For definitions, see note to para 22 below.
References See paras 5.4, 5.6, 17.6.

Duration and renewal of registration

15.—(1) Section 42(1) of this Act (duration of original period of registration) applies in relation to the registration of a mark in pursuance of an application made after the commencement of this Act; and the old law applies in any other case.

(2) Sections 42(2) and 43 of this Act (renewal) apply where the renewal falls due on or after the commencement of this Act; and the old law continues to apply in any other case.

(3) In either case it is immaterial when the fee is paid.

Definitions For definitions, see note to para 22 below.
References See paras 9.1, 9.2, 17.7.

Pending application for alteration of registered mark

16. An application under section 35 of the 1938 Act (alteration of registered trade mark) which is pending on the commencement of this Act shall be dealt with under the old law and any necessary alteration made to the new register.

Definitions For definitions, see note to para 22 below.
References See paras 9.3, 17.7.

Revocation for non-use

17.—(1) An application under section 26 of the 1938 Act (removal from register or imposition of limitation on ground of non-use) which is pending on the commencement of this Act shall be dealt with under the old law and any necessary alteration made to the new register.

(2) An application under section 46(1)(a) or (b) of this Act (revocation for non-use) may be made in relation to an existing registered mark at any time after the commencement of this Act.

Provided that no such application for the revocation of the registration of an existing registered mark registered by virtue of section 27 of the 1938 Act (defensive registration of well-known trade marks) may be made until more than five years after the commencement of this Act.

Definitions For definitions, see note to para 22 below.
References See paras 10.7, 17.8.

Application for rectification, &c

18.—(1) An application under section 32 or 34 of the 1938 Act (rectification or correction of the register) which is pending on the commencement of this Act shall be dealt with under the old law and any necessary alteration made to the new register.

(2) For the purposes of proceedings under section 47 of this Act (grounds for invalidity of registration) as it applies in relation to an existing registered mark, the provisions of this Act shall be deemed to have been in force at all material times.

Provided that no objection to the validity of the registration of an existing registered mark may be taken on the ground specified in subsection (3) of section 5 of this Act (relative grounds for refusal of registration: conflict with earlier mark registered for different goods or services).

Definitions   For definitions, see note to para 22 below.
References   See paras 10.8, 10.10, 17.8.

Regulations as to use of certification mark

19.—(1) Regulations governing the use of an existing registered certification mark deposited at the Patent Office in pursuance of section 37 of the 1938 Act shall be treated after the commencement of this Act as if filed under paragraph 6 of Schedule 2 to this Act.

(2) Any request for amendment of the regulations which was pending on the commencement of this Act shall be dealt with under the old law.

Definitions   For definitions, see note to para 22 below.
References   See paras 11.3, 17.9.

Sheffield marks

20.—(1) For the purposes of this Schedule the Sheffield register kept under Schedule 2 to the 1938 Act shall be treated as part of the register of trade marks kept under that Act.

(2) Applications made to the Cutlers' Company in accordance with that Schedule which are pending on the commencement of this Act shall proceed after commencement as if they had been made to the registrar.

Definitions   For definitions, see note to para 22 below.
References   See para 17.9.

Certificate of validity of contested registration

21. A certificate given before the commencement of this Act under section 47 of the 1938 Act (certificate of validity of contested registration) shall have effect as if given under section 73(1) of this Act.

Definitions   For definitions, see note to para 22 below.
References   See paras 14.10, 17.9.

Trade mark agents

22.—(1) Rules in force immediately before the commencement of this Act under section 282 or 283 of the Copyright, Designs and Patents Act 1988 (register of trade mark agents; persons entitled to described themselves as registered) shall continue in force and have effect as if made under section 83 or 85 of this Act.

(2) Rules in force immediately before the commencement of this Act under section 40 of the 1938 Act as to the persons whom the registrar may refuse to recognise as agents for the purposes of business under that Act shall continue in force and have effect as if made under section 88 of this Act.

(3) Rules continued in force under this paragraph may be varied or revoked by further rules made under the relevant provisions of this Act.

Definitions   For "trade mark", see s 1; for "infringement", see ss 9(1), (2), 10; for "infringing articles", "infringing goods" and "infringing material", see s 17; for "Convention application", see s 35(1); for "certification mark", see s 50(1); for "Convention country", see s 55(1)(b); for "the registrar", see s 62; for "the register" and as to "registered" and "registration", see s 63(1); as to "use" in relation to a trade mark, see s 103(2); for "commencement of this Act", see s 109(2). Note also the definitions in paras 1, 14(1), (3), (6) above.
References   See paras 14.15, 17.9.

SCHEDULE 4

Section 106(1)

CONSEQUENTIAL AMENDMENTS

General adaptation of existing references

1.—(1)   References in statutory provisions passed or made before the commencement of this Act to trade marks or registered trade marks within the meaning of the Trade Marks Act 1938 shall, unless the context otherwise requires, be construed after the commencement of this Act as references to trade marks or registered trade marks within the meaning of this Act.

(2) Sub-paragraph (1) applies, in particular, to the references in the following provisions—

Industrial Organisation and Development Act 1947	Schedule 1, paragraph 7
Crown Proceedings Act 1947	section 3(1)(b)
Horticulture Act 1960	section 15(1)(b)
Printer's Imprint Act 1961	section 1(1)(b)
Plant Varieties and Seeds Act 1964	section 5A(4)
Northern Ireland Constitution Act 1973	Schedule 3, paragraph 17
Patents Act 1977	section 19(2)
	section 27(4)
	section 123(7)
Unfair Contract Terms Act 1977	Schedule 1, paragraph 1(c)
Judicature (Northern Ireland) Act 1978	section 94A(5)
State Immunity Act 1978	section 7(a) and (b)
Supreme Court Act 1981	section 72(5)
	Schedule 1, paragraph 1(i)
Civil Jurisdiction and Judgments Act 1982	Schedule 5, paragraph 2
	Schedule 8, paragraph 2(14) and 4(2)
Value Added Tax Act 1983	Schedule 3, paragraph 1
Companies Act 1985	section 396(3A)(a) or (as substituted by the Companies Act 1989) section 396(2)(d)(i)
	section 410(4)(c)(v)
	Schedule 4, Part I, Balance Sheet Formats 1 and 2 and Note (2)
	Schedule 9, Part I, paragraphs 5(2)(d) and 10(2)
Law Reform (Miscellaneous Provisions) (Scotland) Act 1985	section 15(5)
Atomic Energy Authority Act 1986	section 8(2)
Companies (Northern Ireland) Order 1986	article 403(3A)(a) or (as substituted by the Companies (No 2) (Northern Ireland) Order 1990) article 403(2)(d)(i)
	Schedule 4, Part I, Balance Sheet Formats 1 and 2 and Note (2)
	Schedule 9, Part I, paragraphs 5(2)(d) and 10(2)
Consumer Protection Act 1987	section 2(2)(b)
Consumer Protection (Northern Ireland) Order 1987	article 5(2)(b)
Income and Corporation Taxes Act 1988	section 83(a)
Taxation of Chargeable Gains Act 1992	section 275(h)
Tribunals and Inquiries Act 1992	Schedule 1, paragraph 34.

Patents and Designs Act 1907 (c 29)

2.—(1)   The Patents and Designs Act 1907 is amended as follows.

(2)   In section 62 (the Patent Office)—
   (a)   in subsection (1) for "this Act and the Trade Marks Act 1905" substitute "the Patents Act 1977, the Registered Designs Act 1949 and the Trade Marks Act 1994"; and
   (b)   in subsections (2) and (3) for "the Board of Trade" substitute "the Secretary of State".

(3)   In section 63 (officers and clerks of the Patent Office)—
   (a)   for "the Board of Trade" in each place where it occurs substitute "the Secretary of State"; and
   (b)   in subsection (2) omit the words from "and those salaries" to the end.

(4)   The repeal by the Patents Act 1949 and the Registered Designs Act 1949 of the whole of the 1907 Act, except certain provisions, shall be deemed not to have extended to the long title, date of enactment or enacting words or to so much of section 99 as provides the Act with its short title.

Patents, Designs, Copyright and Trade Marks (Emergency) Act 1939 (c 107)

3.—(1)   The Patents, Designs, Copyright and Trade Marks (Emergency) Act 1939 is amended as follows.

(2)   For section 3 (power of comptroller to suspend rights of enemy or enemy subject) substitute—

"3   Power of comptroller to suspend trade mark rights of enemy or enemy subject

   (1)   Where on application made by a person proposing to supply goods or services of any description it is made to appear to the comptroller—
      (a)   that it is difficult or impracticable to describe or refer to the goods or services without the use of a registered trade mark, and
      (b)   that the proprietor of the registered trade mark (whether alone or jointly with another) is an enemy or an enemy subject,

   the comptroller may make an order suspending the rights given by the registered trade mark.

   (2)   An order under this section shall suspend those rights as regards the use of the trade mark—
      (a)   by the applicant, and
      (b)   by any person authorised by the applicant to do, for the purposes of or in connection with the supply by the applicant of the goods or services, things which would otherwise infringe the registered trade mark,

   to such extent and for such period as the comptroller considers necessary to enable the applicant to render well-known and established some other means of describing or referring to the goods or services in question which does not involve the use of the trade mark.

   (3)   Where an order has been made under this section, no action for passing off lies on the part of any person interested in the registered trade mark in respect of any use of it which by virtue of the order is not an infringement of the right conferred by it.

   (4)   An order under this section may be varied or revoked by a subsequent order made by the comptroller.".

(3)   In each of the following provisions—
   (a)   section 4(1)(c) (effect of war on registration of trade marks),
   (b)   section 6(1) (power of comptroller to extend time limits),
   (c)   section 7(1)(a) (evidence as to nationality, &c), and
   (d)   the definition of "the comptroller" in section 10(1) (interpretation),

for "the Trade Marks Act 1938" substitute "the Trade Marks Act 1994".

Trade Descriptions Act 1968 (c 29)

4.   In the Trade Descriptions Act 1968, in section 34 (exemption of trade description contained in pre-1968 trade mark)12—

    (a)   in the opening words, omit "within the meaning of the Trade Marks Act 1938"; and

    (b)   in paragraph (c), for "a person registered under section 28 of the Trade Marks Act 1938 as a registered user of the trade mark" substitute ", in the case of a registered trade mark, a person licensed to use it".

Solicitors Act 1974 (c 47)

5.—(1)   Section 22 of the Solicitors Act 1974 (preparation of instruments by unqualified persons) is amended as follows.

(2)   In subsection (2)(aa) and (ab) (instruments which may be prepared by registered trade mark agent or registered patent agent) for ", trade mark or service mark" substitute "or trade mark".

(3)   In subsection (3A) (interpretation)—

    (a)   in the definition of "registered trade mark agent" for "section 282(1) of the Copyright, Designs and Patents Act 1988" substitute "the Trade Marks Act 1994"; and

    (b)   in the definition of "registered patent agent" for "of that Act" substitute "of the Copyright, Designs and Patents Act 1988".

House of Commons Disqualification Act 1975 (c 24)

6.   In Part III of Schedule 1 to the House of Commons Disqualification Act 1975 (other disqualifying offices), for the entry relating to persons appointed to hear and determine appeals under the Trade Marks Act 1938 substitute—

       "Person appointed to hear and determine appeals under the Trade Marks Act 1994.".

Restrictive Trade Practices Act 1976 (c 34)

7.   In Schedule 3 to the Restrictive Trade Practices Act 1976 (excepted agreements), for paragraph 4 (agreements relating to trade marks) substitute—

"4.—(1)   This Act does not apply to an agreement authorising the use of a registered trade mark (other than a collective mark or certification mark) if no such restrictions as are described in section 6(1) or 11(2) above are accepted, and no such information provisions as are described in section 7(1) or 12(2) above are made, except in respect of—

    (a)   the descriptions of goods bearing the mark which are to be produced or supplied, or the processes of manufacture to be applied to such goods or to goods to which the mark is to be applied, or

    (b)   the kinds of services in relation to which the mark is to be used which are to be made available or supplied, or the form or manner in which such services are to be made available or supplied, or

    (c)   the descriptions of goods which are to be produced or supplied in connection with the supply of services in relation to which the mark is to be used, or the process of manufacture to be applied to such goods.

(2)   This Act does not apply to an agreement authorising the use of a registered collective mark or certification mark if—

    (a)   the agreement is made in accordance with regulations approved by the registrar under Schedule 1 or 2 to the Trade Marks Act 1994, and

    (b)   no such restrictions as are described in section 6(1) or 11(2) above are accepted, and no such information provisions as are described in section 7(1) or 12(2) above are made, except as permitted by those regulations.".

8.—(1)   The Copyright, Designs and Patents Act 1988 is amended as follows.

(2)   In sections 114(6), 204(6) and 231(6) (persons regarded as having an interest in infringing copies, &c), for "section 58C of the Trade Marks Act 1938" substitute "section 19 of the Trade Marks Act 1994".

(3)   In section 280(1) (privilege for communications with patent agents), for "trade mark or service mark" substitute "or trade mark".

Tribunals and Inquiries Act 1992 (c 53)

9.   In Part I of Schedule 1 to the Tribunals and Inquiries Act 1992 (tribunals under direct supervision of Council on Tribunals), for "Patents, designs, trade marks and service marks" substitute "Patents, designs and trade marks".

Definitions   For "commencement of this Act", see s 109(2). In the Patents, Designs, Copyright and Trade Marks (Emergency) Act 1939, for "the comptroller", see s 10(1) of that Act and for "enemy" and "enemy subject", see, by virtue of that provision, the Trading with the Enemy Act 1939, ss 2, 15(1). In the Restrictive Trade Practices Act 1976, for "agreement", "goods", "information provision" and "restriction", see s 43(1) thereof, and see also as to "information provision" and "restriction", s 9(7) of that Act.
References   See para 16.6.

SCHEDULE 5

Section 106(2)

REPEALS AND REVOCATIONS

Chapter or number	Short title	Extent of repeal or revocation
1891 c 50.	Commissioners for Oaths Act 1891.	In section 1, the words "or the Patents, Designs and Trade Marks Acts, 1883 to 1888,".
1907 c 29.	Patents and Designs Act 1907.	In section 63(2), the words from "and those salaries" to the end.
1938 c 22.	Trade Marks Act 1938.	The whole Act.
1947 c 44.	Crown Proceedings Act 1947.	In section 3(1)(b), the words "or registered service mark".
1949 c 87.	Patents Act 1949.	Section 92(2).
1964 c 14.	Plant Varieties and Seeds Act 1964.	In section 5A(4), the words "under the Trade Marks Act 1938".
1967 c 80.	Criminal Justice Act 1967.	In Schedule 3, in Parts I and IV, the entries relating to the Trade Marks Act 1938.
1978 c 23.	Judicature (Northern Ireland) Act 1978.	In Schedule 5, in Part II, the paragraphs amending the Trade Marks Act 1938.
1984 c 19.	Trade Marks (Amendment) Act 1984.	The whole Act.
1985 c 6.	Companies Act 1985.	In section 396— (a) in subsection (3A)(a), and (b) in subsection (2)(d)(i) as inserted by the Companies Act 1989, the words "service mark,".
1986 c 12.	Statute Law (Repeals) Act 1986.	In Schedule 2, paragraph 2.
1986 c 39.	Patents, Designs and Marks Act 1986.	Section 2.

Chapter or number	Short title	Extent of repeal or revocation
SI 1986/1032 (NI 6).	Companies (Northern Ireland) Order 1986.	Section 4(4). In Schedule 1, paragraphs 1 and 2. Schedule 2. In article 403— (a) in paragraph (3A)(a), and (b) in paragraph (2)(d)(i) as inserted by the Companies (No 2) (Northern Ireland) Order 1990, the words "service mark,".
1987 c 43.	Consumer Protection Act 1987.	In section 45— (a) in subsection (1), the definition of "mark" and "trade mark"; (b) subsection (4).
SI 1987/2049.	Consumer Protection (Northern Ireland) Order 1987.	In article 2— (a) in paragraph (2), the definitions of "mark" and "trade mark"; (b) paragraph (3).
1988 c 1.	Income and Corporation Taxes Act 1988.	In section 83, the words from "References in this section" to the end.
1988 c 48.	Copyright, Designs and Patents Act 1988.	Sections 282 to 284. In section 286, the definition of "registered trade mark agent". Section 300.
1992 c 12.	Taxation of Chargeable Gains Act 1992.	In section 275(h), the words "service marks" and "service mark".

References   See para 16.6.

Appendix 2

Council Directive 89/104/EEC

FIRST COUNCIL DIRECTIVE

of 21 December 1988

to approximate the laws of the Member States relating to trade marks

(89/104/EEC)

Date of publication in OJ: OJ L40, 11.2.89, p 1.

THE COUNCIL OF THE EUROPEAN COMMUNITIES,

Having regard to the Treaty establishing the European Economic Community, and in particular Article 100a thereof,

Having regard to the proposal from the Commission[1],

In co-operation with the European Parliament[2],

Having regard to the opinion of the Economic and Social Committee[3],

Whereas the trade mark laws at present applicable in the Member States contain disparities which may impede the free movement of goods and freedom to provide services and may distort competition within the common market; whereas it is therefore necessary, in view of the establishment and functioning of the internal market, to approximate the laws of Member States;

Whereas it is important not to disregard the solutions and advantages which the Community trade mark system may afford to undertakings wishing to acquire trade marks;

Whereas it does not appear to be necessary at present to undertake full-scale approximation of the trade mark laws of the Member States and it will be sufficient if approximation is limited to those national provisions of law which most directly affect the functioning of the internal market;

Whereas the Directive does not deprive the Member States of the right to continue to protect trade marks acquired through use but takes them into account only in regard to the relationship between them and trade marks acquired by registration;

Whereas Member States also remain free to fix the provisions of procedure concerning the registration, the revocation and the invalidity of trade marks acquired by registration; whereas they can, for example, determine the form of trade mark registration and invalidity procedures, decide whether earlier rights should be invoked either in the registration procedure or in the invalidity procedure or in both and, if they allow earlier rights to be invoked in the registration procedure, have an opposition procedure or an *ex officio* examination procedure or both; whereas Member States remain free to determine the effects of revocation or invalidity of trade marks;

Whereas this Directive does not exclude the application to trade marks of provisions of law of the Member States other than trade mark law, such as the provisions relating to unfair competition, civil liability or consumer protection;

Whereas attainment of the objectives at which this approximation of laws is aiming requires that the conditions for obtaining and continuing to hold a registered trade mark are, in general, identical in all Member States; whereas, to this end, it is necessary to list examples of signs which may constitute a trade mark, provided that such signs are capable of distinguishing the goods or services of one undertaking from those of other undertakings; whereas the grounds for refusal or invalidity concerning the trade mark itself for example, the absence of any distinctive character, or concerning conflicts between the trade mark and earlier rights, are to be listed in an exhaustive manner, even if some of these grounds are listed as an option for the Member States which will therefore be able to maintain or introduce those grounds in their legislation; whereas Member States will be able to maintain or introduce into their legislation grounds of refusal or invalidity linked to conditions for obtaining and continuing to hold a trade mark for which there is no provision of approximation, concerning, for example, the eligibility for the grant of a trade mark, the renewal of the trade mark or rules on fees, or related to the non-compliance with procedural rules;

Whereas in order to reduce the total number of trade marks registered and protected in the Community and, consequently, the number of conflicts which arise between them, it is essential to require that registered trade marks must actually be used or, if not used, be subject to revocation; whereas it is necessary to provide that a trade mark cannot be invalidated on the basis of the existence of a non-used earlier trade mark, while the Member States remain free to apply the same principle in respect of the registration of a trade mark or to provide that a trade mark may not be successfully invoked in infringement proceedings if it is established as a result of a plea that the trade mark could be revoked; whereas in all these cases it is up to the Member States to establish the applicable rules of procedure;

Whereas it is fundamental, in order to facilitate the free circulation of goods and services, to ensure that henceforth registered trade marks enjoy the same protection under the legal systems of all the Member States; whereas this should however not prevent the Member States from granting at their option extensive protection to those trade marks which have a reputation;

Whereas the protection afforded by the registered trade mark, the function of which is in particular to guarantee the trade mark as an indication of origin, is absolute in the case of identity between the mark and the sign and goods or services; whereas the protection applies also in case of similarity between the mark and the sign and the goods or services; whereas it is indispensable to give an interpretation of the concept of similarity in relation to the likelihood of confusion; whereas the likelihood of confusion, the appreciation of which depends on numerous elements and, in particular, on the recognition of the trade mark on the market, of the association which can be made with the used or registered sign, of the degree of similarity between the trade mark and the sign and between the goods or services identified, constitutes the specific condition for such protection; whereas the ways in which likelihood of confusion may be established, and in particular the onus of proof, are a matter for national procedural rules which are not prejudiced by the Directive;

Whereas it is important, for reasons of legal certainty and without inequitably prejudicing the interests of a proprietor of an earlier trade mark, to provide that the latter may no longer request a declaration of invalidity nor may he oppose the use of a trade mark subsequent to his own of which he has knowingly tolerated the use for a substantial length of time, unless the application for the subsequent trade mark was made in bad faith;

Whereas all Member States of the Community are bound by the Paris Convention for the Protection of Industrial Property; whereas it is necessary that the provisions of this Directive are entirely consistent with those of the Paris Convention; whereas the obligations of the Member States resulting from this Convention are not affected by this Directive; whereas, where appropriate, the second subparagraph of Article 234 of the Treaty is applicable,

---

[1]   OJ C351, 31.12.80, p 1 and OJ C351, 31.12.85, p 4.
[2]   OJ C307, 14.11.83, p 66 and OJ C309, 5.12.88.
[3]   OJ C310, 30.11.81, p 22.

HAS ADOPTED THIS DIRECTIVE:

Article 1

Scope

This Directive shall apply to every trade mark in respect of goods or services which is the subject of registration or of an application in a Member State for registration as an individual trade mark, a collective mark or a guarantee or certification mark, or which is the subject of a registration or an application for registration in the Benelux Trade Mark Office or of an international registration having effect in a Member State.

Article 2

Signs of which a trade mark may consist

A trade mark may consist of any sign capable of being represented graphically, particularly words, including personal names, designs, letters, numerals, the shape of goods or of their packaging, provided that such signs are capable of distinguishing the goods or services of one undertaking from those of other undertakings.

Article 3

Grounds for refusal or invalidity

1.   The following shall not be registered or if registered shall be liable to be declared invalid—
- (a)   signs which cannot constitute a trade mark;
- (b)   trade marks which are devoid of any distinctive character;
- (c)   trade marks which consist exclusively of signs or indications which may serve, in trade, to designate the kind, quality, quantity, intended purpose, value, geographical origin, or the time of production of the goods or of rendering of the service, or other characteristics of the goods or service;
- (d)   trade marks which consist exclusively of signs or indications which have become customary in the current language or in the *bona fide* and established practices of the trade;
- (e)   signs which consist exclusively of—
     — the shape which results from the nature of the goods themselves, or
     — the shape of goods which is necessary to obtain a technical result, or
     — the shape which gives substantial value to the goods;
- (f)   trade marks which are contrary to public policy or to accepted principles of morality;
- (g)   trade marks which are of such a nature as to deceive the public, for instance as to the nature, quality or geographical origin of the goods or service;
- (h)   trade marks which have not been authorised by the competent authorities and are to be refused or invalidated pursuant to Article 6 *ter* of the Paris Convention for the Protection of Industrial Property, hereinafter referred to as the 'Paris Convention'.

2.   Any Member State may provide that a trade mark shall not be registered or, if registered, shall be liable to be declared invalid where and to the extent that—
- (a)   the use of that trade mark may be prohibited pursuant to provisions of law other than trade mark law of the Member State concerned or of the Community;
- (b)   the trade mark covers a sign of high symbolic value, in particular a religious symbol;
- (c)   the trade mark includes badges, emblems and escutcheons other than those covered by Article 6 *ter* of the Paris Convention and which are of public interest, unless the consent of the appropriate authorities to its registration has been given in conformity with the legislation of the Member State;
- (d)   the application for registration of the trade mark was made in bad faith by the applicant.

3.   A trade mark shall not be refused registration or be declared invalid in accordance with paragraph 1(b), (c) or (d) if, before the date of application for

registration and following the use which has been made of it, it has acquired a distinctive character. Any Member State may in addition provide that this provision shall also apply where the distinctive character was acquired after the date of application for registration or after the date of registration.

4.   Any Member State may provide that, by derogation from the preceding paragraphs, the grounds of refusal of registration or invalidity in force in that State prior to the date on which the provisions necessary to comply with this Directive enter into force, shall apply to trade marks for which application has been made prior to that date.

Article 4

Further grounds for refusal or invalidity concerning conflicts with earlier rights

1.   A trade mark shall not be registered or, if registered, shall be liable to be declared invalid—
(a)   if it is identical with an earlier trade mark, and the goods or services for which the trade mark is applied for or is registered are identical with the goods or services for which the earlier trade mark is protected;
(b)   if because of its identity with, or similarity to, the earlier trade mark and the identity or similarity of the goods or services covered by the trade marks, there exists a likelihood of confusion on the part of the public, which includes the likelihood of association with the earlier trade mark.

2.   'Earlier trade marks' within the meaning of paragraph 1 means—
(a)   trade marks of the following kinds with a date of application for registration which is earlier than the date of application for registration of the trade mark, taking account, where appropriate, of the priorities claimed in respect of those trade marks—
   (i)   Community trade marks;
   (ii)   trade marks registered in the Member State or, in the case of Belgium, Luxembourg or the Netherlands, at the Benelux Trade Mark Office;
   (iii) trade marks registered under international arrangements which have effect in the Member State;
(b)   Community trade marks which validly claim seniority, in accordance with the Regulation on the Community trade mark, from a trade mark referred to in (a)(ii) and (iii), even when the latter trade mark has been surrendered or allowed to lapse;
(c)   applications for the trade marks referred to in (a) and (b), subject to their registration;
(d)   trade marks which, on the date of application for registration of the trade mark, or, where appropriate, of the priority claimed in respect of the application for registration of the trade mark, are well known in a Member State, in the sense in which the words 'well known' are used in Article 6 *bis* of the Paris Convention;

3.   A trade mark shall furthermore not be registered or, if registered, shall be liable to be declared invalid if it is identical with, or similar to, an earlier Community trade mark within the meaning of paragraph 2 and is to be, or has been, registered for goods or services which are not similar to those for which the earlier Community trade mark is registered, where the earlier Community trade mark has a reputation in

the Community and where the use of the later trade mark without due cause would take unfair advantage of, or be detrimental to, the distinctive character or the repute of the earlier Community trade mark.

4.   Any Member State may furthermore provide that a trade mark shall not be registered or, if registered, shall be liable to be declared invalid where, and to the extent that—

  (a)   the trade mark is identical with, or similar to, an earlier national trade mark within the meaning of paragraph 2 and is to be, or has been, registered for goods or services which are not similar to those for which the earlier trade mark is registered, where the earlier trade mark has a reputation in the Member State concerned and where the use of the later trade mark without due cause would take unfair advantage of, or be detrimental to, the distinctive character or the repute of the earlier trade mark;

  (b)   rights to a non-registered trade mark or to another sign used in the course of trade were acquired prior to the date of application for registration of the subsequent trade mark, or the date of the priority claimed for the application for registration of the subsequent trade mark and that non-registered trade mark or other sign confers on its proprietor the right to prohibit the use of a subsequent trade mark;

  (c)   the use of the trade mark may be prohibited by virtue of an earlier right other than the rights referred to in paragraphs 2 and 4(b) and in particular—

       (i)   a right to a name;

       (ii)   a right of personal portrayal;

       (iii) a copyright;

       (iv)   an industrial property right;

  (d)   the trade mark is identical with, or similar to, an earlier collective trade mark conferring a right which expired within a period of a maximum of three years preceding application;

  (e)   the trade mark is identical with, or similar to, an earlier guarantee or certification mark conferring a right which expired within a period preceding application the length of which is fixed by the Member State;

  (f)   the trade mark is identical with, or similar to, an earlier trade mark which was registered for identical or similar goods or services and conferred on them a right which has expired for failure to renew within a period of a maximum of two years preceding application, unless the proprietor of the earlier trade mark gave his agreement for the registration of the later mark or did not use his trade mark;

  (g)   the trade mark is liable to be confused with a mark which was in use abroad on the filing date of the application and which is still in use there, provided that at the date of the application the applicant was acting in bad faith.

5.   The Member States may permit that in appropriate circumstances registration need not be refused or the trade mark need not be declared invalid where the proprietor of the earlier trade mark or other earlier right consents to the registration of the later trade mark.

6.   Any Member State may provide that, by derogation from paragraphs 1 to 5, the grounds for refusal of registration or invalidity in force in that State prior to the date on which the provisions necessary to comply with this Directive enter into force, shall apply to trade marks for which application has been made prior to that date.

Article 5

Rights conferred by a trade mark

1.   The registered trade mark shall confer on the proprietor exclusive rights therein. The proprietor shall be entitled to prevent all third parties not having his consent from using in the course of trade—

   (a)   any sign which is identical with the trade mark in relation to goods or services which are identical with those for which the trade mark is registered;

   (b)   any sign where, because of its identity with, or similarity to, the trade mark and the identity or similarity of the goods or services covered by the trade mark and the sign, there exists a likelihood of confusion on the part of the public, which includes the likelihood of association between the sign and the trade mark.

2.   Any Member State may also provide that the proprietor shall be entitled to prevent all third parties not having his consent from using in the course of trade any sign which is identical with, or similar to, the trade mark in relation to goods or services which are not similar to those for which the trade mark is registered, where the latter has a reputation in the Member State and where use of that sign without due cause takes unfair advantage of, or is detrimental to, the distinctive character or the repute of the trade mark.

3.   The following, *inter alia,* may be prohibited under paragraphs 1 and 2—

   (a)   affixing the sign to the goods or to the packaging thereof;

   (b)   offering the goods, or putting them on the market or stocking them for these purposes under that sign, or offering or supplying services thereunder;

   (c)   importing or exporting the goods under the sign;

   (d)   using the sign on business papers and in advertising.

4.   Where, under the law of the Member State, the use of a sign under the conditions referred to in 1(b) or 2 could not be prohibited before the date on which the provisions necessary to comply with this Directive entered into force in the Member State concerned, the rights conferred by the trade mark may not be relied on to prevent the continued use of the sign.

5.   Paragraphs 1 to 4 shall not affect provisions in any Member State relating to the protection against the use of a sign other than for the purposes of distinguishing goods or services, where use of that sign without due cause takes unfair advantage of, or is detrimental to, the distinctive character or the repute of the trade mark.

Article 6

Limitation of the effects of a trade mark

1.   The trade mark shall not entitle the proprietor to prohibit a third party from using, in the course of trade,—

   (a)   his own name or address;

   (b)   indications concerning the kind, quality, quantity, intended purpose, value, geographical origin, the time of production of goods or of rendering of the service, or other characteristics of goods or services;

   (c)   the trade mark where it is necessary to indicate the intended purpose of a product or service, in particular as accessories or spare parts;

provided he uses them in accordance with honest practices in industrial or commercial matters.

2.   The trade mark shall not entitle the proprietor to prohibit a third party from using, in the course of trade, an earlier right which only applies in a particular locality if that right is recognised by the laws of the Member State in question and within the limits of the territory in which it is recognised.

Article 7

Exhaustion of the rights conferred by a trade mark

1.   The trade mark shall not entitle the proprietor to prohibit its use in relation to goods which have been put on the market in the Community under that trade mark by the proprietor or with his consent.

2.   Paragraph 1 shall not apply where there exist legitimate reasons for the proprietor to oppose further commercialisation of the goods, especially where the condition of the goods is changed or impaired after they have been put on the market.

Article 8

Licensing

1.   A trade mark may be licensed for some or all of the goods or services for which it is registered and for the whole or part of the Member State concerned. A license may be exclusive or non-exclusive.

2.   The proprietor of a trade mark may invoke the rights conferred by that trade mark against a licensee who contravenes any provision in his licensing contract with regard to its duration, the form covered by the registration in which the trade mark may be used, the scope of the goods or services for which the licence is granted, the territory in which the trade mark may be affixed, or the quality of the goods manufactured or of the services provided by the licensee.

Article 9

Limitation in consequence of acquiescence

1.   Where, in a Member State, the proprietor of an earlier trade mark as referred to in Article 4(2) has acquiesced, for a period of five successive years, in the use of a later trade mark registered in that Member State while being aware of such use, he shall no longer be entitled on the basis of the earlier trade mark either to apply for a declaration that the later trade mark is invalid or to oppose the use of the later trade mark in respect of the goods or services for which the later trade mark has been used, unless registration of the later trade mark was applied for in bad faith.

2.   Any Member State may provide that paragraph 1 shall apply *mutatis mutandis* to the proprietor of an earlier trade mark referred to in Article 4(4) (a) or an other earlier right referred to in Article 4(4) (b) or (c).

3.   In the cases referred to in paragraphs 1 and 2, the proprietor of a later registered trade mark shall not be entitled to oppose the use of the earlier right, even though that right may no longer be invoked against the later trade mark.

Article 10

Use of trade marks

1. If, within a period of five years following the date of the completion of the registration procedure, the proprietor has not put the trade mark to genuine use in the Member State in connection with the goods or services in respect of which it is registered, or if such use has been suspended during an uninterrupted period of five years, the trade mark shall be subject to the sanctions provided for in this Directive, unless there are proper reasons for non-use.

2. The following shall also constitute use within the meaning of paragraph 1—
   - (a) use of the trade mark in a form differing in elements which do not alter the distinctive character of the mark in the form in which it was registered;
   - (b) affixing of the trade mark to goods or to the packaging thereof in the Member State concerned solely for export purposes.

3. Use of the trade mark with the consent of the proprietor or by any person who has authority to use a collective mark or a guarantee or certification mark shall be deemed to constitute use by the proprietor.

4. In relation to trade marks registered before the date on which the provisions necessary to comply with this Directive enter into force in the Member State concerned—
   - (a) where a provision in force prior to that date attaches sanctions to non-use of a trade mark during an uninterrupted period, the relevant period of five years mentioned in paragraph 1 shall be deemed to have begun to run at the same time as any period of non-use which is already running at that date;
   - (b) where there is no use provision in force prior to that date, the periods of five years mentioned in paragraph 1 shall be deemed to run from that date at the earliest.

Article 11

Sanctions for non use of a trade mark in legal or administrative proceedings

1. A trade mark may not be declared invalid on the ground that there is an earlier conflicting trade mark if the latter does not fulfil the requirements of use set out in Article 10(1), (2) and (3) or in Article 10(4), as the case may be.

2. Any Member State may provide that registration of a trade mark may not be refused on the ground that there is an earlier conflicting trade mark if the latter does not fulfil the requirements of use set out in Article 10(1), (2) and (3) or in Article 10(4), as the case may be.

3. Without prejudice to the application of Article 12, where a counter-claim for revocation is made, any Member State may provide that a trade mark may not be successfully invoked in infringement proceedings if it is established as a result of a plea that the trade mark could be revoked pursuant to Article 12(1).

4. If the earlier trade mark has been used in relation to part only of the goods or services for which it is registered, it shall, for purposes of applying paragraphs 1, 2 and 3, be deemed to be registered in respect only of that part of the goods or services.

Article 12

Grounds for revocation

1.   A trade mark shall be liable to revocation if, within a continuous period of five years, it has not been put to genuine use in the Member State in connection with the goods or services in respect of which it is registered, and there are no proper reasons for non-use; however, no person may claim that the proprietor's rights in a trade mark should be revoked where, during the interval between expiry of the five-year period and filing of the application for revocation, genuine use of the trade mark has been started or resumed; the commencement or resumption of use within a period of three months preceding the filing of the application for revocation which began at the earliest on expiry of the continuous period of five years of non-use, shall, however, be disregarded where preparations for the commencement or resumption occur only after the proprietor becomes aware that the application for revocation may be filed.

2.   A trade mark shall also be liable to revocation if, after the date on which it was registered,
   (a)   in consequence of acts or inactivity of the proprietor, it has become the common name in the trade for a product or service in respect of which it is registered;
   (b)   in consequence of the use made of it by the proprietor of the trade mark or with his consent in respect of the goods or services for which it is registered, it is liable to mislead the public, particularly as to the nature, quality or geographical origin of those goods or services.

Article 13

Grounds for refusal or revocation or invalidity relating to only some of the goods or services

Where grounds for refusal of registration or for revocation or invalidity of a trade mark exist in respect of only some of the goods or services for which that trade mark has been applied for or registered, refusal of registration or revocation or invalidity shall cover those goods or services only.

Article 14

Establishment *a posteriori* of invalidity or revocation of a trade mark

Where the seniority of an earlier trade mark which has been surrendered or allowed to lapse, is claimed for a Community trade mark, the invalidity or revocation of the earlier trade mark may be established *a posteriori*.

Article 15

Special provisions in respect of collective marks, guarantee marks and certification marks

1.   Without prejudice to Article 4, Member States whose laws authorise the registration of collective marks or of guarantee or certification marks may provide that such marks shall not be registered, or shall be revoked or declared invalid, on

grounds additional to those specified in Articles 3 and 12 where the function of those marks so requires.

2.   By way of derogation from Article 3(1) (c), Member States may provide that signs or indications which may serve, in trade, to designate the geographical origin of the goods or services may constitute collective, guarantee or certification marks. Such a mark does not entitle the proprietor to prohibit a third party from using in the course of trade such signs or indications, provided he uses them in accordance with honest practices in industrial or commercial matters; in particular, such a mark may not be invoked against a third party who is entitled to use a geographical name.

Article 16

National provisions to be adopted pursuant to this Directive

1.   The Member States shall bring into force the laws, regulations and administrative provisions necessary to comply with this Directive not later than [31 December 1992]. They shall immediately inform the Commission thereof.

2.   Acting on a proposal from the Commission, the Council, acting by qualified majority, may defer the date referred to in paragraph 1 until 31 December 1992 at the latest.

3.   Member States shall communicate to the Commission the text of the main provisions of national law which they adopt in the field governed by this Directive.

Words in para (1) substituted by Council Decision 92/10/EEC of 19 December 1991, Art 1.

Article 17

Addressees

This Directive is addressed to the Member States.

Index